3

Hitler's Admirals

G. H. Bennett and R. Bennett

NAVAL INSTITUTE PRESS
ANNAPOLIS, MARYLAND

Naval Institute Press
291 Wood Road
Annapolis, MD 21402

Library of Congress Cataloging-in-Publication Data
Bennett, G. H. (George Henry), 1967–
   Hitler's admirals / George Henry Bennett and Roy Bennett.
   p. cm.
   Based on extracts of essays written by nine German admirals, translated into English.
   Includes index.
   ISBN 1-59114-061-7 (alk. paper)
   1. World War, 1939–1945—Naval operations, German. 2. Naval strategy—History—
20th century. I. Bennett, R. (Roy), 1928– II. Title.
   D771.B3726 2004
   940.54'5943—dc22

                                                                    2004004854

Printed in the United States of America on acid-free paper ∞
11 10 9 8 7 6 5 4   9 8 7 6 5 4 3 2
First printing

Contents

Preface

This book is based on extracts from English translations of essays written at the request of British Naval Intelligence by nine German admirals who were prisoners of war in British hands in 1945. The admirals' comments have been rearranged into thematic chapters, each covering a particular aspect of the war at sea. Because information has been taken from different parts of the admirals' essays and rearranged as necessary to make a logical narrative, ellipses to indicate omissions have not been used except within sentences.

Apart from this rearrangement, the only editorial changes that have been introduced involve some additional punctuation to clarify the structure of long, complex sentences, an attempt to impose greater consistency in the use of uppercase initial letters, and spelling changes from British spelling (e.g., *colour*) to American (*color*). Certain passages have been omitted on the grounds that they are repetitive, of little interest, obscure in meaning, or are irrelevant to the overall purpose of this book.

The 1945 translations were probably done rather hastily, and it is likely that they adhere rather too closely to the conventions of German sentence structure. The meaning of many sentences could be clarified by some rearrangement of subordinate clauses, but no attempt has been made to introduce changes of that description at this stage.

Linking passages of text and additional information inserted by the editors are printed in bold type so they may easily be distinguished from passages written by the admirals.

The British National Archives (Public Record Office) file numbers, and the dates when the English translations were circulated by the Naval Intelligence Division of the Admiralty are listed below. Each report was accompanied by a brief résumé of the admiral's career and a summary of the most important points, prepared by E. G. N. Rushbrooke, director of Naval Intelligence.

Grand Admiral Karl Dönitz [PRO ADM 223/688, 24 September 1945]

General Admiral Herman Boehm [PRO ADM 223/692, 26 October 1945]

Admiral Theodor Krancke [PRO ADM 223/689, 2 October 1945]

Vice Admiral Hellmuth Heye [PRO ADM 223/690, 15 October 1945]

Rear Admiral Hans Meyer [PRO ADM 223/691, 16 October 1945]

Vice Admiral Eberhard Weichold [Part I, PRO ADM 223/797,
    26 November 1945] [Part II, PRO ADM 223/695, 28 December 1945]

Rear Admiral Otto Schulz [PRO FO 371/47018, 1 November 1945]

General Admiral Otto Schniewind and Admiral Schuster
    [PRO ADM 223/696, 10 November 1946]*

We are grateful to the British National Archives (Public Record Office) and the controller of Her Majesty's Stationery Office for allowing us to reproduce the admirals' words. If history is written by the victors then the essays show that the losers can also be just as instrumental in its writing. They qualify many of the judgments about the history of the war at sea in which Anglo-American historians since 1945 have been so predominant.

---

*The main contributor to this joint essay appears to have been General Admiral Schniewind, with Admiral Schuster checking and confirming the opinions expressed. Sometimes the writer uses the first person singular, sometimes the first person plural, and in one or two places one gets the impression that probably Admiral Schuster was the primary contributor on certain topics. Who contributed what cannot now be identified with any certainty in most instances.

Hitler's Admirals

Introduction

A LITTLE BEFORE 0800 hours on 1 May 1945 the commander of the German navy, Grossadmiral Dönitz at his headquarters in Flensburg, northern Germany, received a cryptic message from the Führer bunker in Berlin. It advised him that Adolf Hitler's political testament had come into force. Communicated a few hours earlier, the testament appointed Dönitz as Hitler's successor. The message on 1 May meant, without actually saying it, that the Führer was dead and Dönitz was the new head of state. Other contenders such as Goering and Himmler had disqualified themselves from the succession by plotting to overthrow Hitler. Dönitz's sole duty, the only course remaining for Germany, would be to negotiate the surrender of the German armed forces. Everywhere German resistance was crumbling and Dönitz's only hope was to prevent needless bloodshed, and to save as much of Germany as possible from occupation by the Russian army. The position of the German navy (Kriegsmarine) was as precarious as the rest of Germany's armed forces. As had been reported to Hitler on 18 April at the final Führer conference on naval affairs, the handful of surface vessels remaining in operation were busy covering the evacuation of civilians and military personnel from the advancing Red Army in the Baltic region. The crews of damaged and decommissioned ships were being thrown into the land fighting.[1]

The U-boat campaign, with which Dönitz had been closely associated from the 1930s onward, had proved a costly failure. In north German ports like Kiel and Wilhelmshaven, the heartland of the German navy, sat the rusting and blackened hulks of battleships, cruisers, destroyers, and submarines.

In Kiel, the pocket battleship *Admiral Sheer* lay bottom up in one of the dock basins. Nearby, in another basin, lay the heavy cruiser *Admiral Hipper.* She had been heavily damaged by Allied bombing. Farther afield the seas of the world were littered with the wreckage caused by the destruction of the German navy. Battleship *Bismarck* lay at the bottom of the Atlantic. Her capsized sister *Tirpitz* could be found in a Norwegian fjord, and the old battleship *Schleswig Holstein,* which had led the assault on Poland in September 1939, had been scuttled at Gydnia in the Baltic. Defeat was inevitable, but at the end of this world war the German navy would not mutiny as it had done at the end of the first. Discipline remained good, and morale, under the circumstances, was extremely good. Before his appointment as Germany's last Führer, Dönitz contemplated leading his remaining forces out into the Atlantic in a last glorious charge. Plans for a similar sortie in 1918 had led the high seas fleet to mutiny, but a reprise was not anticipated in 1945. Ironically just as the navy and Germany were forced to concede defeat, they had acquired the weapons that, with a little more time, could have turned the tide completely. The final charge might be glorious, but it would not be completely suicidal. A new generation of U-boats was entering service, and their performance was much improved on that of the type VII and type IX U-boats that had been temporarily withdrawn from the Atlantic because of heavy losses in the spring of 1943. On 30 April veteran U-boat commander Korvettenkapitän Adalbert Schnee took U-2511 on her maiden voyage.[2] U-2511 was a 1,600-ton type XXI oceangoing electro-boat. The submarine represented a quantum leap in ship design. The old type VII U-boat struggled to operate off the North American Atlantic coast from the French ports, and under attack while submerged it was reliant on electric motors whose endurance, 100 miles at 2 knots, was less than electrifying. The new type XXI had an underwater attack speed of 17 knots and could travel for almost 300 miles at 6 knots while remaining submerged. Underwater, while attacking a convoy, it could outpace most escort vessels. On 4 May, along with the rest of the U-boat command, Schnee received orders to cease hostilities. The new Führer had decided that his appointment as head of state called him to a rather different course of action than leading the German navy into a final battle. Even though he had received the order Schnee could not resist launching a dummy attack against an escorted cruiser that he encountered near the Faeroes. Approaching the enemy warships at high speed underwater he was able to penetrate the screen of escorts and get into a perfect position from which to torpedo the cruiser. That he was able to stage the attack and escape without detection indicated that, just at the point of capitulation, the navy had, at long last, acquired the weapons capable of severing the North American lifeline that had prevented the capitulation of Britain after 1940 and that after June 1944 had carried an unceasing flow of men and material to the battles on the western front.

For many members of the German navy, especially its senior officers, this was the second time in their careers that Germany had been defeated in a major war. At the end of the First World War they had analyzed the conflict carefully to learn lessons for the future. In 1945 it was clear that the process of reflection would have to begin again. This time the German Admiralty would not be left to its own in its reflections. At 1530 on 21 May 1945 the advance elements of a British Admiralty mission arrived in Flensburg. The British Admiralty mission, temporarily housed on the Hamburg-America liner *Caribia* in Flensburg harbor, was eventually to number 38, including 19 naval officers, supported by interpreters and secretaries. The task of the mission was twofold: "To interrogate senior officers in the German Admiralty . . . [and] to obtain details of technical development and equipment from the appropriate departments of the German Navy."[3] Essentially the mission was intended to secure as many of Nazi Germany's technical secrets as possible and to begin the process of trying to understand the strategic thinking, and decision-making process behind Germany's prosecution of the war at sea. The latter was motivated partly by historical curiosity and partly by a desire to see what lessons could be learned for future wars. Some questions were particularly urgent: were there any German naval units still at large that had not received or were refusing to obey the surrender order? Admiral von Friedeberg, who had become head of the German navy on Dönitz's appointment as Führer, was supplied with lists of surrendering U-boats as it rapidly transpired that the surrender order was being followed, although some commanders preferred to scuttle their vessels rather than hand them over to the allied powers. Some U-boat commanders like Peter Cremer, who had distinguished himself in U-333, were interrogated about their tactics in attacking convoys.

In part the Admiralty was motivated by the postwar desire to ensure a proper accounting on both sides. Admiralty officials and German commanders worked jointly to try and piece together the fate of particular U-boats during the war as apparently inconclusive depth charges were reconciled with last known positions. The process worked both ways: U-boat officers were not above asking the Admiralty for a precise accounting of their successes against a particular convoy. Some of these questions became less than purely historical during 1945 as the West slowly began to prepare for a possible war against the Soviet Union.

The enquiries of the Admiralty mission were also concerned with war crimes. At the Nuremberg war trials in 1946 Grossadmiral Raeder and Grossadmiral Dönitz would find themselves on trial on a number of counts including planning a war of aggression. Investigations would also be held into the widespread suspicion that German submariners were not beyond machine-gunning the survivors of sunken ships as they swam in the water or attempted to escape on rafts or lifeboats. Heinz Eck, commanding U-852, would be executed after the war for his massacre of the crew of the Greek steamer *Peleus,* which he sank in the South Atlantic on 13 March 1944. U-852 then cruised around in darkness machine-gunning survivors. Three men, who survived the massacre and another twenty-five days adrift, were able to relate their account of the massacre. At the end of hostilities war crimes investigators went through the German naval records, a substantial proportion of which was captured by American forces near Tambach and then flown to London, to see whether Eck had been alone in the actions he took against survivors. They found that he was, although at Nuremberg Dönitz would be called to account for an order he issued on 17 September 1942, which became known as the Laconia order. Issued after U-156, U-506, U-507, and the Italian submarine *Comandante Cappellini* endangered themselves by rescuing a large number of survivors from the British liner *Laconia,* sunk by U-156 on 12 September 1942, the wording of the Laconia order was ambiguous enough to invite a variety of interpretations:

1. No attempt of any kind must be made to rescue members of ships sunk, and this includes picking up persons in the water and putting them in lifeboats, righting capsized lifeboats, and handing over food and water. Rescue runs counter to the most elementary demands of warfare for the destruction of enemy ships and crews.
2. Orders for bringing back captains and chief engineers still apply.
3. Rescue the shipwrecked only if their statements will be of value to your boat.
4. Be harsh. Bear in mind that the enemy takes no regard of women and children in his bombing attacks on German cities.[4]

The Laconia order was intended to guard against U-boat commanders risking their crews because of their humanitarian instincts toward shipwrecked fellow mariners, but it could also be read as an incitement to murder Allied crews. Eck's interrogators would later try to get him to admit that he was acting on the instructions contained in the Laconia order when he murdered the crew of the *Peleus*. Eck would steadfastly refuse the invitation to implicate his former commander in exchange for life imprisonment rather than the death penalty, and at Nuremberg the allegation that Dönitz had licensed his crews to commit atrocities would be thrown out. However, in 1945 all this was in the future as Allied officers investigated Dönitz and Raeder and other senior figures within the German Admiralty for possible trial as war criminals.

The Admiralty faced serious problems in its attempt to obtain statements from the German naval high command. The British arrested most, but not all, of the surviving German naval officers after the unconditional surrender in 1945. Grand Admiral Raeder, head of the German navy from 1933 until 1943, was arrested by the Russians and taken to Moscow along with his wife. Raeder who had overseen the prewar build up of the German navy was a key figure, and his detention in Moscow put him beyond the reach of the Naval Intelligence Department until the start of the Nuremberg war trials. Admiral von Friedeberg, the final head of the wartime German navy after Dönitz was appointed Führer, was another figure whom the Admiralty looked to for help and cooperation. In the immediate aftermath of the surrender he had proved cooperative, even helpful to Naval Intelligence. On 23 May he was collected from a prisoner of war cage in Flensburg by a detachment from the 1st Battalion, the Cheshire Regiment. He was to be allowed to return to his home to collect some belongings before being taken to brigade headquarters for further questioning. While packing at home he asked to visit the toilet, to which the escorting officer agreed providing he leave the door open. In his later report Captain Davies of the Cheshire Regiment related:

> I followed him to the bathroom and he entered rather slowly, then suddenly closed the door and turned the key. I called the escort and we immediately forced the door. . . . I did not fire the lock as I thought the Admiral's behaviour natural in the circumstances and did not wish to shoot him on the inside. On my entering, he was heaving by the wash basin, half turned round and fell into the bath backwards, striking his head at the bottom of the bath. I first thought he had [had] a heart attack. I ordered his son to fetch a doctor immediately, then with the escort and his servant, lifted him from the bath, loosened his clothing and tried first to make him cough up anything he'd swallowed, then to drink without success.[5]

Despite the frantic attempts to save him Admiral Friedeberg died from the poison he took. Friedeberg's suicide was not only a needless death at the end of a costly war but also a loss in terms of potential intelligence. It was also an indicator of the difficulties of interrogating the surviving leaders of a defeated nation that was coming to terms with its immediate past and possible future. The full horror of the immediate past was just coming to light. Von Friedeberg had been deeply affected by pictures of Buchenwald concentration camp, which he had seen in an American newspaper in early May 1945. The true nature of the regime he had served was further exposed shortly thereafter when a ship carrying concentration camp inmates evacuated from the east had docked in Flensburg. Added to the horrors of the concentration camp for men like von Friedeberg was the fact that they had commanded thousands who had met their deaths in the Atlantic in the cause of a fruitless struggle. Their future and the future of their country were uncertain. Did a Germany that had unleashed two world wars have a future in the postwar world, and might the former German naval high command find itself on trial for war crimes either individually or collectively? Undoubtedly many other former admirals contemplated von Friedeberg's course of action.

Members of the Admiralty delegation met with a variety of responses after their arrival on 21 May. The situation was initially somewhat confused. Germany had surrendered, but senior naval officers remained free, and German troops continued to guard military buildings. Officers of the Admiralty delegation managed to conduct a number of interviews with German naval officers before they were formally detained as prisoners of war by the British army on 23 May. Those arrests and the death of von Friedeberg on 23 May changed the attitude of some naval officers who had previously talked openly to the Admiralty delegation. Vice Admiral Hellmuth Heye was due to be interrogated on 23 May, but was arrested before the interview. When the captive admiral was interviewed on the following day he proved "entirely non-co-operative."[6]

He began by stating that although he had previously given all information requested and had even offered it without demand, he had been arrested and for the last 36 hours had been treated like a criminal. He demanded an explanation before entering into any further discussions. He complained that no charge had been made against him, and if he were to be arrested he considered that a naval officer should have undertaken the duty and not a junior military officer. He also complained of the conditions under which he was accommodated.[7]

Hitler's Admirals

Interviewed along with Admiral Meisel, chief of naval operations, and three other staff officers, Heye was sufficiently truculent to result in his removal from the interview room under armed guard. Meisel and the other officers proved more cooperative once Admiral Heye had departed.

Most of the officers interviewed during May 1945 were slow in venturing information. Their interrogators put this down to depression induced by their arrest. This was despite the fact that members of the Admiralty delegation had tried to foster a relationship with those that they wished to interrogate. For example, one member of the delegation, Captain Gilbert Roberts, the head of the anti-U-boat school, had arranged to have personal possessions returned to Admiral Godt after they had been seized by British soldiers. He also arranged to reunite U-boat Ace Otto Kramer with his wife. Roberts found Kramer wandering through the dockyard at Kiel after arriving back from the final cruise of U-333. Roberts was pleased to find that the relationship was not one-sided as Godt and Kramer proved willing to talk to him. He also discovered an enlarged photograph of himself labeled "This is your enemy, Captain Roberts, Director of anti-U-boat Tactics" in the operations room in Kiel.[8]

While Godt, Kramer, and others proved willing to talk others did so only reluctantly. Rear Admiral Meyer, the deputy chief of naval operations in 1945, talked freely while maintaining an atmosphere of "veiled hostility in all that he said." He also gave nothing more than "a very sketchy" response to key questions, such as the nature of the German assault plan against Britain in 1940.[9] In various ways, from Heye's outright aggression to Meyer's hostile forgetfulness the German admirals under interrogation continued to resist the enemy. At the same time, as prisoners of war possibly facing investigation for war crimes, their vulnerability compelled a degree of cooperation with their interrogators.

Meanwhile Admiral Weichold, the former naval liaison officer to Italy, was fully cooperative. In his interview he talked freely and in great detail about the Mediterranean war. He was no doubt motivated by the fact that the war in the Mediterranean had been over for almost two years and he was little more than a bystander to Italian naval operations against the British. He could talk about the events of 1940 to 1943 with little concern that he was in some way betraying his country or his fellow officers in the Kriegsmarine. He provided detailed and revealing information about Axis naval intelligence in the war in the Mediterranean. He was also absolutely scathing about the Italian navy:

The Italians had no tactics and they could not operate at sea. They had learnt no lessons from the last war as they had no naval engagements. The commanders of Major Units were unable to handle their ships unless an Admiral was present. . . . I do not think the Italians are afraid but they lack experience. Some of the Italian Admirals are good friends of mine and they are capable men but they have the Latin temperament. The Italians cannot handle ships.[10]

Despite the willingness of figures like Weichold to cooperate with Allied interrogators the British Admiralty Mission was judged a failure. Useful technical information was gathered, but the uncooperativeness of most of the German admirals meant that little of real strategic interest or value emerged. It was unsurprising that with a multirole function, in a confused and chaotic aftermath of a major war, the British Admiralty Mission was not wholly successful in securing the cooperation of men who feared they might be handed over to the Russians or put on trial by the Western Allies.

The Admiralty, particularly the historical section charged with writing the official histories of the recent conflict, was unsurprisingly less than satisfied by the results of the British Admiralty Mission. Thus, in the autumn of 1945, the Naval Intelligence Department began reinterviewing admirals such as Heye and Meyer, and interrogating other figures who had been identified as pivotal in German naval policy from 1933 onward. Dönitz and Raeder, as indicted war criminals, were subject to ongoing interrogation about naval and political manners. Dönitz's initial interrogations at the hands of the British and Americans were rather more systematic and detailed than that of Raeder at the hands of the Russians. The latter expected to execute their man come what may, so there was little point in wasting too much effort on his interrogation. From 15 August onward both were interrogated by American teams in preparation for the Nuremberg trials. The work of interrogating those officers of lesser rank was done by junior officers who toured the prisoner of war camps. On behalf of Naval Intelligence and the Admiralty Historical Branch they conveyed a request to the admirals: would they write individual essays examining German naval policy from 1933 onward? The perspective of each essay would be determined by the personalities and positions held by each admiral. Thus the essayists were selected on the basis of the commands they had held and also on their personalities and political attitudes.

Getting the admirals to write essays was predicated on the idea that more information would be forthcoming if they were free to talk about those issues they were prepared to discuss. An interrogation was, by its very nature, a confrontational event that had military and legal overtones. Interrogation invited a defensive response on the part of those being interrogated even if it also compelled answers. As Richard Overy has noted on the interrogations for the Nuremberg trials, "Silence might have protected them, but it seems to have occurred to none of them to refuse co-operation."[11] The process of writing an essay had more of the resonance of historical understanding about it—of equals sharing their view of the past in a nonconfrontational manner. The admirals were reassured that nothing they wrote would be used in the preparation of war crimes cases. They would not have access to German Admiralty papers, although some, like Weichold, retained a considerable number of his private papers while in captivity. Writing essays, rather than undergoing further interrogations, was also functionally more efficient. A proper interrogation required an interrogator, a translator, and a secretary. Translating and analyzing an essay written in German took considerably less time and made fewer demands on personnel. Even at the high-profile Nuremberg trials, securing the services of enough interpreters and secretaries was not easy.

Acquiring essays from the admirals was somewhat difficult because of the conditions in which many were held in late 1945, early 1946. The responsibility for prisoner of war camps was an army, American and British, rather than a navy responsibility. As the officers of the Naval Intelligence Department visited the various admirals selected for approach they became concerned about the conditions in which they were being held. In part their motivation was humanitarian. In part they identified with fellow naval officers, even if they came from a defeated nation. The two officers charged with speaking to Admiral Schuster, who had been head of the German Admiralty Historical Section from October 1943 onward, disapproved of the lack of military bearing of the American guards at the Allendorf prisoner of war camp: "The American Officers at this camp appeared to be very ignorant and uninterested in their responsibilities, and the discipline among the U.S. Army Guards, particularly the orderlies in the guard room, was extremely lax, even for an American unit. The men sat playing cards and smoking while their officer spoke to them on duty, and seemed to be doing him a favor in answering his questions."[12]

Alarmed by what they saw, the two Royal Navy officers enquired about food, accommodation, and medical treatment available to the inmates of the camp. On each point they were reassured, but they remained unhappy about the general running of the camp.

Royal Navy visitors to other prisoner of war camps were even less satisfied. One such visit to Camp 2226 near Ostende in Belgium resulted in a full investigation and report to the Admiralty. The camp held 4,496 officers including 35 admirals under the command of Admiral Foerste and his deputy, Vice Admiral Ruge. While living conditions were adequate in the summer, during the winter the camp was extremely damp. Concerns about the future and the fate of families and friends were exacerbated by inadequate recreational facilities. Foerste said that he was having "great difficulty in trying to keep up the morale of some of the older German officers." Vice Admiral Ruge confirmed that certain officers "just seemed to sit down and waste away." The deaths of two admirals at the camp in December 1945 confirmed the views of Foerste and Ruge. The findings of the inspection team were supplemented by other evidence. In February 1946 one of Admiral Heye's friends approached the British naval authorities in Germany with a copy of a letter he had received from him in Belgium. In the letter Heye related: "The camp is a marsh . . . accommodation suitable for cattle: no beds, tin roof, no W.C., no ablutions in the barracks: cold and extraordinarily damp, so that many people are always sick . . . : 18 Admirals all in one room: no mail from one's family, etc."[13] Heye mentioned that Weichold was among the sick. Details about the contents of the letter were immediately telephoned through to the Admiralty in London. The wives of the captive admirals, who received mail from them every two weeks or so, also passed on their concerns to Royal Navy officers in northern Germany. Some of those concerns involved physical abuse as well as poor conditions. In particular, the Admiralty learned that in north Germany allegations were circulating to the effect that Admiral Heye had been beaten by Allied soldiers while on his way to the camp in Belgium.

Information from released former inmates of the Belgian camp added further to the Admiralty's concerns. Kapitän zur See Loffler was released from Camp 2226 in early 1946 and was promptly interviewed by the Naval Intelligence Department. He commented that "[c]onditions there were very bad. Many of the guards seemed to be Jews and the German working staff appeared to have received anti-Officer instructions. High German officers . . . had the impression that they had been sent to a Straflager (punishment camp)."[14] Almost every inmate of the camp had a distressing story to tell that merely confirmed the general picture. Kapitänleutnant Johann Heinrich

Fehler would later recount: "We had no coal nor heating of any kind, and our diet consisted mostly of white bread and thin soup. Any complaint on our part was met by the moral reflection that we were not alone in our misery: all Europe, they said, was starving."[15] Fehler also observed that other ranks were better fed than their superiors but could offer no explanation why this was so. Other evidence reaching the Admiralty suggested that the conditions in the Belgian camp were by no means exceptional. One inmate transferred to another prisoner of war camp near Hamburg, so that he could be nearer his family, likened the conditions in the new camp to that of a "Concentration Camp, the horror of which is unsurpassable." Food, heating, and living conditions were described as intolerable. Foerste was warned not to allow any more naval personnel to be sent to the camp and to try and secure the return of those who had already been transferred.[16]

Faced with considerable evidence about the poor conditions that German naval officers were being held in, even though they had clearly improved since late 1945, the Admiralty decided to press the British army of the Rhine to secure an improvement. Stung by the suggestion that German prisoners of war were being treated inadequately, Major General A. A. B. Dowler replied on behalf of headquarters, the British army of the Rhine, that conditions were improving and that they had always been as good as shortages of various kinds would allow.[17] Not satisfied with the response, on 4 April Vice Admiral H. T. C. Walker wrote back. He acknowledged that improvements had been made but that "conditions in these camps are still such as to warrant very drastic and urgent action to improve them, lest we should lay ourselves open to very grave charges of holding prisoners in conditions akin to those of BUCHENWALD and BELSEN."[18]

The emotive language used by Walker indicated the extent to which a relationship had developed between British and German naval officers since Germany's capitulation. That relationship was typified by mutual respect and a sense of mutual need. The Admiralty wanted additional intelligence from their former enemies; the German admirals were eager to secure an improvement in their conditions. The relationship between the two shifted from that of interrogator and interrogated in May 1945 to the mutual pursuit of naval history later that same year. In May 1945 the Royal Navy was eager to engage the Kriegsmarine in battle. By February 1946 the Royal Navy was happy to engage the British army of the Rhine in a rather different battle on behalf of the former members of the German Admiralty. German and British sailors identified with each other.

Dönitz, meanwhile, was awaiting trial at the International Military Tribunal at Nuremberg on charges of conspiring to wage an aggressive war and for specific war crimes, including ordering the killing of shipwreck survivors. His situation was altogether different. On trial for his life along with Raeder and the rest of the surviving leadership of the Third Reich, Dönitz was repeatedly interrogated about his actions. And despite his status as a prisoner of war he believed he still had a role to play in leading Germany and the navy. In the hours before he was incarcerated on 23 May he drafted an address to the officer corps. It revealed an astute political awareness of Germany's position and the navy's, together with an understanding of what he and the officer corps could contribute to the future of Germany. The address was further evidence of what his wartime opponents had known since 1939: Dönitz was extremely cunning.[19] The first priority, Dönitz argued in his address, was to cooperate with the Western powers in order to prepare the ground for the rehabilitation of Germany and the reclamation of the parts of Germany then under Russian occupation: "It is clear that we have to go along with the Western powers and work with them in the occupied territories in the west, for it is only through working with them that we can have hopes of later retrieving our land from the Russians."[20]

The address also recognized that such preparation would involve securing the correct interpretation of the history of the Third Reich. After its defeat in the First World War the German military had fostered the notion of the "stab in the back" that had cost them victory. The myth that was established suggested that German forces, unbeaten on the battlefield, had been forced to agree to an armistice because of the outbreak of a revolution at home that had been fostered by Communists, Socialists, Jews, and others. In 1945 a new narrative was needed. Part of it was the heroism of the German military in a lengthy and bloody struggle. As Dönitz stated in his address to the officer corps: "Our fight against the British and Americans can be viewed with pride and glory. We have nothing to be ashamed of."[21] The omission of the Russians from the sentence was quite intentional, because the second element in the new narrative would be to stress the danger to civilization of world communism so as to convince the Western powers that Germany had to be revived as a bulwark against communism. The final element in the new narrative would be to convince the Western Allies that the concentration camps were unknown to the vast majority of the Germans, who would not have tolerated such outrages. Dönitz put forward this view strenuously from his capture onward. In his memoirs he put the case forcefully: "Every decent German today is ashamed of the crimes which the Third Reich committed behind the nation's back. To hold the people as a whole responsible for the misdeeds of a small minority is contrary to every canon of justice. Men cannot be condemned for things of which they did not even know."[22]

By the time Dönitz's memoirs were published in 1958 the new narrative of defeat had proven a spectacular success. Germany was rehabilitated back into the Western camp and an East-West cold war was in full swing. The majority of Western scholarship had been happy to conclude that knowledge of the camps by ordinary Germans was minimal, that Hitler had been uniquely responsible for the war and its evils, and that the German nation had been led astray. Some of those men who had been admirals in the German navy in the Second World War had risen to prominence in the Federal German Republic, and some of their wartime protégés were admirals in the new Bundesmarine. Dönitz was already out of prison, having been sentenced in 1946 to 10 years imprisonment for war crimes and for waging an aggressive war.

Dönitz was determined to establish the new narrative of defeat, and he was prepared to cooperate with the Admiralty in order to establish it. If they wanted an essay, he was quite prepared to give it to them. His call to cooperate was not lost on his subordinates who were also approached to write essays. Even in prison Dönitz maintained close links with his former admirals and former U-boat commanders. The admirals maintained links among themselves through their wives and associates and to Dönitz and Raeder through their attorneys. Under Allied direction, the minesweeping forces of the German navy continued to operate after the surrender, and its officers also helped to maintain connections between the members of the old officer corps. An underground network was established in 1945, and in 1946 it helped to organize documents and experts for the defense of Dönitz and Raeder; then it lobbied against their sentences. Both of the grand admirals called on their immediate subordinates to provide affidavits and testimony to back up their cases. For example, Admirals Lohmann and Boehm provided affidavits to help Raeder's case, and Admiral Wagner gave testimony on Dönitz's behalf. Not surprisingly, the British Admiralty grew alarmed in 1946 at what it saw as the continued existence of the Kriegsmarine as a recognizable and functioning entity, especially considering that the conviction of its two wartime leaders might lead to an organized response.

Anticipating the possibility that he might be found guilty, Dönitz wrote a letter to Rear Admiral Kraus, head of the minesweeping service, instructing him to do all in his power to prevent a reaction. Given the role of the minesweeping service in maintaining links between the old comrades of the Kriegsmarine, Dönitz's instruction extended well beyond ensuring that German minesweepers remained operational. Dönitz knew it, Kraus knew it, and so did the British. Dr. Kranzbuhler, Dönitz's attorney at Nuremberg, visited Vice Admiral Walker, commanding British naval forces in Germany, on 23 August 1946 with a copy of the letter, which he asked the British Admiralty to endorse and publicly release. Kranzbuhler stated that his warnings of the trouble within the ranks of the former Kriegsmarine was backed by "several senior ex-German Naval Officers."[23] Walker refused Kranzbuhler's request because "it would have the appearance of Dönitz still being at the head of his men and indicate a 'fleet in being.'"[24] Appearances notwithstanding the reality was that the upper echelons of the German navy did indeed remain a fleet .

Given the existence of a network between former German admirals spread across prisoner of war camps in Western Europe, one cannot rule out the possibility of collusion between those figures who were asked by the Naval Intelligence Department to write essays. Nor can one rule out the possibility that on a subconscious level at least their essays were influenced by the need to produce a new narrative of defeat that Dönitz had identified in May 1945. Other senior figures in the Nazi regime were also involved in putting forward the new narrative in 1945 and 1946. Hjalmar Schacht, who had been Germany's minister for the economy before falling from Hitler's graces in 1937 over the level of military spending, put forward views similar to those of Dönitz in interrogation. He cautioned the Western Allies: "In Versailles the German nation, which at that time, with clean hands and honorably, had entered a war not of its own making, had been morally maligned and had been treated as unworthy. Hitler profited by the feeling of despair which had the German nation in its grip. I beg and advise most earnestly that there be no repetition of this mistake. Let all really guilty men be punished. . . . One may belittle and scold the German nation for its political stupidity and frivolity but one should refrain from the moral defamation of the entire nation."[25] The question of Germany's future was undoubtedly on the minds of a number of Dönitz's contemporaries both within the German navy and within the ranks of the former leadership of the Third Reich. The future, individually, collectively, and nationally was a subject pondered and discussed by many of those at Nuremberg and in the prisoner of war camps. The formation of the new narrative of defeat was one of many responses to Germany's prostration and questions about the future. Some military figures, like von Friedeberg and Goering, chose suicide. Von Ribbentrop, Hitler's foreign minister, tried to secure a deal in which some leading figures of Nazi Germany would be saddled with responsibility for the war and for war crimes in exchange for clemency for the German people as a whole.[26]

Dönitz and his former admirals may have hoped to use the essays to put forward the new narrative. Certainly after 1945 some of them regarded "putting the record straight" as a continuing duty. Dönitz and Raeder published their memoirs in the 1950s. More junior admirals, including some of those who agreed to write essays for the Naval Intelligence Department, published memoirs and historical accounts, and could be relied upon to help vet and influence some of the early accounts of the war at sea. The sections dealing with the war in the Mediterranean in Anthony Martienssen's 1948 work *Hitler and His Admirals* relied heavily on the essay that Admiral Weichold wrote for the Naval Intelligence Department.[27]

The former admirals were also prominent in trying to influence the direction of the Bundesrepublic. Thirty former admirals and generals gathered in Bonn in July 1951 for a two-day conference on the question of German rearmament. T. H. Tetens, who had been war crimes investigator for the United States and who tended to regard every senior officer of the Third Reich as a Nazi, was later to write with disgust: "Surveying the entire political structure of the Bonn Republic, one comes to the inescapable conclusion that the Nazis have had a quiet comeback almost everywhere."[28] Undoubtedly Admiral Heye, who in 1953 entered the Federal German Parliament as the Christian Democrat Deputy for Wilhelmshaven, was the kind of figure that had aroused Tetens's anger. In the postwar period a discrete veil was drawn over some passages of history, while it became politically useful to stress the gallantry of German forces from 1939 to 1945. In the cold war old enemies became new friends.

The publication of *Swastika at Sea: The Struggle and Destruction of the German Navy, 1939–1945* in 1953 was an important step in the changing history of the Kriegsmarine. Written by former Kriegsmarine sailor Cajus Bekker, it had the full cooperation of a number of former admirals. The tone of the book was particularly significant. Throughout, the German navy was depicted as proud and professional, but there was also a note of defiance and determination. On the final page Bekker recalls the encounter between Fregattenkapitän Gunther Hessler, Dönitz's son-in-law, and representatives of the British Admiralty mission to Flensburg in May 1945. Asked for his thoughts on the likely operational performance of the type XXI electro-boat,

Hessler responded: "Perhaps I may refer you to what your Prime Minister has said. We had the opportunity to read the summary that Mr. Churchill gave in his broadcast of 13th of May. If I remember aright, he said: 'The Germans had prepared a new U-boat fleet and novel tactics which, though we should have eventually destroyed them, might well have carried the U-boat warfare back to the high peak days of 1942.'" One of Hessler's interrogators went on to counter that he thought Churchill was "slightly at fault" in his analysis and that "by comparison 1942 would have been child's play."[29] As early as 1953 the assertion that but for the failure of the land forces the German navy might have secured victory for Germany had been added to the new narrative of defeat.

Also noteworthy in the book is the foreword in which Bekker recorded his "special thanks . . . to Admiral Theodor Krancke and Konteradmiral Gerhard Wagner, who by reason of their all-embracing knowledge of the events described have watched over the historical accuracy of the whole."[30] Indeed, Krancke and Wagner provided testimonials to support the historical accuracy of the book. Those same admirals, together with General Admiral Wilhelm Marschall, Admiral Werner Fuchs, Vice Admirals Wegener and Ruge, and Rear Admirals Godt and Meyer, also supported Edward Von Der Porten's *The German Navy in World War Two* published in 1969.[31] Dönitz provided the foreword and a testimonial to the book. The testimonials provided by the likes of Dönitz and Krancke were written at a time when the endorsement of books by major figures in a particular field was less than common. They were also at pains to support the veracity of the account being presented—as if they were giving a seal of approval to a particular narrative of history.

The guiding hand of the old admirals could still be found as late as 1971 with the publication of *Hitler's Naval War*. Written by Cajus Bekker this was the first popular history of the WWII German navy to be written after naval records seized in 1945 were returned to Germany. Dönitz's longevity (he lived until Christmas Eve 1980) meant that he was a major force shaping the understanding of historians on the wartime period for more than 35 years after its conclusion. By the time of his death a consensus had been established on the German navy in the Second World War and the navy's role in the evolution and eclipse of the Third Reich. Dönitz and his admirals had played a major role in that process, and the result was not wholly unfavorable to them.

The admirals called on to write essays by the Department of Naval Intelligence can be divided into roughly two groups dependent largely on their political fortunes in the German navy. With the exception of Schulz (1916), they had entered the navy in or before 1914, and during the First World War they saw combat in a variety of roles.[32] Dönitz served aboard the cruiser *Breslau* in the Mediterranean before transferring to the U-boat service in 1916. He commanded the mine-layer UC-25 from 1917 to 1918, and then UB-68 before she was forced to surface on 23 October 1918. Dönitz was a POW until his release in 1919. Heye and Schuster similarly served in U-boats, and Krancke and Schniewind in torpedo boats. Their later contemporaries like Raeder and Canaris, who would serve as head of German military intelligence from 1935 to 1944 until implicated in the Hitler bomb plot, served in cruisers.[33]

During the 1920s they rose slowly through the ranks of a much-reduced Kriegsmarine with Dönitz commanding surface vessels and Heye being appointed to command a torpedo boat in 1926. With the expansion of the German navy after 1933 the chances of promotion increased dramatically. In 1937 Schniewind was appointed rear admiral: two years after Schuster had been awarded that rank. Dönitz was appointed to command the first U-boat flotilla in 1935 and became a rear admiral in 1939. The start of the war would see the promotion of some of the younger officers such as Krancke, who became Kapitän zur See in command of the *Admiral Scheer*. Heye would hold the same rank and would command the *Admiral Hipper*. During the war they continued to climb the promotions ladder, but sea commands rapidly gave way to shore-based work. In 1941 Krancke, who acquired something of a public profile because of the commerce-raiding success of the *Admiral Scheer* while under his command in 1940, was promoted to rear admiral and took up the appointment of Admiralty Staff Division for Supplies. In 1943 he became admiral and commander in chief west. He also became a star of the newsreels when he inspected the defenses of *Festung Europa* and received visitors such as Dönitz. Heye, meanwhile, held a shore command on the Black Sea before becoming a rear admiral in 1942. After Dönitz took control of the navy in 1943 a wave of retirements and semiretirements followed including that of Boehm, Schniewind, and Schuster.

If the admirals as a group are interesting, on an individual basis they are fascinating. For example, though Heye was of comparatively junior rank for much of the 1930s and the war period, his impact on the German navy was noteworthy. In 1938 Heye, then Kapitan zur See, was asked by Raeder to write a plan for waging naval war against Britain.[34] That the youngest staff officer should be commissioned to write such a paper was evidence of his considerable capabilities. Heye's plan caused consternation among the older admirals, for it suggested that the navy should move away from a preoccupation with big gun surface actions like Jutland and Dogger Bank. Instead the German navy was to concentrate on the war on trade as the means to bring Britain to the point of surrender. Heye's plan provoked heated debate in the planning committee of the German Admiralty headed by Vice Admiral Guse. The resulting compromise, envisaging a war on trade and the development of 56,000-ton battleships capable of hunting down elements of the British fleet spread across the oceans by the war on trade, was enshrined in the naval building program, which became known as Plan Z.[35] Heye was one of the rising stars of the German navy and one of its principal theoreticians. However, in 1938 he remained skeptical of the value of the submarine, believing that the countermeasures developed toward the end of WWI had much reduced its value as a weapon in the trade war he envisaged. Later on he was to sharply revise his opinions.

From April 1939 to September 1940 Heye commanded the heavy cruiser *Admiral Hipper*. He took part in the Norwegian campaign including *Hipper*'s engagement with the destroyer HMS *Glowworm*. *Hipper* was damaged as the British destroyer rammed the far larger German vessel. After this he served as chief of staff, Naval Group North. In February 1943 Dönitz pressed his chief of personnel, Rear Admiral Baltzer, to secure Heye's release from his position as chief of staff to the admiral commanding the fleet. Dönitz wanted Heye to head a new department responsible for commando attacks, assault frogmen, and midget submarines. Baltzer refused to allow Heye's transfer. However, Baltzer's replacement, Admiral Weichold, was unable to prevent the transfer, and in April 1944 Heye assumed a new command, the small battle units command (Kleinkampfverbande). Influenced by the successful attack on the battleship *Tirpitz* in September 1943 by British x-craft midget submarines, Heye's task was to oversee the development of a range of midget submarines for operation in inshore waters against the anticipated cross-channel invasion. He wanted recruits to the new organization to show initiative and daring. As he later recalled: "The K-force aimed at the idea of Nelson's 'band of brothers'—a concept that was not so easy to achieve in the last phase of the war, when suitable leaders were at a premium, and operational conditions increasingly severe."[36] Yet again Heye was being called on to be Kriegsmarine's principal innovator, and Dönitz was prepared to give him an unusual degree of power. The Kleinkampfverbande was freed from the complicated hierarchy into which other Kriegsmarine units fitted. Heye was given considerable autonomy over every aspect of his unit, with the exception of operational control. In part, this arose out of a recognition that the invasion was imminent and that the small battle units might prove a decisive weapon if they could be developed in time. Heye still faced massive problems of supply, design, and personnel. However, he proved equal to the task. As Mallmann Showell has commented: "The amazing thing about the Midget weapons Unit was that it started as just a collection of quick-thinking, unconventional men without weapons and in a few months it was organized and had a variety of ingenious devices."[37]

In all, seven different kinds of attack craft were developed including six types of midget submarines manned by one to three men. The Small Battle Units Group also developed an explosive, radio-controlled motorboat code-named Lentil (Linsen). The human pilot would take the boat close to its target then jump overboard, allowing control to be assumed by a command boat via radio. The Lentil was developed from Italian explosive motorboats that had proved less than successful in the Mediterranean from 1940 onward. Hitler was an enthusiastic supporter of the Kleinkampfverbande, which he felt certain would inflict massive damage on the Allied invasion fleet. However, not until late June 1944 did the first elements of Heye's command begin arriving in the channel to confront an already successful invasion. As the Allied foothold in France expanded, the Kleinkampfverbande was forced to operate farther and farther from Normandy. The remaining elements of the small battle units command finished the war fighting in the Scheldt estuary and on the Dutch coast. Considering Heye's reputation as a technical and strategic innovator it was not surprising that at the end of the war the Royal Navy should have been eager to interrogate him.

If the career histories of the German admirals selected by the Department of Naval Intelligence to write essays help explain the particular interest in them, they also help explain the literary approaches of some of the admirals. Admiral Weichold served as the commandant of the Naval Academy and principal staff officer to the admiral of the fleet. From 1940 onward he served as liaison officer with the Italian navy. In February 1943 he was relieved of his command; Dönitz sent Rear Admiral Meendsen-Bohlken to replace him. The evacuation of Axis forces from North Africa called for the practical combat experience that Weichold lacked. Back in Germany, Weichold, on the suggestion of Rear Admiral Baltzer, the chief of personnel for the Kriegsmarine, was appointed head of the navy's Kleinkampfverbande. Dönitz replaced him just over a year later because he felt Weichold lacked the necessary aggressive spirit. As Dönitz commented rather acidly in his memoirs during his time in charge of the Kleinkampfverbande, "Vice-Admiral Weichold confined himself mainly to working out theoretical principles."[38] Weichold had been handicapped by interdepartmental rivalry, and Dönitz fully expected his replacement, Vice Admiral Heye, to overcome such problems with stronger leadership. Weichold had a reputation as a thinker, rather than a man of action, and for much of his career he was only too ready to encourage this impression. In all probability he was flattered to be interrogated by British Naval Intelligence at the end of the war and reasonably happy to write an essay giving his thoughts on the war at sea.

Inevitably, there are deficiencies in the essays. They were for the most part, as Grossadmiral Dönitz pointed out in the preface to his essay, "written from memory without any kind of documentary support."[39] Dönitz did get Admiral Wagner, who had served on the Operations Division of the naval staff throughout the war, to confirm as many of the dates and details as possible. Inaccuracies were, nevertheless, inevitable. Vice Admiral Heye complains in the preface to his essay about the "short time" at his disposal to write the essay, which limited the range of topics on which he felt able to write.[40] Vice Admiral Weichold similarly complained at the rush to write an essay "in the allotted time of two weeks."[41] He decided to restrict himself to "particular spheres and problems." As scholarly history the essays were clearly deficient, and the reader should view them as a form of oral history, with all the consequent pitfalls of memory, embroidery, and personal bias.

This bias is particularly evident in the diversity of opinion within the German Admiralty between 1933 and 1945 on strategic and, occasionally, tactical questions. Despite popular conceptions, the Nazi state was no totalitarian monolith under the direction of one all-seeing individual. Rather it was a competitive anarchy in which the fortunes of groups rose and fell. A man like Albert Speer could rise to become minister for industrial production even though he was an architect by trade. Likewise, Hellmuth Heye could rise quickly through the ranks because he, like Speer, was extremely good at getting the job done. Competition for favor and influence was acute but individuals of real merit could advance. "Office politics," as a term describing the interactions between individuals in the workplace, might have been invented after 1945, but it has relevance to the world of the German admiral from 1933 onward. Their workplace extended across a range of commands scattered across Europe and the high seas but the political struggles were fought within the German Admiralty. The admirals were by no means of one mind and the essays highlight that fact as well as the changing fortunes of some of the key figures of the German navy. Hermann Boehm had been one of those in favor until Dönitz replaced Raeder in 1943. Forced to make way for younger men like Krancke and Heye, he finished his essay with the events of March 1943. He commented that after this "I had no further influence in the war."[42] Evident within the conclusion to his essay is the pain of a career sailor sidelined in the midst of a war. He was not prepared to comment on the strategies of those who had succeeded him.

The navy was also prey to the "high politics" of the Nazi regime. Herman Goering the head of the Luftwaffe was an empire builder by nature. As the essays reveal, he had a long-running and highly detrimental struggle with the navy over the question of naval aviation. Plan Z called for the development of two aircraft carriers, but Goering was determined that the Luftwaffe should control all aviation. Thus the aircraft for the proposed carriers were to be adaptations of existing types flown by Luftwaffe personnel. Of far greater significance was the routine failure to cooperate between naval and air operations. The potential for Luftwaffe aircraft to direct submarines toward convoys was never realized owing to operational and technical difficulties. Similarly the cooperation between Luftwaffe and Kriegsmarine in bringing all arms to bear in the Mediterranean and against the North Russian convoys left something to be desired. Raeder feared the ambitions of Goering. His final act as commander in chief in 1943 was to ask Hitler to protect his successor and the navy from Goering's ambitions.

Goering was not the only threat to the navy. Reinhard Heydrich, who became second in importance to Heinrich Himmler in the SS organization, had a particular loathing of the navy and of Raeder in particular. In 1922 he had entered the navy, but his promising career had come to an end in 1931 when Raeder had forced him to resign for "conduct unbecoming an officer and a gentleman." His dreams of becoming an admiral had foundered on a sexual relationship with the daughter of a shipyard director and his subsequent refusal to marry her. Later that same year he had joined the SS and his progress had been meteoric. In government and party circles from 1933 until his assassination in 1942 Heydrich was an outspoken critic of Raeder and the navy. The essays capture something of the essence of the high politics of the Nazi dictatorship.

Unsurprisingly the essays have considerable autobiographical value in what they reveal of their authors not only in terms of their fluctuating careers but also in terms of their personalities. While Boehm is embittered, Weichold emerges as loftily academic in his opinions. He seems determined to help shape how historians would write about the war in the Mediterranean and his role in it. Dönitz shows his overwhelming interest in the submarine campaign, and Heye his skills in improvisation. The essays reveal as much about the personalities of their writers as they do about their subject matter. In every sense they give unique insights into the war at sea and into the thinking of some its principal architects.

Notes

1. Fuehrer Naval Conference, 18 April 1945, reproduced in J. P. Mallmann Showell, *Fuehrer Conferences on Naval Affairs, 1939–45* (London: Greenhill, 1990).

2. L. Peillard, *Geschicte des U-Boot Krieges 1939–1945* (Munich: Wilhelm Heyne Verlag, 1970), 374.

3. Report on visit of Naval Representative to the German Admiralty at Flensburg, 21–24 May 1945, TNA: PRO ADM 1/18222.

4. International Military Tribunal, *Trial of the Major War Criminals* (Nuremberg: Tribunal Secretariat, 1948), 8:278.

5. Report on Admiral Friedeberg's death by Captain H. Davies, 1st Battalion, Cheshire Regiment, TNA: PRO ADM 1/18362.

6. Report on visit of Naval Representative to the German Admiralty at Flensburg, 21–24 May 1945, TNA: PRO ADM 1/18222.

7. Interview with Vice Admiral Heye and his staff contained in report on visit of Naval Representative to the German Admiralty at Flensburg, 21–24 May 1945, TNA: PRO ADM 1/18222.

8. M. Williams, *Captain Gilbert Roberts, R.N., and the Anti-U-boat School* (London: Cassell, 1979), 144.

9. Interview with Rear Admiral Meyer contained in report on visit of naval representative to the German Admiralty at Flensburg, 21–24 May 1945, TNA: PRO ADM 1/18222.

10. Interview with Admiral Weichold contained in report on visit of naval representative to the German Admiralty at Flensburg, 21–24 May 1945, TNA: PRO ADM 1/18222.

11. R. Overy, *Interrogations: The Nazi Elite in Allied Hands, 1945* (London: Allen Lane, 2001), 86.

12. Visit to prisoner of war camp at Allendorf (near Marburg) on 20 March 1946, TNA: PRO ADM 228/67.

13. Extracts of a letter from Vice Admiral Heye telephoned to Admiralty, 6 February 1946, TNA: PRO ADM 228/67.

14. Report on statements made by Kapitan-zur-See Loffler, February 1946, TNA: PRO ADM 228/67.

15. Quoted in A. V. Sellwood, *The Warring Seas* (London: White Lion, 1956), 226.

16. Letter from Rudolf Stange, 14 February 1946, TNA: PRO ADM 228/67.

17. Major General A. A. B. Dowler, Headquarters British Army of the Rhine, to Vice Admiral H. T. C. Walker, 31 March 1946, TNA: PRO ADM 228/67.

18. Vice Admiral H. T. C. Walker to Headquarters BAOR, 4 April 1946, TNA: PRO ADM 228/67.

19. For an interesting assessment of Dönitz's personality see Peter Kemp, "Grand Admiral Karl Doenitz," in *The War Lords: Military Commanders of the Twentieth Century,* ed. Michael Carver (London: Weidenfeld and Nicolson, 1976), 483–84.

20. Address to the officer corps, 22 May 1945, in P. Padfield, *Dönitz: The Last Fuehrer* (London: Victor Gollancz, 1993), 432.

21. Ibid., 433.

22. K. Dönitz, *Memoirs: Ten Years and Twenty Days* (London: Weidenfeld and Nicolson, 1959), 477.

23. Vice Admiral Walker to Commander in Chief British Zone of Occupation, 26 August 1946, TNA: PRO FO 1030/150.

24. Ibid.

25. Interrogation report, 7 September 1945, reproduced in R. Overy, *Interrogations,* 555. Schacht, who finished the war in Dachau, would eventually be found not guilty on all charges.

26. R. Overy, *Interrogations,* 163.

27. A. Martienssen, *Hitler and His Admirals* (London: Morrison and Gibb, 1948).

28. T. H. Tetens, *The New Germany and the Old Nazis* (London: Secker and Warburg, 1961), 37.

29. C. D. Bekker, *Swastika at Sea: The Struggle and Destruction of the German Navy, 1939–1945* (London: William Kimber, 1953), 207.

30. Ibid., 6. Wagner continued to give his help to Bekker after this. See for example C. D. Bekker, *Verdammte See* (Berlin: Ullstein, 1971), 9.

31. E. Von Der Porten, *The German Navy in World War Two* (London: Arthur Baker, 1970).

32. See H. H. Hildebrand and E. Henriot, *Deutschlands Admirale, 1849–1945,* 3 vols. (Osnabruck: Biblio Verlag, 1988–90).

33. A. Brissaud, *Canaris* (London: Weidenfeld and Nicolson, 1970).

34. See C. Bekker, *The German Navy, 1939–45* (London: Chancellor Press, 1997), 34–38.

35. Plan Z originated from Hitler's conclusion in the summer of 1938 that reluctantly Germany had to prepare for war against Britain. He therefore asked Raeder to make the necessary preparations. The plan went through various evolutions from the summer of 1938 onward, but it had been finalized by February 1939. The German navy would consist of: 6 battleships of 56,000 tons; 2 battleships (*Bismarck* and *Tirpitz*) of 42,000 tons; 2 battleships (*Scharnhorst* and *Gneisenau*) of 31,000 tons; 3 battle cruisers of 31,000 tons; 3 pocket battleships; and 2 aircraft carriers. The fleet would be supported by cruisers, destroyers, and submarines. Raeder intended to operate the major surface units in three groups: the *Bismarck-* and *Scharnhorst*-type battleships would remain in home waters; the battle cruisers and pocket battleships would be sent into

the Atlantic to attack British trade; and the 56,000-ton battleships would operate as a hunter-killer group tracking down elements of the British fleet deployed to try and protect the trade routes. Plan Z was a recognition, heavily influenced by Heye, that to defeat Britain the war on trade would probably be more effective than major surface engagements. It was also a recognition of the inadequacy of Germany's shipbuilding infrastructure. Big ships required considerable know-how, facilities and specialist skills. Each ship that was built expanded the infrastructure to the point where bigger projects could be undertaken. Thus there was to be no leap from pocket battleship to the 56,000-ton type envisaged under Plan Z. Developmental difficulties were to seriously affect the development of the German fleet, especially with regard to the development of propulsion units for large surface vessels. "Engine problems" sharply limited the efficiency of a number of ships including the *Admiral Scheer* and the *Hipper*.

36. H. Heye, preface to C. D. Bekker, *K-Men* (Maidstone: George Mann, 1968), 5.

37. J. P. Mallmann Showell, *German Navy Handbook, 1939–1945* (Stroud: Sutton Publishing, 1999), 164.

38. K. Dönitz, *Memoirs: Ten Years and Twenty Days* (London: Weidenfeld and Nicolson, 1959), 369–70.

39. Essay by Grand Admiral Karl Dönitz, 24 September 1945, TNA: PRO ADM 223/688.

40. Essay by Vice Admiral Heye, 15 October 1945, TNA: PRO ADM 223/690.

41. Essay by Vice Admiral Weichold, 26 November 1945, TNA: PRO ADM 233/797.

42. Essay by General Admiral Herman Boehmn, TNA: PRO ADM 223/692.

1

The Prewar Period

THE GERMAN ADMIRALS who, as prisoners of war, sat down in
1945 to write essays for their British captors were weighed down by the experience of being on the losing side in two World Wars. As young officers
they had joined the powerful German navy built up by Admiral Tirpitz
before 1914, and their memories went back to the Battle of Jutland, the
shameful mutinies of 1918, the flight of Kaiser Wilhelm II, and the scut-
tling of the fleet at Scapa Flow on 21 June 1919 in one last gesture of defiance. Vice Admiral Heye sums up what that previous defeat had taught
the men who were to lead the German navy in the Second World War.

Admiral Raeder and all expert naval officers held the opinion that the
1914–18 war was lost because of Anglo-American sea power. The outcome
of land battles was only the result of Anglo-American superiority at sea.

**Vice Admiral Weichold considers that, outside the navy, that view was
not widely shared.**

Germany lost World War I, 1914–18, because she failed to break British sea
power. All the successes of the German army on the Continent were negated
by the course of the war at sea. Every means of pressure used by the Allies,
which led to the collapse of the central powers in 1918, [depended on] British
sea power. Moreover, the last decisive battle that was fought on the continent
was only made possible by the exercise of sea power. The outcome of the
1914–18 war taught, therefore, that a European war in which Great Britain

participated must essentially be a sea war and would be decided by sea power. Germany, in her geographical position on the continent, did not understand this lesson, and instead made the Revolution of 1918 responsible for the loss of the war.

Accordingly, in the twenty years following the First World War the continental outlook of the German people did not change much. German leadership carried on a policy without regard for world powers and sea power.

Among the humiliating clauses imposed by the victorious Allies in the Treaty of Versailles in 1919 were a set of severe limitations on the size and equipment of the postwar German navy. Heye explains the difficulties of the tiny force allowed to the Weimar Republic.

In 1919 the small German navy consisted of fifteen thousand men [and] a few obsolete vessels without all the special craft that comprise a fleet. . . . Internal confusion, repeated attempts at revolution, and the lack of modern material considerably hindered the building up of the small navy.

When minesweeping was completed, training and the development of the simplest tactics had to be begun practically from scratch. Similarly, new methods of education and discipline were introduced. As a result of the 1918 disarmament, the navy had lost many valuable officers and, in the first few years after 1919, bore the characteristics of a navy in training. Preparations for a speedy expansion could not be made at that time. Money for material and government assent were not forthcoming. The position of the ratings was at first very difficult.

Although the Treaty of Versailles explicitly prohibited Germany from acquiring U-boats, General Admiral Schniewind and Admiral Schuster in their joint essay admit that the tiny navy continued to take an interest in that weapon.

Those small sea powers, who owing to their financial capabilities or international position were unable to build a large fleet, did not renounce the U-boat as "a defensive weapon for weak sea powers." It was, therefore, understandable if the conception was repeatedly expressed in studies, war games, and maneuvers in the German navy, that even a weak U-boat arm would improve the already threatening naval strategic position of the Reich in the Baltic (Poland, Russia, and plans for breakthrough by French naval forces). Naval forces operating against an opponent from whom they had absolutely no fears of U-boat attack possess resources and freedom of action that would be considerably prejudiced by the mere sight of a periscope or of a U-boat torpedo track.

These—and not questions of prestige and/or the attainment of equal rights—were the reasons why the German navy, even in the years when it was most restricted from the political, financial, and personnel point of view, did not abandon its connection with the development of the building and employment of U-boats.

Heye shows how the Versailles restrictions forced the German navy into innovations in surface ship design in order to make the best possible use of the permitted tonnage, and he makes the important point that the navy was able to select personnel of very high quality.

The new construction allowed under the Treaty of Versailles began with the *Emden*. In order to have at least one more or less modern ship, she was built according to plans of 1918. New plans were drawn up for subsequent ships; here arose the first major difficulties in shipbuilding. Attempts were made to install all modern improvements in the few ships allowed. They had at the same time to be training ships, experimental ships, and warships. In consequence, very complicated and overloaded types resulted since, instead of more ships being built, all reserve materials were carried in one ship. The widespread choice of officers and men, which was aided by growing unemployment, made it possible to obtain well-educated personnel who were fit to serve in more complicated ships.

The building up of the navy within the limits allowed by the peace treaty was at that time based only to a small extent on practical requirements and definite operational intentions. The fundamental idea was to put the best possible armament on these ships by using to the fullest the permitted tonnage and by saving weight, for example, by welding. New paths were explored with armored ships, whose construction was chiefly made possible by the use of motors. The greater endurance gained thereby at first played a smaller role than armor and armament. The construction of the armored ships then led to the development of new "tip and run" tactics. It was, however, clear that these tactics were only possible against an enemy whose superiority did not appear too great. These armored ships were at first frequently criticized until their teething troubles were overcome.

The three armored ships (*panzerschiffe*) were nicknamed pocket battleships by the British, but at a nominal 10,000 tons and with 11-inch guns as main armament, they were not true battleships of the type found in

other navies. Schniewind and Schuster claim that the decision to go ahead with the pocket battleships was a victory for those German naval officers who wished to retain an oceangoing capability over those who would have preferred to see the permitted tonnage expended on vessels more suitable for limited roles in the Baltic and southeastern waters of the North Sea.

The largest ship that the Versailles Treaty allowed Germany was a type of 10,000 tons. It was discussed in German naval circles for a long while as to what type of vessel of 10,000 tons should be built. Opinions varied between a minor type of vessel corresponding roughly to the *Schleswig-Holstein* and a type similar to the armored ships. It was decided on the latter because it was believed that, with it, the idea of a *sea*faring navy could most easily be achieved and furthered; to retain the navy at that time was considered to be the most important ideal aim. That these armored vessels had a comparatively heavy armament and their engines a good speed and wide cruising range was naturally very welcome. No definite strategic, operational, or tactical purposes were proposed in the planning. These came later when the value of the vessels was realized (blockade war, group tactics). . . . The opinion often expressed to me that the armored vessels were obviously built from the beginning for surface blockade war—clearly against England—is false.

The continued hostility of Poland and France forced the navy of the Weimar Republic to make contingency plans for a defensive war, but General Admiral Boehm is at pains to point out that, at that period, the Germans assumed that Britain would not be an enemy.

The foreign policy of a great state is most clearly expressed in its naval policy and naval construction. If the development of the German war machine is to be dealt with, something must be said about German foreign policy and (this has to be included) naval policy.

Following the early years of naval reconstruction, the building of pocket battleships gave the first indication of naval policy that arose from the threat of the then very strong Poland (as far as land forces were concerned when compared with Germany), and particularly in view of her alliance with France. The naval command had no illusions in regard to the limited military possibilities but, on the other hand, realized quite clearly that military operations might be necessary.

The naval high command was, however, perfectly aware that a conflict with Poland would also probably bring about a war with France and that we could not carry this on alone. The aim of our efforts was therefore . . .

to build up our small fighting forces and to make them [so] efficient as to bring [an] alliance within our reach. At that time, therefore, the basic idea of the naval high command was to prepare for a short counteraction against any Polish aggression and, by securing supplies from overseas, also against France. In this connection there was the assumption from the beginning that French forces would also be tied down elsewhere and that, above all, England would show toward us a benevolent neutrality. Such ideas may have been called utopian, but there appeared no other possibilities for us. We were not prepared to resign ourselves to our fate, but meant to use what small power we had. However this may be, one thing is certain: in the period up to 1933 the naval policy depended entirely on coming to an understanding with England and on the efforts of the German government and the Foreign Office to secure this end. [On] this there was complete agreement.

The German navy had to exist amid the recurrent financial and political crises that marked the short life of the Weimar Republic in Germany. Heye suggests rather tentatively that most of the more experienced officers in the German navy were inclined to remain aloof from the political tensions and that, while they accepted the need for stable government, the senior officers were not, at that time, committed supporters of Hitler's Nazi Party.

The internal unity of the navy, especially of the officer corps, was very good. As with many other Germans, the opinion was held in the navy too that a consolidation of the internal policy was of primary importance. Without this, no thought of foreign policy could be entertained. The radical parties did not gain many friends among the middle classes and the officer corps as a whole, but through public demonstrations they won favor with the youth, workers, and younger members of the officer corps. With the failure of the middle-class parties, German youth saw no other possibility open to it. The naval staff, and especially Grossadmiral Raeder, had great hopes of Brüning's government, until the events of the winter of 1932–33 permitted no other solution than the formation of a government under Hitler with all parties except the Communists included. The presidency of Hindenburg was a guarantee of continued development. These matters did not affect the navy as much as the home front.

Grand Admiral Dönitz asserts that, at the time Adolf Hitler rose to power in Germany, the German armed forces on land and sea and in the air, were effectively condemned to impotence.

When the Führer, Adolf Hitler, assumed power on 30 January 1933, the German Wehrmacht found itself in a position of impotency, in accordance with the stipulations of the Versailles Treaty. The strength of the German army was one hundred thousand men; there was no German air force. The navy had not yet attained even the modest strength allowed it in the Versailles Treaty. With a total strength of fifteen thousand men, there were six new light cruisers available, each of 6,000 tons; the torpedo boats had been brought up to the permitted number of twenty-four by the construction of twelve new ships; of the pocket battleships of the *Deutschland* class, only one ship— the *Deutschland* itself—had been completed, while two more, *Scheer* and *Graf Spee,* were building. The three other pocket battleships, which could have been built under the treaty, had not yet been ordered.

Heye looks at the first consequences of Hitler's rise to power and describes the technique adopted by Grand Admiral Raeder, commander in chief of the Kriegsmarine since 1928, in his dealings with the new chancellor.

Rearmament was not at first affected to any marked degree when Adolf Hitler took over the government. The armed forces expected the authority of the state, and with it the state's armed potential, that is, the armed forces, to be strengthened. The abolition of unemployment promised by the new government and a few other social principles were, in the eyes of most Germans, capable of forming the basis of a uniform way of thinking in Germany and of removing class distinctions.

Adolf Hitler did not at first play any part at all in the internal building up of the armed forces and in their organization. His opinion was that this task should be left to professional experts. Apprehension within the navy that its interests and those of the sea would suffer under the new government was soon dispelled. From Hitler's earlier statements one had to assume that the navy would be put at a disadvantage. Grossadmiral Raeder attempted from the very beginning, just as he had done with former chancellors, to arouse an understanding for shipping and the navy. With his age and impartiality, he succeeded in increasing measure, but did not fully achieve his real aim. He gained the confidence of Adolf Hitler and also of [War] Minister Blomberg by limiting himself to his own task. His statements always proved their point. Very often, against the wishes of the officer corps, he refused to exploit his influence with Adolf Hitler in order to deal with questions not connected with the navy. He only attempted conferences when ordered to do so, and, when answering questions, limited himself to those put to him directly. Only in rare and decisive cases did he seize the initiative and get his

Hitler's Admirals

proposals and ideas accepted. During this period his leadership of the navy was very centralized and unified. In consequence the navy was to the very end more compact than was the case with the army, for example.

After the retirement of Blomberg—and later too—Admiral Raeder's aim was to succeed in unifying the navy, even at this difficult time, and to build it up organically into an instrument of war. To this aim he sacrificed wishes that to him, as commander in chief, did not seem attainable. He attempted to keep the navy clear of all political difficulties.

Schniewind and Schuster set out the reasons why Germany needed a bigger fleet in those days, but they emphasize that even planning for expansion took time.

Especially after 1933 it was the unbiased opinion of the well-informed leading personalities that [a fleet] was indispensable in view of the increasing overseas trade and the interests representing Germany abroad, added to which it was hoped to regain colonies within a reasonable space of time— to my knowledge several discussions with England had taken place—and this too was scarcely conceivable without a navy. Furthermore . . . friction leading to war could result from Germany's position in Europe and thus endanger her home coastline and the German sea communications. [This possibility] was not altogether out of the question (Poland, Russia). For that purpose the existence of a fighting German navy was essential.

A navy of the strength laid down by the Versailles Treaty seemed sufficient against Poland and perhaps Baltic Russia. However, it no longer corresponded to the Reich's prestige at sea and the German interests, investments, and complications abroad. It was, in no case, sufficient for a warlike discussion with France, who had already reacted to the building of the armored ships by building the ships *Dunkerque* and *Strasbourg*.

It was announced in the Führer's speeches, after his advent to power and in official and semiofficial statements, that the Führer intended to place at the forefront of his program of government the re-creating of Germany as a well-respected, independent power, freed from all the military and territorial ties of [the Treaty of] Versailles, and having some independent and esteemed position in the world; and furthermore, to bring the German-speaking peoples of central Europe into closer contact with the Reich. In these aims he was fulfilling the earnest desires and strivings of all honor-loving and self-respecting nations, and he felt himself to be in complete accord with the right of self-determination of the nations that has been proclaimed since 1918.

A strong army, in conjunction with a healthy progressive home policy and economic life, should form the basis upon which the road toward the self-realization of these aims is built.

The rearmament plans and the measures preparatory thereto were, therefore, to come in immediately after the 1933 swing-round to National Socialism, without being based on premeditated warlike intentions. From statements made by the Führer and from his book *Mein Kampf*, and from things that he said to me personally, it was particularly made known that he would endeavor to pursue his political aims without, under any circumstances, bringing about a warlike conflict with England.

In the first stages after the advent to power (1933–35) the only real progress toward the arming of the navy was on the planning and theoretical side, because it was in connection with the navy that the conditions of the Treaty of Versailles were particularly rigid and narrow, as it was in the sphere of naval affairs that friction with England appeared to be most likely to occur, and such possibilities of friction before work had commenced on the rebuilding had to be removed by means of an agreement with England (naval treaty, 1935).

Practical expressions of the rebuilding of the navy before 1935 only took the form of:

> strengthening the personnel complements in all categories;
> intensifying and enlarging the activities of the [naval training] schools;
> preparing for the building of U-boats.

Rear Admiral Schulz draws attention to the manpower problem.

[After 1933] the first concern was to ease the acute shortage of personnel in the navy since, in consequence of the numerical limitation to fifteen thousand men and in the face of the manifold tasks of a modern navy, a serious shortage of manpower was evident all round.

Dönitz explains why Hitler wished to expand the German armed forces, and he emphasizes the importance attached to maintaining good relations with Britain.

It was part of the Führer's policy to create again for the German people, along with the restoration of their honor, an adequate Wehrmacht, which would be in a position suitably to represent the interests of the Reich. The central position of Germany in the heart of Europe compelled her to place the emphasis on rearmament first on the weapons of land warfare, that is on the army and air force, as only these latter were in a position to secure the extended and unprotected land frontiers against the large number of hostile continental neighbors, thus creating the first prerequisite for domestic reconstruction. Consequently the navy had, of necessity, to modify its armament demands.

That was all the more possible as the Führer was striving for a political agreement with England, having always regarded Bolshevik Russia as the arch enemy of Germany and Europe; none of the great naval powers, therefore, was considered to be among the future opponents of Germany.

This policy of the Führer found its consummation in 1935 with the conclusion of the naval agreement with England. . . . This clearly showed that Germany did not reckon with a war against England, as she voluntarily renounced arming against English sea power.

The Anglo-German naval agreement of 1935 is also cited by Boehm as evidence that, even under Hitler, German naval policy was not preparing for war with Britain.

As is known, Germany left the Disarmament Conference . . . and also the League of Nations, as the discrimination of the latter was not acceptable. Being, from her point of view, free of any further restrictions, Germany could have commenced the construction of larger and more heavily armed ships. This, however, would have upset our relations with England and, as I have already mentioned, was not carried forward in compliance with the views of the Führer. It was thus that German shipbuilding policy—for example the building of *Scharnhorst* and *Gneisenau*—was influenced out of consideration for England.

In spite of all [Hitler's] endeavors to loosen the bonds of Versailles, the English mentality was taken into account during the construction of our fleet. Thus, it was due to Hitler's own decision that the first battleships . . . were limited to a displacement of 26,000 tons and [main armament of] a caliber of 28 cm. This was a great disappointment to the navy, who doubted the later effect of this political gesture and because the ships would always be burdened by this weakness.

In March 1935 Germany made her declaration of suzerainty over her armed forces [*Wehrhoheit*]; in June of the same year came the Anglo-German naval treaty with its voluntary limitations.

The strongest expression of Hitler's attitude toward England is shown in the treaty . . . of which the chief points are recognition of the fact that England's existence depended on her having the strongest sea power;

on this account, Germany's voluntarily limiting herself to one-third of England's sea power;

Germany's guaranteeing the British Empire with all her then strong forces.

This treaty was concluded without any counterdemands by Germany, solely to clear the air. I am of the opinion that never was a more generous offer made, nor more honorably meant.

According to the position in 1935, England had a total tonnage of about 1.2 million tons; thus Germany could build up to 400,000 tons, of which 180,000 tons was for battleships.

The views of the great majority of German naval officers on the Anglo-German naval agreement are summed up by Schulz.

The conclusion of the Anglo-German naval treaty was at that time cordially welcomed both by me and by practically the whole corps of German naval officers. If Germany could thereby achieve only the standing of a second-class naval power, such as France or Italy, it was none the less fully appreciated that England, by virtue of her imperial requirements, was fully entitled to a considerably stronger navy, whereas Germany, with her central position and unprotected frontiers, based her defenses primarily on the army and the air force, relegating the navy to a secondary position. This was more particularly so since the security of German sea communications could be far better achieved by a political agreement with England, such as the naval treaty appeared to establish and that conformed to the permanently expressed wish of the German national leaders, than by a far more extensive naval rearmament.

In a major departure from the restrictions imposed in the treaty of Versailles, the Anglo-German naval agreement provided for Germany to begin building U-boats once more. Schniewind and Schuster explain how that was negotiated.

In accordance with earlier statements by the Führer, the readiness of Germany to renounce all U-boat building—naturally with the proviso *si omnes* [i.e., if everybody does the same]—was once again put forward.

The head of the German military delegation had strongly endorsed this interpretation during the oral negotiations, when Britain for her part had

expressed doubt as to any necessity for the German U-boat arm or the justification, in case of necessity, for exceeding the 35 percent (or the 45 percent
agreed for U-boats alone) beyond and up to the British tonnage, which had
been expressly agreed upon for U-boat tonnage of other powers (in contrast
to that of other ships). At this confidential discussion of experts, the standpoint of the Reich's equal right was only touched upon from the German
side. The fact, however, was pointed out that Germany, with the possibility
of a war on two fronts and at sea (Russia with her rapidly increasing naval
strength in the Baltic, together with France in the North Sea, drawing ever
more closely to her politically) must quickly produce part of her embryo
naval armament, or at any rate the U-boat arm.

This could be soonest accomplished by a large number of small U-boats
(which would be unsuitable for attacks on the ocean routes of a sea power
like England) with relatively high fighting power. In order to emphasize the
German aim and to relieve public opinion as to the justification of the agreement, since the British Admiralty and Parliament had been sensitive about
the U-boat arms of other powers ever since World War I, the German delegation already in London made the recorded declaration that Germany was
ready to agree not to use unrestricted U-boat warfare.

> Among German naval officers there were sharp differences of opinion on
> how the navy ought to be expanded within the tonnage limits established
> in the Anglo-German agreement. Rear Admiral Hans Meyer points to
> Grand Admiral Raeder as the decisive influence.

In the battle of arguments relative to the merits of a U-boat fleet or a surface fleet, a decision was made in accordance with the views of Grossadmiral
Raeder for a "healthy mixture" of the whole fleet, a view that was agreed to
by all but a few officers (among whom was Dönitz, later Grossadmiral).

> Dönitz mentions the same decision without actually expressing an opin-
> ion on its merits, although there appears to be a hint of regret that his
> U-boats did not receive a larger share of the available funds.

Apart from the fact that the composition of the projected German fleet was
already extensively fixed by the percentage figures of the treaty, the building
of a fleet was based on the conception of creating a small, homogeneous,
well-balanced fleet, which would be in a position to counter successfully
the fleets of continental neighbors, [such as] France [or] Russia, and which,
moreover, would considerably improve Germany's ability to ally herself with

the great naval powers. This was, at the same time, a reason why Germany, on the basis of experience gained in the First World War, did not at once proceed to build a large U-boat fleet, but on the other hand constructed a symmetrically balanced fleet of all types, conceding only a small part to the U-boat arm.

One of those who had doubts about the doctrine of building up a balanced fleet was Vice Admiral Heye, who sets out the arguments in favor of a weaker naval power departing from orthodox and traditional thinking.

The tremendous difficulties of actually building a fleet became apparent even in the preparatory stage. Opinion in the navy differed even on the manner of creating a fleet. The aim, however, was to have completed blueprints and clear plans ready in case it was permitted by treaty to strengthen the fleet, as in fact later happened as a result of the London conferences.

Questions of correct shipbuilding will always lead to different points of view in all navies. These differences of opinion will increase as the influence of innovations and inventions on warfare, and therefore on shipbuilding, increases. The submarine, the mine, and even to a greater extent, the aircraft, were bound to set shipbuilding policy greater tasks than before 1914. Since before 1933 Germany had practically no fleet, the possibility existed of building a modern fleet according to quite new conceptions.

I personally, along with other officers, held the opinion that the composition of a fleet and the types of ship in it must vary according to the geographical position of the country, the possible strength of its fleet, and its dependence on sea routes. In the definition of the types in a fleet—as laid down at the Washington conference—I saw one of the strongest drawbacks by which a smaller navy would be bound. With the standardization of the world's fleets, the state that engaged the enemy with an inferior number of ships was bound to remain inferior. The difference in the individual types used by different nations could never, in view of the same technical level of these nations, be so great that it could make up for inferiority in numbers. An engagement between a battleship and three enemy battleships, for example, must normally lead to the destruction of the inferior side. By the loss of this ship it loses 100 percent of its forces, while the enemy might lose . . . 30 percent or, at most, 60 percent. I therefore supported the idea of trying other ways. I should have considered it correct not to take over all the Washington types but to search from the first for types that were suitable for another kind of warfare. Since the construction of the German fleet was bound to take many years, a small fleet consisting solely of types similar to those laid down in Washington could, in my opinion, scarcely gain success in defensive engagements.

Quite clearly we had to give up the idea of fleet engagements and to operate against the enemy's weak spots. This would have meant, for example, building first of all a modern U-boat service. For this purpose we should have had to reject the normal types laid down in the Washington treaties and to build special ships with great endurance in accordance with the principle "speedier against the stronger enemy," in order to carry on warfare against merchant shipping. It was clear that, with a fleet of this kind, we could cause damage to the enemy but could [protect] our own sea communications.

Germany had, therefore, to limit her defensive activities to the Baltic and the areas near her coast. Here, with the help of E-boats, the air force, and mines, we could defend our own sea communications even against stronger enemies. Such trains of thought did not prevail, although Admiral Raeder agreed with them to some extent. Within the navy there were strong champions of the classical battleship.

Even Adolf Hitler appeared increasingly interested in shipbuilding. In every case he was in favor of the largest and most strongly armed ship. A certain number of modern ships were, moreover, required very quickly. It would at that time have been possible to construct the "armored ship" [pocket battleship] types, without real alteration in size, [but] with increased speed and more powerful engines. Plans also existed for cruisers and destroyers designed to operate against trade with great endurance, greater speed, and more than one form of propulsion (cruising motors). Instead the heavy 10,000 ton cruisers were built, which in my opinion had little value in view of our geographical position. As a result of the policy of building larger armored ships, *Scharnhorst* and *Gneisenau* were built as an [intermediate] type, and only *Bismarck* and *Tirpitz* could be considered the beginning of a battle-fleet. It was clear that, after the long years when we had no shipbuilding, numerous other naval craft such as E-boats and so on could have been built instead of these types, which at the beginning of the war were only available in small numbers in the German navy.

Heye goes on to spell out some of the logistical problems faced by any country that seeks to pursue a policy of naval rearmament.

Construction [of new naval vessels], ordered to begin but hindered by frequent changes and hesitancy over the types, soon made the difficulties apparent. It was not a question of simply building the ships. The expansion of the navy required the changeover of commercial shipyards to warship production, new harbors, new dock installations, tugs, schools for the personnel, increased recruitment of cadet-officers and ratings, and so on. Large-scale construction was in no way possible, because the material requirements, for example, steel and other raw materials, including even labor, were not available for the complex tasks. They had to be obtained by constant negotiations with other branches of the armed forces and civil departments such as those responsible for building the motorways [autobahnen]. A tremendous amount was planned and begun. Nevertheless progress could not be made so quickly in the case of the navy as, for example, in the case of other branches of the armed forces. As far as I can remember, we could not expect to have a fleet in the terms of the Washington standard of about eight battleships before 1947 or 1948. Construction was made more difficult by overhasty introduction of technical innovations that lacked slow organic development. Motors were rejected and high-pressure steam introduced; this led at first to many setbacks. The navy was still hampered with the task of coastal defense. The relationship between sea and land [postings] therefore had to remain unsatisfactory. Admiral Raeder set great store by a good basic training of sailors ashore especially because of the experiences of the 1918 revolution.

It was clear that a large expenditure on personnel and material was necessary. Closely connected with shipbuilding was the building of schools and arsenals, which alone meant an extensive program. Apart from the difficulties of the actual building of a fleet and its auxiliaries, that is, shipyards, docks, schools, arsenals, and so on, there was the very great difficulty of holding trained officers and men in readiness. On this question Admiral Raeder held the point of view that personnel should be increased only to such an extent that its basic training still appeared guaranteed. The mobilization of former active service and Merchant Marine officers, and of the gradually increasing number of officer cadets and candidates for P.O. [petty officer] rating could not, however, cover requirements. In my opinion, this became especially and decisively noticeable during the war. The shortage of well-trained officers of intermediate rank could not be made up because of the large numbers of U-boats lost. Even the quality and seniority of U-boat commanders and officers in other important posts decreased to a marked degree. All this emphasized the point of view put forward repeatedly by Admiral Raeder that the building of a fleet requires many years.

Thus this whole period 1933–39 was one of great pressure to make up in a short time for the many years of inactivity in naval construction. This was not understood in all departments, neither by commanders in chief nor by other branches of the armed forces. Settled conditions and time for experience were lacking in many of the navy's plans. Of course there was internal friction, too, which could only be overcome by austere leadership and a concentration by the navy on purely naval affairs. One remembers, for example, the Roehm putsch, the dismissal of Generaloberst Fritsch, and the retirement of Blomberg.

That expanding the German navy involved far more than merely building more ships is also mentioned by Dönitz.

Technical development, which before 1933 was retarded through lack of means, was extended and pushed forward energetically. The technical establishments of the navy believed they had produced superior weapons (of first class performance) as regards both mines as well as torpedoes, in spite of the short time for development at their disposal. . . . The significance of shortwaves for locational purposes [i.e., radar] was recognized, their investigation and exploitation were pushed forward, but we did not succeed, as late[r] experience was to show, in attaining the degree of development reached by our enemies in this sphere. . . . In all other spheres of naval war technique we in fact succeeded in making good to some extent the fateful effects of disarmament and military impotence before the outbreak of war. We were convinced that the German U-boat types, especially, represented the best of their kind in the world.

Both Krancke and Weichold obviously feel the navy was something of a Cinderella when it came to financing rearmament, but Krancke is able to detect a possible advantage in this.

Krancke: When our budget was allocated, the navy took second place to the other two branches of the armed forces, since only potential conflicts with neighboring countries were still regarded as politically possible. The slow construction of the fleet that resulted created an opportunity for consolidating discipline and training.

Weichold: After the failure of the Treaty of Versailles, large estimates were made for the building of an army and an air force, but the navy was left to the last. German policy only reckoned on having to deal with difficulties arising from continental neighbors. For such conflicts the creation of sea power did not appear necessary.

The admirals reveal some differences of opinion on the subject of the German navy's deployment off the Spanish coast in support of General Franco's nationalist forces during the Spanish civil war.

Dönitz: Internal reorganization of the navy went hand in hand with the construction of the ships. The navy of fifteen thousand men had provided a good nucleus of fully trained petty officers and seamen, who were of great value. The existing ships were almost exclusively used for training purposes, so as to have crews ready for the new ships in good time. Difficulties did not arise to any great extent. Certain difficulties, however, were caused in home training by the dispatch of strong units of the German fleet to Spain to protect German interests there in the years 1935–39, but they were partly mitigated by the advantage of sea experience, which a large part of the crews there were able to obtain and which was not available to the same extent in home waters.

Boehm: The training of the limited German forces was considerably prejudiced on account of the dispatch of single units to Spanish waters to protect our interests there during the civil war; I myself was busy there in three different sectors. At the same time, we considered, apart from political necessity, that this had some value, as it gave our men some experience far away from home stations and in unusual tasks.

Meyer: All foreign cruises, with the exception of the Spanish civil war and excluding, of course, certain special ceremonial cruises, were made for training, although, naturally, one also expected from them an increase in Germany's international prestige.

The operations of the German navy during the Spanish civil war were carried out with limited means, nothing else being available. Thus, for example, on account of the shortage of efficient destroyers, the torpedo boats (*Wolf* and *Möwe* classes) were used. It was quite a risk to let these go into the Atlantic. Several breakdowns that, had the weather been bad, could have led to serious consequences, showed this very clearly.

The systematic peacetime training became curtailed during the Spanish civil war owing to the lack of ships; the same ones had to do continual duty on the Spanish route. On this account it was the general opinion that the navy was in no way strong enough for these tasks.

Schniewind and Schuster: The Spanish civil war for years kept a large portion of the growing German fleet off the coast of Spain and excluded them from any regular unit or weapon training.

Many of the admirals express their frustration with the inadequate way in which the program of expansion for the German navy made provision for the important contribution that air power could make to future naval operations.

Dönitz: The complete abolition of the air force under the Versailles Treaty and the consequent necessity of developing it afresh from the beginning had led, despite the navy's vigorous efforts to build up its own naval air force, to the Führer's decision to form the flying units required for the navy within the framework of the Luftwaffe. In this way a closer concentration in the development of aircraft types and in all other aeronautical questions was to be attained.

Schniewind and Schuster: After the formation of our own naval air arm had been rejected against the vote of the navy, the navy's demands for aircraft had to be met from general Luftwaffe sources. The navy regarded this as an unsatisfactory state of affairs and even the Führer himself later referred to this as a "historic mistake." It was perhaps right at the time of the building up; in the interests of the concentration of forces and of production potentialities and to guard against any splitting up, an organization such as the navy was endeavoring to get was rather pointless. These arrangements thus ordered were never able, therefore, in any phase of the war to place at our disposal enough [air]craft to satisfy the needs of the navy, neither with regard to the number of units and the suitability of the types of aircraft, nor as regards training and experience of the units in naval warfare. In particular, the aerial torpedo arm, from the point of view of numbers, of technique, and in operation, had not been sufficiently developed and trained. This inadequacy has not been able to be leveled out on account of the transfer of personnel from the navy to the air force, which was at times very considerable (especially officers and W/T [wireless telegraphy] personnel), and because of the intensive cooperation of the navy with the training of air force potential officer material. It must be remembered, too, that the time at our disposal for the completion of these tasks [was] extremely short. The significance of a good naval air arm in modern naval warfare and the difficulties of aerial warfare over the sea and in cooperation with naval forces were, indeed, fully appreciated by the navy, and [were] submitted to high quarters. The authorities, however, did not accept these opinions.

Meyer: The matter of navy–air force cooperation at sea is a story in itself. From the start the navy considered that a naval air force was the only correct and possible solution to operations at sea: the naval air force to be assisted, in case of need, by the land air forces. The navy lost the long battle against the high command of the air force—Göring—and the only thing that came out of all these arguments was a "sea air force," which was to come under the direction of the navy purely for tactical sea operations. In all other matters, such as personnel, material, training, ground organization, and so on, the air force had control. In short, the sea air force was simply a part of the general land air force, which adopted a stepmotherly attitude toward it. Had any economies to be made, or were any cancellations to be enforced, the sea air force was the first to be hit. During the course of the war, the sea air force became more and more shrunken. Its aircraft became obsolete; personnel generally were ill trained for sea duties. Again and again attempts were made to carry out sea operations with personnel borrowed from the land air force. It was mainly due to this general unsuitability, particularly of personnel, that, apart from a few partial successes, the whole thing collapsed.

Heye: Especially difficult was the problem of the aircraft carrier. There was reason for great doubt as to whether this type was necessary at all for a nation in our position. Certainly it was not necessary for the Baltic and the North Sea, but very necessary for the Arctic. But the aircraft carrier was always dependent on the protection of stronger naval forces and escorts so that at first there was, in my opinion, no question of our using aircraft carriers for a war in the Atlantic. The construction of two aircraft carriers was decided upon. The construction plans were delayed because of the lack of experience and the difficulty of arranging the question of command.

Since, in spite of many attempts, Admiral Raeder had not succeeded in establishing a separate fleet air arm, two departments of the armed forces were interested in the aircraft carrier. In the navy, construction of this type of ship was welcomed, perhaps less for operational reasons than because it provided the possibility of keeping naval aircraft separate from the independent air force. Large carriers were planned, contrary to the original intention.

The naval expansion program after 1935 must have been an exciting time for the admirals and future admirals. Instead of the limited opportunities provided by the "token navy" permitted under the Treaty of Versailles, the officers of the Kriegsmarine found themselves running a "growth industry," with wider opportunities for power, prestige, and promotion. In their postwar essays they insist that the primary motive for rearmament was

essentially defensive and that there was certainly no intention of preparing for a war against Britain.

Boehm: The main idea in all [the Führer's] writings—an understanding with England—was to be made a fact.

Krancke: To my knowledge the Führer was always emphasizing the fact that war with England was politically out of the question, as there were no grounds for conflict, hence the naval treaty, which by its balance of power prohibited such a conflict.

Meyer: For me it is beyond question that Hitler had never wished a quarrel with England, and that everything he ever said in his speeches or in his book *Mein Kampf* with regard to coming to arrangements with England was seriously meant. . . . To my knowledge, Hitler had expressed himself several times during the period 1933 to 1938 to Grossadmiral Raeder, to the effect that any idea of competing with England at sea was completely wrong. Even were we to find it necessary, for political reasons, to augment the navy, we should always be a good deal behind England for the simple reason that, because of the necessary extension of our land and air forces, we had not the material strength to do the same with the navy. Doubtless the unfavorable geographical position of Germany vis-à-vis England also played an important role.

Heye: The high command strove from the beginning at all costs to avoid enmity with England. In my opinion this hope existed right up to the day England declared war on Germany. There is no better proof of this than the fact that the navy was forbidden until shortly before the war—1938, I believe —to carry on studies and make plans in case of war with England.

Admiral Raeder and the German navy held after 1933 that our foreign policy should be designed to prevent any question of a war with a greater naval power, and especially with England.

Schniewind and Schuster: The possibility of events developing into a war with England was quite outside the consideration and intentions of the policy of the Reich government.

Schulz: The support given to this [Washington naval] treaty by England was universally regarded by the German navy as an English breach of faith toward Germany, since it involved a considerable restriction of our rights under the Anglo-German naval treaty.

Although a certain distrust of English intentions was called forth among some German naval officers, this incident had no further repercussions on the general attitude of the corps of German naval officers.

At all events England was never, even then, considered a possible enemy by the German navy and, furthermore, as far as I know, the supreme political leaders of the Reich continuously impressed on Grossadmiral Raeder that a conflict with England would be avoided at all costs.

The admirals call attention to various pieces of evidence in their efforts to "prove" that Germany's naval rearmament was not aimed at Britain. Their anxiety to clinch this point may well have arisen from their concern about the possibility of being indicted—as war criminals—for "waging aggressive war."

Boehm: Corresponding to [the] political judgment of the leaders of the state was the intellectual preparation of the navy. None of the war exercises of the naval staff were, to my knowledge, based on a war with England, and no maneuvers were carried out with this in mind.

Dönitz: The Naval Intelligence Service was . . . mainly directed against the European continental powers, less importance being attached to the collation of intelligence from England.

Schniewind and Schuster: The arms potential of Germany during these years was by no means utilized to its fullest extent. Considerable reserves that might have been drawn upon to bring about adequate rearmament were directed to the building of state motor roads [*Reichsautobahnen*] and [Nazi] Party buildings.

Meyer: Until almost directly before the outbreak of war, the navy had not even thought of the possibility of a sea war against England. In view of the comparative strength of England and Germany and their geographical position[s] the idea was absurd. A proof of this is the fact that in the "Battle Instructions," which were issued annually by the high command, no hint appeared of the possibility of a war with England; war exercises were never based on such a hypothesis, and even up to the day of the outbreak of war, no orders had been issued by the high command for this purpose. Germany's political leaders had never calculated on such a war and even forbade any kind of preparation, so that no rumors of such preparations could trickle through with the possibly dangerous effect of creating a war psychology.

Another thing that shows that the war against England was unthought of is the fact that, in the plans for the creation of operational staffs in the event of war, that is, those that would have to deal with the various war sectors, no arrangements were made for west group. There was the east group—for the Baltic—which had been in existence since 1937, but the west group, which would deal with operations toward the west, was only created in the early days of the war in Wilhelmshaven.

During the 1938 crisis, operations in the North Sea were limited to a few weak patrol positions held by U-boats, and this was a very clear indication of the absurdity of war against England. The German navy was simply too weak.

Schulz: From a naval point of view, the relative strength of the two navies was hopelessly unfavorable to Germany. As a result of this, a construction policy based on war with England was never envisaged, far less put into effect. This was carried so far that for about a year no U-boat orders at all were placed, since differences of opinion existed as to the best types, and Germany wished to make the best possible use of the U-boat tonnage allowed her under the Anglo-German naval treaty.

Had it not been for this construction pause, the number of German U-boats would have been correspondingly higher in the first and, for the conduct of the U-boat war, most favorable war years.

Likewise, so hazardous a step as the change over to high-pressure superheated steam for all new destroyers would certainly not have been taken, if consideration had been given to the possibility of war with England in a [foreseeable] future and preparation had been made accordingly.

The most striking illustration that the German navy did not prepare in any way for war with England was the indisputable fact that not only the construction but even the design of any force of invasion craft was entirely neglected.

In the summer of 1938 international tension grew as Germany put pressure on Czechoslovakia to cede the Sudetenland frontier areas populated by ethnic Germans. At the end of September the British, French, Italian, and German leaders met in conference at Munich and compelled the Czechs to agree to the German demands. Despite that apparent success, after the Munich crisis the German navy could no longer feel so confident that Britain could be safely excluded from consideration as a possible opponent in a future war. Various admirals make frank acknowledgment of the significant reappraisal that occurred at that time. Schniewind (as chief of staff to the naval war staff) and Boehm (as commander in chief fleet) were most likely to have been privy to the planning at the highest level.

Schulz: Even the Sudeten crisis, which took the German navy completely by surprise, and temporarily gave rise to the possibility of an Anglo-German conflict, had no immediate effect on the construction policy or the general attitude of the German navy. The Munich Agreement, the Chamberlain-Hitler mutual nonaggression declaration, and the agreement with France concluded in the winter appeared to remove all danger of a European war, and furthermore, the political leaders impressed upon the navy, now as ever, their desire for an understanding with England.

From March–April 1939 onward it became increasingly obvious that the trend of events pointed to war and the navy had, therefore, seriously to face the possibility of a showdown with England, although the supreme political leaders continued to assure the navy, now and until immediately before the outbreak of the war, that there would be no war with England.

Krancke: In 1938, for the first time, during the Sudetenland crisis, the navy was suddenly faced with the problem of a possible war with England. After the Munich Agreement, and England's subsequent rearmament, the [German] navy was also granted more facilities for rearmament and began to make psychological preparations for war with England. In the grand strategy, with the forces at our disposal, it could only be a defensive war, which could be augmented by an offensive with raiders and mines, directed against enemy merchant shipping. The employment of U-boats, heavy cruisers, and auxiliary cruisers against enemy merchant shipping was planned, as well as very active mine warfare in the North Sea.

In view of our enormous numerical inferiority, the only thing that we could aim at was to avoid lying useless in harbor. In contrast to 1914–18, the strategy of a "fleet in being" was meaningless, as the German fleet was much too weak to be able to tie up substantial parts of the English fleet. (Even the French fleet alone was far superior.)

Schniewind and Schuster: [Following the events of 1938 and early 1939,] the Führer obviously became convinced then that a further strengthening of Germany's position politically and economically, seen from a long view in its military aspect . . . would be opposed by the increasing resistance of England. To combat the dangers resulting from this he wanted to strengthen Germany's power at sea.

A new situation arose after the announcement of the [revoking of the 1935 Anglo-German naval agreement in April 1939, by which time Czechoslovakia had broken up and Germany had established a "protectorate" over the Czech provinces of Bohemia and Moravia]. It was clear that each and every possibility of friction was not to be avoided, and that new plans for the building up of the fleet as regards numbers of ships and their size must be in line with this new situation. At the outbreak of war these plans were still in progress and turned out to be very difficult because, for the stronger fleet that was necessary in view of the new and bigger tasks ahead, some agreement had to be reached with the other branches of the armed forces about the utilization of the production sites and, because of this buildup, new production potentials would have to be created and the existing ones enlarged.

I myself, as chief of staff of the naval war staff (SKL) was responsible for part of this planning. The construction of a strong type of battleship and a type of battle cruiser (together with heavier commerce raiders) with 42-cm (16-in) guns, 10,000-ton cruisers with 15-cm (6-in) armament, fast small-type cruisers with greater endurance, smaller aircraft carriers, faster supply ships, a considerable increase in the number of U-boats and destroyers were all provided for by these construction plans. The final decision on the strength of the units and the construction periods of the ships were not determined at the outbreak of war.

Together with these plans for the building of the fleet, proposals were also put forward for a corresponding increase of production facilities by enlarging existing shipyards and harbors and opening up new ones.

Boehm: It was only during 1938 that the Führer began to consider for the first time the possibility that England would come into a war on the opposing side. In April 1939 the Anglo-German naval treaty was canceled by him. Even if the new constructional plans for the fleet showed a considerable increase over former plans and, for example, the so-called Z Plan foresaw the creation of a fleet that, in size and strength, would be more compatible with the size of Germany and her position as a power on the high seas, these still constituted no threat to England. To my knowledge, Hitler did not foresee before 1948 a larger number than ten large battleships and battle cruisers, while England already had fourteen of these in 1939 if I remember correctly. The proportion of cruisers and destroyers was even more unfavorable for us.

Meyer: The aim of the latest German shipbuilding plans was not to prepare for an attack on England but to create a *Risikoflotte* [risk fleet] in the Tirpitz-sense, that is, a fight against Germany would at least constitute some risk for England and prevent her from interfering or at least make intervention less probable.

Despite the reappraisal of the likelihood of Britain's becoming embroiled in hostilities against Germany, Hitler seems to have been convinced that it was a development that would not arise for several years, giving time

for the large naval expansion plans to come to fruition. He obviously did not think it was likely to arise as the result of his plans to launch an attack on Poland in 1939. The admirals are virtually unanimous in depicting the outbreak of war as a miscalculation rather than something deliberately provoked by the German government, but Krancke is the only one who attempts to justify the attack on Poland. Schulz's comments on the timing and significance of the Russo-German pact of August 1939 are interesting; although he does not relate it specifically to Anglo-German relations, he clearly appreciates that Ribbentrop's diplomacy had virtually deprived Britain of the blockade weapon that had been so effective against Germany in the First World War.

Schniewind and Schuster: When, round about the end of 1938 and the beginning of 1939, it appeared to Admiral of the Fleet [*Grossadmiral*] Raeder, who at that time was commander in chief of the navy [*Oberfehlshaber der Kriegsmarine*], that the development of the political situation was becoming serious, and the question arose as to whether there was sufficient time left to build up a homogeneous and modern fleet with all types of ships, or whether it would not be more advisable, in view of the increasing tension, to concentrate on the building of U-boats, [Admiral Raeder], in a statement on this question, referred to the Führer's decision. It was as follows: that the navy had sufficient time to build up a homogeneous fleet, that Germany's foreign policy would be able to avoid any serious developments toward war, and that the navy could continue to carry out the program of building up the fleet, systematically and according to plan, without laying any special emphasis on the U-boat arm.

Boehm: It is not possible in a few short years to produce a powerful fleet from nothing; this is the work of several decades. At the beginning of the war the German navy was in the first stage of its development and expansion. It was in no way comparable to the British fleet. We had to reckon in every way, everywhere, and in whatever we undertook, with absolutely superior powers, and we were by no means armed sufficiently to enter battle against England or against the two greatest sea powers in the world.

This was well known to the leaders of German policy. Anxious regarding the coming war, in which I counted upon the participation of England, I myself asked the C in C [Raeder] during the summer of 1939, on board my flagship, whether he had made fully clear to the Führer our position at sea, and whether he fully realized what war at sea with England would mean.

The Grossadmiral confirmed that he had done so and added, "I told the Führer that, in such a case, the navy could do nothing but die gracefully." As, in spite of this, war developed between our two countries, I do not see that the key to the puzzle lies in the fact that the leaders of German policy, especially the Führer himself, had insufficiently calculated the military situation at sea, but in the fact that Hitler never wanted a war with England and did not believe that England would come in as a result of the Polish campaign "because England did not want war."

Also, although during the last year before the war the danger of England coming in [was] raised by statesmen and the naval staff, a member of the naval high command said to me as late as August 1939 that "in Berlin one did not anticipate any intervention by England in the event of war with Poland." As C in C fleet I had other opinions and expressed them and took the necessary steps.

I bring forward these points in order to show how little a war with England was desired by authoritative circles and how disinclined they were to cause one, thus contradicting the idea that they made efforts to obtain mastery in Europe.

The strength of Hitler's adhesion to [the idea of avoiding war with England] is shown in the speech that he made just before the Polish campaign. This speech was to the service chiefs and I was present. Of this speech, which lasted several hours, there are two sentences that have remained fixed in my mind, that is, "England has no need to make war against us" and "I cannot imagine that, in this situation, an English statesman would lead England into war." Even if these words of Hitler's indicate a fundamental political error, the historical fact remains that the leader of Germany, and with him the German people, never wanted a war with England, to say nothing of a world war. On the contrary, to the very last moment he hoped to avoid it; he wished solely to clean up the eastern frontiers, and not to gain the mastery of Europe. That was the basic political attitude of Germany toward England.

Meyer: When, in 1939, Hitler moved into Poland, he reckoned that England (and for this reason also France) would not take any very serious steps. Only a few days before the outbreak of war, he spoke to a gathering of the leading military personalities at Berchtesgaden somewhat as follows: "If it comes to war with Poland, England and France will perhaps mobilize and they may, perhaps, deploy troops against us—but all that would be merely to make a show. Neither will let it come to war in the west. If I thought it would come to a war, I should not maintain my attitude toward Poland, as this Polish business is not worth a world war. But quite obviously, we shall have to take steps to protect ourselves in any case." (Source of information: my chief, Admiral Saalwächter, when speaking to me a few days after the Berchtesgaden speech.)

From remarks made by officers who, at the time, were serving in the high command, I learned that Grossadmiral Raeder had expressed to Hitler his doubts as to the accuracy of Hitler's views on the probable attitude of England in the event of a war with Poland. The navy, or at least the greater part of the officer corps, was during the prewar years unanimous as to the attitude that England would take. Their judgment was based on their continuous study of the great sea powers, on their practical contact with the outside world, and on their experiences in the First World War. For this reason, the general trend of German politics toward England until 1938 was especially welcomed by the navy. Further, the large shipbuilding program of 1938, which planned to have built (by 1945) thirteen battleships (including those already built), four aircraft carriers, and corresponding flotillas of other vessels, caused a good deal of anxiety in the officer corps.

Heye: I know from [a] reliable source that Adolf Hitler was convinced the day before England's declaration of war that it would not take place. I know from hearsay, moreover, that on the day after England's declaration of war, Grossadmiral Raeder pointed out that our tasks at sea could not be performed by the fleet available in 1939. I am convinced that, relying on [the] political leadership, he had himself not reckoned with the possibility of war with England.

Krancke: When the conflict with Poland came to a head in 1939, our political leaders did not believe there would be a war with the western powers. In order to avoid any visible provocation, no mobilization measures were taken in the North Sea area. I did not share this view, as it was apparent from the radio talks given by English statesmen that, at the outbreak of hostilities with Poland, England had made her sympathies unmistakably known. How it was possible so seriously to misinterpret the political situation can only be explained by the fact that the Führer was completely misinformed on the question of the English mentality. Further, the atrocities to which the Germans were submitted in Poland before the outbreak of war (they were fleeing from Poland in thousands over the German border) influenced the decision of the high command, who regarded them as a conscious provocation of war and was convinced that they could avoid a world war by means of the pact with Soviet Russia.

As a precautionary measure, however, two heavy cruisers and some U-boats were sent to sea ready for action but were instructed that they were only to take offensive action on receipt of special orders. The North Sea was being patrolled by patrol vessels as yet unarmed, otherwise no preparations for war were made.

Schulz: All naval officers who had a sense of responsibility and a general appreciation of the situation viewed the outbreak of war with the greatest misgiving, as everything pointed again to an overwhelming world coalition against Germany that would have to be faced at sea by a totally unprepared German navy under conditions of hopeless inferiority.

All contentions that the German navy or its corps of officers had striven for war are not only untrue but, in view of comparative strength, so senseless that they could not be taken seriously.

The unexpected nonaggression pact concluded with Russia at the end of August [1939] and the Russo-German pact of friendship and consultation that followed in September, were naturally greeted by the navy with considerable relief, although from a purely naval standpoint the situation showed no such marked improvement for the conduct of the war at sea as in the sphere of the army and air force. On the other hand, the blockade, which had been so fatal to Germany during the First World War, was from the outset so effectively broken by these treaties and the parallel commercial agreements that its effectiveness was ultimately completely nullified; furthermore the whole Balkan economic sphere could be utilized without interference for the supplying of Germany.

Schniewind and Schuster: A war on such a tremendous scale—or even [just] with England—was in 1939 quite beyond the range of the preparations and intentions of the government. But the policy of the government and its political negotiations did not make any provision for this idea, as subsequent developments showed. They had gone too far. They completely failed to realize the determination, on the part of those who were later to become their enemies, to declare war in the event of Germany carrying out any further activities similar to the occupation of Austria, Sudetenland, or Czechoslovakia. Germany, her armed forces—and especially the navy—were therefore taken unawares and had to enter the war inadequately equipped.

2

The First Year of War

WRITING IN 1945, when their thoughts were, no doubt, heavily colored by their country's disastrous defeat, the admirals present a cumulative picture of a German navy that had found itself committed prematurely, on 3 September 1939, to a war that it neither wanted nor expected, for which it was ill prepared and ill equipped, and for which its vessels were inadequate both in numbers and design. After interviewing Grand Admiral Dönitz about his essay, the British Naval Intelligence Department summarized his personal verdict:

The war was in one sense lost before it began because . . . Germany was never prepared for a naval war against England. The possibility of having England as an antagonist was not envisaged until 1938, because the government was ill advised politically. Hitler had never been abroad.

In the main body of his essay Dönitz is no more enthusiastic about Germany's prospects at that time:

The navy at the outbreak of war was in an extraordinarily bad position . . . [and] was in no way suited to fight England's sea power numerically, nor was the composition of naval war material adapted to a war with England.

General Admiral Schniewind, chief of staff to the naval war staff in 1939, and Admiral Schuster also claim to have been pessimistic, and they outline the case for departing from conventional concepts of naval strategy.

The outbreak of the war in September 1939, in view of the enormous superiority of the enemy, presented the German navy with tasks that, when reviewed in the traditional and customary manner of considering the prospects of a naval war, must have appeared insurmountable. This conclusion was expressed by the C in C of the navy [*Oberbefehlshaber der Kriegsmarine*] in a statement made to the Führer when the war began. He stated therein that the German navy, which was just beginning its reorganization, would have no chance of success against the combined fighting power of the enemy naval forces in a struggle for the mastery of the sea, if the problem were considered from the conventional point of view and according to traditional principles. In this struggle, so full of fate and significance for Germany, the navy, if it was to be able to make any use at all of its latent fighting strength, would have to free itself completely from the tactical and operational rules and principles that had up till then held sway in naval warfare. It would have to try and make up for its weakness by a bold conduct of the war and, if it should prove necessary, would have to know how to meet defeat while fighting gallantly to the last.

General Admiral Boehm who, as commander in chief fleet when the war began, had the heavy responsibility of being the most senior German admiral afloat, does not seem to have been filled with confidence at that time.

The German "war machine" at sea, the fleet under my command in 1939, was anything but a powerful instrument of force among the nations, particularly where England was concerned. It consisted, in the main, of two battleships of inadequate caliber, three pocket battleships, five light cruisers, and two heavy cruisers (these latter still being under test and training conditions). There was a correspondingly small number of destroyers, U-boats, and other small craft. . . . At the beginning of the war the German navy was in the first stage of its development and expansion. It was in no way comparable to the British fleet. We had to reckon, in every way, everywhere, and in whatever we undertook, with absolutely superior powers and we were by no means armed sufficiently to enter battle against England or against the two other greatest sea powers in the world.

Other admirals write in a similar vein:

Weichold: When England entered into the war against Germany in 1939 and added sea warfare to the continental war, Germany possessed no sea power. She lacked an efficient fleet air arm such as other great navies had created as an indispensable part of their fleets. Accordingly, the seagoing state of the [German] fleet was much worse in the Second World War than in 1914.

Krancke: The navy, therefore, entered into the war, which was forced upon it against its will, insufficiently armed and without a real battle fleet, and the naval high command, in spite of incomplete numbers and complement, had to open the offensive against enemy merchant shipping with all the means at their disposal and in every way possible, and consciously ignoring many proven principles of strategy.

Schniewind and Schuster: The war . . . caught the navy unawares in the very early stages of building up the fleet, and thus it was only natural that when war broke out it felt itself totally unprepared for the tasks and responsibilities of war that were now to be expected. The position was this: the fleet had not been built up in order to carry out certain strategic plans that the supreme command had deputed to it and to which the strength of the fleet was equal, but that strategic and operational planning had of necessity to be adjusted to fit in with the actual unsatisfactory strength of the fleet.

On the results of their interview with Dönitz, the British Naval Intelligence Department reported that in his view, "A realistic policy would have given Germany a thousand U-boats at the beginning of the war." No doubt that was an unrealistic and wildly exaggerated statement made out of exasperation with the questions of his interrogators, but it also reflects, perhaps, his disillusionment with the list he provides of the actual warships available for deployment on the outbreak of war and those then in the course of construction:

At the beginning of the war the German fleet was still in its initial reconstruction stage. The numerical strength permitted by the London naval treaty had not yet been attained by a long way. We did not yet possess a single real battleship; *Bismarck* and *Tirpitz* were building. The following ships had been newly commissioned since 1933:

> the two transitional battleships *Scharnhorst* and *Gneisenau*
> the pocket battleships *Scheer* and *Graf Spee*
> the heavy cruiser *Hipper*
> 22 destroyers of the 1934 and 1936 classes
> some torpedo boats of the 1935 class
> about 48 U-boats of classes II, VII, and IX

At the outbreak of war the following were in production:

the battleships *Bismarck* and *Tirpitz*

the aircraft carriers *Graf Zeppelin* and B

the heavy cruisers *Blücher, Prinz Eugen, Lützow,* and *Seydlitz*

8 destroyers

some torpedo boats

some U-boats

A fleet of that size was more than adequate to establish complete control of the Baltic and to set up defensive minefields in the North Sea.

Dönitz: The Polish war made only slight demands on the navy. The modern Polish destroyers had, before the outbreak of war, broken out of the Baltic and gone to England. We were not able to prevent this as a state of war did not exist. The other Polish surface craft did not put in an appearance. The Polish U-boats were actually at sea, but had no success of any kind and later allowed themselves to be interned in neutral countries.

Schniewind and Schuster: The operation of sealing Poland off from the sea, together with the capture of Gotenhafen and the Hela peninsula, came to a close before the end of September. The Baltic was from then on safe against any threat of attack from the sea. Certain defensive measures were maintained at the entrances to the Baltic against a breakthrough by Allied forces, the possibility of which—if perhaps not so much the probability—had already been taken into account at the outbreak of war (such defensive measures as sea and air patrols, minefields, and mine carriers in a constant state of readiness). After the defeat of Poland, merchant shipping and naval exercises (U-boats) could be resumed and continued in the Baltic under almost peacetime conditions. . . . An important part of the navy's responsibilities became redundant with the fall of Poland. The naval forces on duty in the Baltic could, for the most part, be transferred to the North Sea battle area.

In this area the most pressing responsibility of the navy was the defense of the North Sea territorial waters—roughly bounded by the longitude of Terschelling [5.20 E] and the latitude of Horns Reef [55.35 N]. The protection of this area was achieved by a series of minefields that were laid along the western limit of the area by cruisers and minelayers during September 1939. Continuous patrolling by air reconnaissance of the North Sea, the east coast of Britain, northward to the Orkneys, and as far as the Norwegian coast was carried out, and at the same time light naval forces were in a permanent state of readiness for action.

Heye, who was commanding a heavy cruiser when war broke out, gives his own expectations of how he thought the war might develop in the long run.

It may be that in our estimation of the prospects of war, not only the belief that England would not engage in this continental war, but also overestimation of the air force played a part. The concept of the blitzkrieg, in my opinion, did a very great deal of damage, and resulted from a wrong appreciation of a war with sea powers.

In such a war, irrespective of the state of armament at the beginning of the war, time was to the advantage of the side that possessed the largest manpower and the greater wealth of materials. Well-informed officers in the navy were convinced from the beginning that America would one day come into the war on Britain's side. In any case, the industrial support of America must in the long run have a tremendous effect in England's favor, just as it did in the last war. A series of victorious battles has not the same [significance] as the final battle in such a war as this.

At the beginning of the war I was captain of the heavy cruiser [*Admiral*] *Hipper.* She was still undergoing trials. I was convinced, nevertheless, on the day war broke out that [with] the German navy, as it then existed, only the U-boats could play a decisive role in offensive warfare. I was also convinced that the war would be a long one.

Meyer echoes the views expressed by Heye on both the priority given to U-boat construction and his lack of confidence in the contribution the Luftwaffe was likely to make to the war at sea.

After the outbreak of war . . . the whole of the shipbuilding program was turned upside down and a new plan was evolved that foresaw exclusively the construction of a vast U-boat fleet. There were certainly a number of people who saw in this one-sided program an error, but the greater part of the officer corps were in agreement, for it was impossible during a war to build a surface fleet anything like the size of the British fleet. On the other hand it was possible to produce U-boats in large quantities comparatively quickly and to send them into action. It was with U-boats that the navy had the only chance against England, but even the building of U-boats would demand a tremendous armament potential and, further, the tremendous difficulties connected with the manning and training problem were not underestimated. Looking back on events, the decision to concentrate on the production of U-boats must be considered to have been the correct one; a fleet of U-boats could do the job, but a surface fleet could never have become strong enough to have done it.

When at the end of July 1939 the preliminary discussions took place in regard to the possibility of a war at sea with England, we were faced with a problem that was practically insoluble. How could the tiny German fleet possibly fight against the powerful British fleet? It was clear to us that the air force could not be counted upon as a substitute for the general lack of ships of all kinds.

The high command decided on a massed operation of all U-boats and two pocket battleships in the Atlantic. These forces were to be directly under the command of C in C U-boats, who would receive his instructions from the naval high command.

Schniewind and Schuster, like so many of the admirals, are inclined to be scornful of the Luftwaffe's contribution, although they are fair minded enough to recognize certain mitigating circumstances.

The air force, in so far as it was able to do so without having to draw upon units that might be required for other duties that appeared important, turned its attention to the task by laying mines in the sea channels and also by direct attacks on ports of discharge, inland communications, and the actual shipping itself. The intensity of this cooperation by the air force in this most important task in the war against England did not reach the standard hoped for by the navy. (At the beginning of the war it is true that in the matter of the use of aircraft mines there was a considerable lack of material to be reckoned with.) But England was not the only enemy.

Boehm adds further criticism of the German air force and identifies Göring as a major obstacle to interservice cooperation. Boehm obviously feels that the navy was at a disadvantage because most of the leading figures directing the German war effort had an insufficient understanding of the nature of sea power.

The navy was in no way prepared for war with England, particularly where material was concerned, as it was only in the first stages of its expansion. Correspondingly there was not the best distribution of ships—surface or submarine, offensive or defensive—available; and the navy was not in a position to execute any prepared and large-scale plans. Naturally, the navy was perfectly clear about the basic purpose of any war at sea, that is, the protection of one's own sea [lanes] and attack on the enemy's. There [could] be no argument about the impossibility of keeping open our sea-lanes or maintaining supplies via the Atlantic because of our geographical position and our military situation vis-à-vis England.

For this reason the navy concentrated on the attack on the British sea-lanes with all the means in its power. . . . Although, following the law of the concentration of force, the navy threw in everything possible against England, this cannot be said of the German air force. Complete and thorough cooperation between the two services was lacking, in the endeavor to hit England to the utmost through her overseas supplies. In my opinion the reason for this lay primarily in the C in C of the air force [Göring] and, further, in the fact that the navy had not its own air arm, so often asked for. How far the high command expected to go toward a resounding success in order to compel a real peace offer by this means of operating, or where they erred, is not known to me.

The German navy was not so land-minded as to desire to fight to a successful conclusion a sea power like England. It knew quite well that a world war is, in essence, a sea war and that no matter what great battles might occur on land, sea power is the deciding factor. Whether the leading German statesmen and war leaders were equally clear about this I somewhat doubt: my view is rather to quote Tirpitz, that "they didn't understand the sea."

Within the German government there seems to have been a certain amount of optimism that the long maritime war, which the admirals viewed so apprehensively, would not actually need to be fought. The alternative would have been for Britain and France to accept the partition of Poland as a fait accompli; and it was on that basis that, in October 1939, Hitler had made his offer to enter into peace negotiations, referred to above by Boehm and mentioned by other admirals.

Krancke: When, at the end of the Polish campaign, our attempt to settle our differences with the western powers failed, the naval forces received their orders to open hostilities.

Heye: The measures that had been taken shortly before, in case of a possible war with England, were largely defensive as far as the navy was concerned. U-boats alone had the task of carrying on offensive warfare by attacks on trade and by minelaying. In the first few weeks the armored ships were to operate against trade in order to tie down enemy forces. It was estimated that this war against trade would soon have to cease when defensive measures had been organized. Valuable time was lost because, as far as I know, attacks on trade were only allowed after some time had elapsed, since the [German] government clearly had hopes of coming to an understanding with England, or at least with France.

> Heye's final sentence above is, in fact, incorrect. The first British merchant ship, the passenger liner *Athenia*, was torpedoed by U-30 on the day war was declared. By the end of the first month twenty-five other British merchant vessels had suffered the same fate, with three more lost to mines. From the earliest days, therefore, the German navy determined to strike at what it identified as the most vulnerable aspect of British sea power. Directing U-boat operations was Karl Dönitz, a U-boat commander from the First World War, who had been in charge of training the new U-boat service since 1936. At the outbreak of war he was promoted to rear admiral with the title *Befehlshaber der U-boote*. His 1945 essay recalls the thinking on which German strategy was based.

England was in every respect dependent on seaborne supply for food and import of raw materials, as well as for [the] development of every type of military power. The single task of the [German] navy was, therefore, to interrupt or cut these sea communications. It was clear that this object could never be attained by building a fleet to fight the English fleet and in this way win the sea communication. The only remaining method was to attack sea communications quickly. For this purpose only the U-boat could be considered, as only this could penetrate into the main areas of English sea communications in spite of English sea supremacy on the surface.

Therefore, when the war with England became an [actuality] in September 1939, the navy had to convert its armament to this opponent. Thus the former program for building a homogeneous fleet [was] altered, and only those ships that were nearly ready were completed. In lieu of this a considerably increased U-boat construction program was ordered. Whereas previously the monthly output was only about two to four U-boats, in the new U-boat construction program ordered in September 1939 it was intended to reach by stages twenty to twenty-five U-boats a month.

> Dönitz describes the U-boat types that, apart from small boats designed for coastal waters, were available to him to conduct a campaign against Britain's ocean supply routes.

Mainly U-boat types VIIC and IXC were under construction. Type VIIC was a comparatively small, therefore very handy, boat of 517 tons with a high action radius for its size and a comparatively high number of torpedoes (12–14). In the opinion of the U-boat command it was the ideal combination of tactical usefulness in attack—light and easy to handle, difficult to see at night, small turning circle—and the necessary fighting strength, expressed in radius and armament. As a second type of boat the type IXC . . . of about 740 tons was ordered. Though less handy and more complicated to handle, it had a larger action radius and more torpedoes. Both types of boats were already available in the small U-boat arm and had proved themselves in peacetime operation.

A construction period of about twenty-one months was envisaged for the U-boats ordered in September 1939, so that they could not be counted on operationally for two years. Therefore it was clear that the armament of the navy, only commenced at the beginning of the war with England, would be very late, if not too late, for a successful U-boat war.

The type VIIC enabled the war to be carried to the north coast of Spain and the type IXC to Gibraltar. All these distances were reckoned with outward and inward passage round the north of England. This long journey took up a considerable part of the action radius of the boat. So in November 1939 the U-boat command attempted to send U-boats through the Channel on their way to the Atlantic. They failed in this, however. The losses, apparently through mines in the narrow Dover-Calais Strait, were too high so that this route had to be abandoned as too expensive.

Partly frustrated in his eagerness to enjoy the maximum success before Britain could organize properly the defense of her maritime trade, Dönitz sets out the restrictions under which his boats had to operate in those early days.

The orders of the Operations Division of the naval staff were authoritative for carrying out the U-boat war. Merchant ships were, in accordance with these orders, only to be attacked in accordance with the rules of international law. Over and above this, the Führer expressly and additionally forbade that any passenger ship [or] ships of French nationality should be attacked or stopped. The reason for this was obvious. The Führer hoped, in spite of England's and France's declaration of war, to limit the war to Poland, and wished in this way above all to prevent an actual active participation by France in the war.

Only when England placed her ships outside the preconditions of international law as laid down at the Hague convention, by arming merchant

Hitler's Admirals

ships and by orders to use those weapons for defense and attack against U-boats, was the U-boat command allowed to attack any merchant ship whose armament was officially recognized or whose armament was recognized with certainty. In the same way the U-boat arm was given permission to attack darkened merchant ships by night, as the recognition of these ships as merchant ships—and therefore the corresponding treatment—was made impossible by this English precaution. The declaration of an operational area around England and freedom of attack on all British merchant ships followed this gradual change of orders after England had publicly declared that all English merchant ships had been armed. Very soon after the beginning of the war the convoy system was instituted by England to an ever increasing degree. By this, merchant ships lost the protection of all international rules, as [sailing] under the protection of their own warships had put them outside the prize law. The U-boats were given freedom of attack on all merchant ships escorted by enemy warships.

With the very small number of U-boats that were available . . . it was clear to the U-boat command that they could only inflict pinpricks on England's trade and conduct of the war at sea. The U-boats at sea in operational areas during the winter [of] 1939–40 never exceeded ten in number and at times it sank as low as two. It was clear to the U-boat command that they could only achieve anything if they took the bull by the horns and attacked, as far as possible, the concentration point of traffic in or near harbors.

The U-boats also showed that they were capable of securing impressive successes against even the most powerful units of Britain's surface fleet. The aircraft carrier HMS *Courageous* was sunk by U-29 on 17 September; and on 14 October U-47 penetrated into the main British fleet anchorage at Scapa Flow and sank the battleship HMS *Royal Oak*. The latter success was a serious blow to Britain's naval prestige, and it did much to enhance the reputation of the U-boat arm in Hitler's eyes. Nevertheless, Dönitz expresses some disappointment. He obviously feels that weapons failures had robbed his U-boats of even greater triumphs.

The operation against Scapa Flow, carried out by Kapitänleutnant Prien, required a previous air reconnaissance so that the U-boat command could determine the possibilities of penetration. The successful penetration by the boat proved the correctness of the view that the boom could be passed here. I had expected very much more of the operation against Scapa Flow. Kapitänleutnant Prien was denied further successes by torpedo failures.

The operation against the Firth of Forth carried out by Kapitänleutnant Frauenheim resulted in damage to the cruiser *Belfast* and the operation against Loch Ewe in damage to the battleship *Nelson*. An operation against the Clyde had to be given up after two fruitless attempts.

Basically these operations were carried out with a mixed outfit of mines and torpedoes. In this respect the magnetic mine had proved itself an effective weapon in the first month of the war when it was actually laid in the narrows of harbor channels. In contrast to this, the U-boat arm's experience with torpedoes during these months [was] both surprising and unpleasant. It appeared that the magnetic firing of torpedoes had not been mastered, as had been thought in peacetime. The torpedoes usually exploded before reaching the target or did not detonate at all. As magnetic firing had been relied on in peacetime, depth keeping had been neglected and was also not fully understood. The same applied even to contact firing. These circumstances had a marked influence on the success of the U-boat arm in the first months of the war. For example, in November 1939 [when] a German U-boat west of the Orkneys fired at the [British battleship HMS] *Nelson* from very close range, the torpedoes hit but did not explode.

The losses of U-boats during this period were comparatively heavy, although English defenses were still very weak. Besides the general inexperience of the crews under war conditions, the reason lay in technical defects that could only become apparent in war, for example, leaky exhaust valves in type VII boats, which when submerged for long periods or when being chased resulted in the gradual flooding of the boat aft, finally forcing it to surface, where it was destroyed.

> Even though the U-boats could be assumed to have by far the best chance of inflicting serious losses on both the Royal Navy and Britain's merchant fleet, Germany's naval war staff had no intention of merely preserving their own surface warships by leaving them in the safe Baltic harbors. Those ships, too, were expected to make a contribution to the war on commerce, even if that meant taking considerable risks. Dönitz explains the reasoning that determined the employment of the German surface fleet.

Planning the use of surface forces was governed by the fact that they could not embark on a battle for sea supremacy, on account of their inferior numbers and strength compared with the overpowering sea power of England, which had been strengthened by the addition of the French fleet, in itself far superior [to Germany's]. . . . On the other hand, a direct attack by enemy fleets in German home waters was not to be expected, taking into account the air position and the forces available on the coast. All sections of the German fleet were free, [therefore], for offensive action. When the focus of the war at sea turned to shipping, it was obvious that, as far as possible, the surface forces had to be devoted to this task as well [as the U-boats]. Here only was there a chance for the navy to play an important, perhaps even decisive, part in the general conduct of the war.

The weakness of our surface forces had to be compensated for by boldness and constant changes of tactics. Where previous tactical views stood in the way of such an operation, they had to be abandoned and replaced by the tactic of surprise. The greater our own weakness was, the more daring our operations had to be if the fate of the First World War was to be avoided, when the fleet, without any decisive losses but also without any strategic value, was locked up in German waters. It was obvious (and was taken into account) that in this type of operation great risks at times—and the heaviest losses—had to be reckoned on, and the change to the U-boat building program meant such a reduction in other construction that any possibility of replacing battleships and cruisers, if losses occurred, was out of the question.

Work was continued on the nearly completed *Bismarck, Tirpitz,* and *Prinz Eugen* . . . but the other [major] new constructions . . . were stopped. A newly planned program for surface ships envisaged merely construction of destroyers, torpedo boats, minesweepers, R-boats, and E-boats, and these in only limited numbers.

Some of the other admirals add their own comments on the employment of surface vessels.

Meyer: In spite of, or rather because of, the limited means at our disposal, we in Germany realized clearly that it would only be by throwing everything we had into an outright offensive that we could achieve any success against the great British fleet. Space does not permit me to give details of all the various measures that were taken. I can mention the U-boat offensive, the operations of the pocket battleships in the Atlantic, the three operations of the battleships *Scharnhorst* and *Gneisenau* in the North Sea, the destroyer operations, and the use of special vessels in and west of the Skagerrak against enemy merchant ships and their successes on occasions against warships, and finally the numerous mining operations by destroyers along the British coasts.

Schniewind and Schuster: Tackling the problem of offensive action—the

attacking and/or paralyzing of enemy shipping traffic—was much more difficult and presented considerable risks. In this task the goal aimed at by the
C in C of the navy—namely to make up for our undeniable inferiority as far
as possible by bold and daring undertakings—was achieved. Among these
undertakings can be included the attacks by surface forces taking part in
mercantile warfare . . . off the Norwegian coast and in the Skagerrak against
shipping sailing for England, the attack made by battleships in Icelandic waters [including the sinking of the armed merchant cruiser HMS *Rawalpindi*
on 23 November], the countless minelaying operations off the east coast of
Britain in the months from October 1939 to February 1940, as a result of
which the sea routes in that area from Hoofden to the Tyne were made unsafe
and the highly important approaches to the Thames, the Wash, the Humber,
and the Tyne were endangered. These destroyer operations were supplemented by minelaying operations and attacks by U-boats. . . . At the same
time, after the outbreak of war, commerce raiding had begun, with pocket
battleships (*Deutschland* and *Graf Spee*) in the north and south Atlantic,
and with U-boats on the high seas in the North Atlantic west of England
and Spain.

In estimating the successes of the pocket battleships *Spee* and *Deutschland*, which were operating in the Atlantic from the outbreak of war onward,
one must bear in mind that for a time quite early on in the war these pocket
battleships had a few weeks of inactivity imposed upon them (in the mistaken assumption of the high command that the western enemies had only
halfheartedly entered the war and that they would probably retire from the
field once Poland had been defeated), that, moreover, their operations took
place in the middle of the unfavorable season of the year, that information
was yet to be obtained as to the enemy's methods and performance, and
finally that the last operation of the *Graf Spee* against the important sea area
round the River Plate fell very short of the intentions of the naval war staff
since, although it is true that there was a heavy concentration of shipping
there, at the same time a strong enemy defense force was to be expected.

Krancke: The war against merchant shipping was successfully started in
the Atlantic with U-boats, heavy cruisers, and auxiliary cruisers. The loss
of the *Graf Spee* in December 1939 made no fundamental change, as it only
affected the tonnage war, and the heavy cruisers were better suited to act as
commerce raiders than as escort vessels. (The mistakes made by the *Graf
Spee* during the battle were due to the fact that the captain was wounded in
the head, which affected his vision and powers of decision.) Also the *Graf*

Spee captured about the same amount of tonnage as the famous *Emden* in 1914.

The sympathetic reference to Captain Langsdorff of the *Graf Spee* was, no doubt, influenced by Krancke's own experience of commanding the pocket battleship *Admiral Scheer* on a successful commerce raiding cruise in 1940–41. In all, the pocket battleship *Graf Spee* sank a total of nine British merchant vessels in the south Atlantic and Indian Ocean before she was brought to action on 13 December 1939 by the British cruisers *Exeter, Ajax,* and *Achilles* in the battle of the River Plate. After taking refuge in neutral Montevideo, she sailed again on the seventeenth and, on orders from Berlin, was scuttled in the estuary of the River Plate rather than renew the battle with the waiting cruisers. The other pocket battleship at large in 1939, the *Deutschland,* sank only one British merchant vessel in the North Atlantic before being recalled to Germany in November. Their ability to cause disproportionate alarm, disruption, and distraction to more powerful opponents is indicated by the fact that, by the end of October, the British and French navies were employing a total of 4 battleships, 3 battle cruisers, 5 aircraft carriers, and 16 cruisers in reinforcing convoy escorts or forming special task forces to hunt down the pocket battleships. By the end of 1939, in addition to the 10 victims of the pocket battleships, a total of 51 British merchant vessels had been sunk by U-boats, 30 by mines, and 1 by aircraft attack, while 4 other losses were attributed to enemy action but the cause could not be established. Losses due to mines might, of course, have been either in minefields laid by surface vessels, U-boats, or aircraft. In the same period the German navy had lost the *Graf Spee* and 9 U-boats. In the first three months of 1940, the Germans lost 9 more U-boats while another 58 British merchant vessels were sunk. Of those, the Luftwaffe sank 10; mines claimed 28; 6 were lost to unknown causes. None were lost due to surface raiders and a mere 14 to Dönitz's U-boats. No doubt the changing pattern of losses was brought about by a variety of causes such as bad weather, malfunctioning of German torpedoes, and the arming and convoying of British merchant vessels, but many of the available U-boats and all the surface warships were being prepared for a bold attack on a new objective. Dönitz explains the strategic considerations that led to the selection of that objective.

The attitude of the navy regarding the policy to be adopted toward Norway was based on the conviction that Norway's neutrality would be the happiest solution, but only if Norwegian territorial waters were also respected by the enemy. The reason for this was that they considered it almost impossible to effectively protect shipping in Norwegian coastal waters with the limited means at their disposal, because it would be easy for the English navy, from its nearby bases, to interfere with this shipping at suitable points and at any time. On the other hand, all possible means would have to be employed to prevent Norway becoming an English sphere of influence, as this would also lead to the blocking of the North Sea and constitute a threat to the entrance to the Baltic.

The attack on the German supply ship *Altmark,* in spring 1940, by the British destroyer *Cossack* in Norwegian territorial waters, and contrary to international law, showed that England was not prepared to respect Norwegian neutrality in all circumstances. Various reports from Norway that England was planning to attack that country confirmed this impression. It therefore seemed advisable to make careful preparations for the occupation of Norway. These were ordered by the Führer, at the suggestion of Grossadmiral Raeder, and immediately put into action. All possible measures were taken to ensure secrecy and these, regarded as a whole, were apparently successful.

When, at the beginning of April 1940, the reports of an imminent English expedition against Norway increased, our own preparations were complete so that April 9 could be fixed as the beginning of the operation. In view of the inferiority of the German fleet, this undertaking was one of the boldest in naval history. Every risk was, however, justified by the enormous strategic importance of Norway as the cornerstone of a blockade against Germany or alternatively as a jumping-off place for German surface forces [and] particularly U-boats. The decision to throw into the attack all the German navy that could fight was made with the full realization of the implications.

Other German admirals recognize the very risky nature of the operation but consider the risks fully justified.

Schniewind and Schuster: An occupation [of Norway] by the enemy, which by March 1940 was a possibility that had to be seriously taken into account, would have been a decisive setback (far more serious than in 1914–18) to Germany's chances of continuing the war at sea. That Norway—and perhaps Sweden too—might enter the war on the side of the enemy, thereby reopening the naval war in the Baltic, did not seem at that time to be out of the question. This would have meant a very serious crisis that might have decided the issue of the war. If Germany occupied the Norwegian coast, this danger would be averted and, at the same time, it would increase the range of operations in a manner most desirable for the conduct of the war.

Heye: The preparations for this operation were kept very secret and were influenced strongly by Adolf Hitler himself. Admiral Raeder was quite aware that one mistake in this undertaking could have meant [the] inevitable loss of all our fleet units. In the eyes of the high command the occupation of Norway was worth such a risk.

Meyer: During the years after 1940, Grossadmiral Raeder said that the idea of occupying Norway had been passed by him to Hitler. The ideas of the navy . . . were strongly influenced in this direction by a book written by Vice Admiral Wegener, in which he examined critically the naval operations during the war [of] 1914–18 and came to the conclusion that Norway ought to have been occupied in order to create the proper base, from the geographical point of view, for a fight against Britain. During the first six months of the [Second World] War there was very great anxiety in the navy that Britain would occupy Norway and thus close every outlet to the open seas.

Krancke: The danger that England would, as in 1918, close the entrance routes to the Atlantic, and perhaps settle forces in Norway in order to obtain bases there for the air force, led to our decision to counteract this measure by occupying Norway and thus gain access to the Atlantic.

The German plan was to land troops at several points in Norway on 9 April. Many were to be put ashore from warships, but to accommodate all the troops, weapons, and equipment, a number of slower merchant ships had to be sent on ahead of the various naval task forces. Schniewind and Schuster point out the inevitable disadvantages of employing merchant ships in that way.

It was assumed that no serious resistance or prepared defenses would be met with in Norway, and events justified this assumption. All branches of the armed forces—even the navy—would have preferred to have had stronger forces at their disposal for the first assault, and above all light guns that could be speedily mounted to provide temporary artillery for coastal defense (particularly Narvik). The lack of fast transport ships rendered this out of the question. The necessity for secrecy also enforced the exclusion of everything except what was absolutely essential. Slow merchant vessels were used, laden with artillery equipment, fuel, and other supplies, but they were first held up by the English mining operation on the night of 8–9 April, and later, when they attempted to continue their passage, some of them fell victim to the English forces (off Narvik and Stavanger). [In particular, refueling tankers failed to reach Narvik and Trondheim as planned.]

Dönitz lists the order of battle adopted by the German navy for these operations.

For the carrying out of the expedition the fleet was divided into different forces made up somewhat as follows:

Narvik—ten destroyers, under the command of Commodore Bonte, [the] senior officer, destroyers

Trondheim—*Hipper, Königsberg,* training ship *Brummer,* [and] torpedo boats, under the command of Vice Admiral Schmundt

Kristiansand—*Karlsruhe* [and] torpedo boats, under the command of the [captain] of the cruiser

Oslo—*Blücher, Scheer, Emden,* [and] torpedo boats, under the command of Rear Admiral Kummetz

The greatest possible number of troops were embarked on these ships. To cover the expedition the two battleships *Scharnhorst* and *Gneisenau,* under the command of Rear Admiral Lütjens, were standing by west of West Fiord.

In March 1940 the U-boats were withdrawn from the operational spheres . . . so that they would be available should the occupation of Norway become necessary. They took up position off different fiords as a defensive measure against the penetration of English ships.

The expedition was entirely successful, although at some places initial difficulties and serious losses were experienced, including the *Blücher* in the Droebag [Dröbak] Straits south of Oslo, the *Karlsruhe* in the Skagerrak, and damage to [the] *Königsberg* while running into Bergen.

Heye recalls being more directly involved:

As captain of the heavy cruiser *Hipper* I had command of the group, consisting of *Hipper* and four destroyers, intended for the occupation of Trondheim. We set out in company with [the] *Scharnhorst* and *Gneisenau* and the Narvik group, and later proceeded independently. We experienced heavy weather on the way, as a result of which the torpedo boats lost men and materials; the maintenance of secrecy was, however, made easier by the weather. The *Hipper* group had an action with [HMS] *Glowworm,* which put up a brave fight, and after that [we] successfully occupied Trondheim after a short duel with the coastal batteries. There was no fighting ashore except round the coastal fortifications that had to be captured after [the] *Hipper* had entered the harbor. The oil ships were not in position as intended and single U-boats were placed as a rearguard before the entrance to the fiord. Attacks by the British fleet and from the air and, in certain circumstances, landings north and south of Trondheim were continually to be reckoned with. *Hipper* received orders to return to Wilhelmshaven two days later, leaving the torpedo boats behind. She joined the battleships on the way.

The very bold German plan achieved complete success. All the target ports were occupied. Resistance by the mainly obsolescent coast defense vessels of the Norwegian navy was brushed aside, and the small Norwegian army was forced into retreat. Reinforcements were rushed into southern Norway by air, and the German air force lost no time in establishing itself on key Norwegian airfields. The only serious reverse occurred at Narvik—the most distant objective—where, after landing their consignments of troops, Commodore Bonte's destroyers found themselves trapped. An attack by a British destroyer flotilla on 10 April led to the loss of two destroyers on each side, and three days later, a further attack by the battleship HMS *Warspite* and British destroyers led to the remaining eight German destroyers and a U-boat being hunted down and sunk in Narvik and the neighboring fiords. Dönitz and Schulz both consider the losses to have been acceptable.

Dönitz: The attack by the English navy on Narvik cost the German navy ten of their latest destroyers, which were unable to repel the attackers' superior strength, especially as their fighting power was seriously reduced by extreme shortage of fuel. On the other hand, the destroyers' personnel formed a welcome reinforcement to the land forces and, according to Colonel-General Dietl, the holding of the Narvik area for so long would have been impossible without them.

Schulz: Had this Narvik position been once lost, it would have been difficult, if not impossible, to recapture it, even after the Allied reverses on the western front. Narvik in Allied hands would have so seriously prejudiced the German position in Norway—among other reasons because of the undisturbed Allied communications with Sweden that would have resulted—that however painful the loss of approximately half her destroyers was to the German navy, yet from the point of view of the overall conduct of the war, the possession of Narvik was of greater importance.

Within two months of the first landings, the Germans had succeeded in making themselves masters of the whole of Norway. An ambitious plan to recover Trondheim by a direct naval assault up the fiord was never attempted. Instead landings at Namsos and Andalsnes with inadequate and ill-equipped troops ended in humiliating and costly evacuations after two or three weeks in the face of the rapid buildup of German military and air power in southern Norway. A British and French expedition to recapture Norway, after making slow progress initially, managed to take the port briefly at the end of May, but had to be withdrawn on 8 June. The inadequacy of the British response came as both a surprise and a relief to the Germans.

Boehm: Norway, lying as it does in the Arctic, in the Atlantic, and at the gateway to the Baltic, was to us of great strategic importance. I have never been able to understand (and this was my greatest worry) why the British fleet did not attack with large forces at least as far as Trondheim and Bergen, . . . destroy our few light forces and supply vessels, and so cut off our troops in the enemy country with the most serious consequences. Norway might then not have fallen into our hands, or only at a much greater cost of men and time; further operations in France would have been delayed and the whole face of the war might have been changed to the benefit of England. My personal judgment is that this was a great loss of opportunity on the part of the British high command.

Meyer: The general opinion in the German navy at that time was that had England wished and concentrated on it, it would have been an easy matter to have thrown the Germans out of north and central Norway at least.

The German admirals are naturally—and justifiably—inclined to see the occupation of Norway as a naval triumph, but Schniewind and Schuster are less than generous in their assessment of the contribution made by the Luftwaffe.

The reconnaissance units of the naval air arm put in some good work in the Norwegian campaign. They were also sufficiently well trained for sea service, but the naval war staff did not have an equally good opinion of the units of the operational air force that were attached for this operation, although their leadership and performance were spirited.

In fact, off Norway the German air force destroyed the British antiaircraft cruiser *Curlew*, four destroyers (two British, one French, one Polish), one

British sloop, and two Norwegian torpedo boats. Those results may be compared with the Royal Navy's other losses: one cruiser by accidental stranding plus five destroyers and an aircraft carrier in surface action with German naval vessels. The most serious loss was the aircraft carrier *Glorious* and her two escorting destroyers during the final withdrawal from Narvik, when they had the misfortune to encounter the *Scharnhorst* and *Gneisenau*. Dönitz expresses his great disappointment that his U-boats achieved little during the campaign:

The naval staff and the U-boat command had expected great results from the use of U-boats. Because of the confined waters and the probable counteraction, it seemed likely that there would be frequent contact with the enemy, but the result of the U-boat activity was extraordinarily disappointing. The chief reason for this was torpedo failures. If a torpedo shortage had been evident in the early months of the war, it was now their ineffectiveness in the Norwegian expedition that became disastrously apparent. As a result of being in contact with the enemy for long periods, the U-boats were forced to remain submerged for a very long time, causing excess pressure in the boat, which penetrated the depth chamber of the torpedo and considerably increased the depth setting. Thus, for example, Leutnant Prien was able to fire at close range at the big British transports near Harstad, but again the torpedo went too low. The reason for the increasing number of torpedo misses was only understood by the German navy at a very much later date, when the individual technical faults of the torpedo were ascertained by systematic testing. It was actually true that, despite numerous opportunities to fire, there were few, if any, successes. The effect on the crews was marked; they lost confidence in the weapon, and the personal influence of the C in C U-boats was necessary to restore their morale. At the same time everything possible was done to overcome torpedo faults.

The small German navy paid a heavy price for its success in Norway. In all it lost three cruisers, ten destroyers, a minelayer, three minesweepers, a torpedo boat, and two U-boats. Those losses might, indeed, have been very much heavier. The *Hipper* had been rammed and damaged by the sinking HMS *Glowworm*. The *Scharnhorst* and *Gneisenau*, with their 11-inch caliber main armament, had been fortunate to escape in bad weather on 9 April from the 15-inch guns of the British battle cruiser HMS *Renown*; and on 8 June the *Scharnhorst* was damaged by a torpedo from HMS *Acasta*, one of the destroyers escorting the *Glorious*. The pocket battleship *Lützow* (ex-*Deutschland*) was damaged on 10 April by a torpedo from the British submarine *Spearfish*. Nevertheless, Schulz quite justifiably sees the whole operation as a triumph achieved against the odds.

The difficulties of this task imposed on the German navy can only be appreciated in their entirety by a naval officer, and any British naval officer will therefore understand that the German navy is proud of having successfully carried out this task and regards the Norwegian campaign as one of its greatest achievements.

This is in no way altered by the heavy shipping losses incurred, since these had been anticipated from the outset in view of the difficulties of the operation.

By the occupation of Norway, Germany had for the first time broken out of the "wet triangle" of the inner North Sea and secured herself a strategic position offering greater operational scope and would now exploit to the utmost the weak naval forces at her disposal.

With benefit of all the hindsight that came from writing of these events five years later, Heye identifies, in the success of the Polish and Norwegian operations, the seeds of a problem that would eventually bring about Germany's defeat.

During the preparations for the Norwegian operation, I attended a single address by Adolf Hitler: he stressed the importance of the occupation of Norway for the prosecution of the war and said that he was the only man who could take the responsibility for such an operation against the advice of his specialists. During the course of the war he frequently acted, it is true, against the advice of the services and on a few occasions with success. This may have led him and certain officers to regard himself not only as a statesman but as supreme war lord. His interference with military operation in any case became noticeably stronger. There were consequently more failures, as a result of orders that he gave contrary to the advice of the service chiefs, than successes, for example in Poland and Norway, which he achieved against their advice.

In 1940, however, Hitler's war machine still rolled on unchecked. On 10 May, only a month after launching the invasion of Norway and Denmark, German forces invaded Holland, Belgium, and Luxemburg. Within a week they were sweeping into France; and by the end of the month Britain was reduced to ever more desperate expedients in evacuating by sea the bulk

of the British expeditionary force and large numbers of French troops from the port of Dunkirk and the open beaches to the east. Schniewind and Schuster reveal that the German navy had been rather frustrated in their efforts to discover the full extent of the army high command's intentions in launching this land campaign in the west.

Long before the opening of the campaign in the west the naval war staff established liaison with the army general staff so that they could keep them informed of the efforts of the naval war staff to gain bases in the western approaches to the Channel or, better still, on the Atlantic coast. This liaison at the same time served the purpose of providing the naval high command with information and confirmation as to how soon and to what extent the high command hoped to make a breakthrough to the French-Belgian coast. On this information depended the degree and the timing of the navy's cooperation. Preparations for taking over the defense of the coastline, making the ports serviceable for military and supply purposes, and preparing the naval forces for those tasks would be conditioned by this.

In April 1940 the high command of the army was still unable to give any definite promises or predictions ("It is quite impossible to state whether a breakthrough to the coast can be made, when the coast will be reached, and how far westward the spearhead can be extended. It is equally possible that the attack may be carried right up to the coast as that it may come to a standstill on the Sambre or the Dyle.") Thus, even only a few weeks before it began, the army general staff expressed its opinions on the prospects of the campaign in the west with the greatest reserve.

The navy's preparations and arrangements for this campaign in the west were correspondingly dilatory, because at that time circumstances necessitated taking very strong measures in matters of supplies and personnel, in view of the weakening of the home and Norwegian fronts. Then, when the great successes in the west during the second half of May began to make themselves felt, the required cooperation of the navy had to be set in motion with great efficiency and speed. The utilization of seagoing vessels, some of which were still tied down in Norway or had been weakened by the Norwegian campaign, had at first to be restricted to the use of U-boats in Hoofden and off the Dutch-Belgian coast, and of E-boats in the same area. As far as the author can remember, no targets of great importance presented themselves for attack to these naval forces in this sector of the western campaign.

Dönitz also acknowledges that the German navy did not have the resources to interfere significantly in the Dunkirk evacuation.

The navy only played a small part in the campaign in the west, as its forces were tied up in Norway. The campaign developed with such astonishing rapidity that it was not possible to make available sufficient fighting forces to attack the English retreating from Dunkirk. The few E-boats that took part did not have much success.

The E-boats sank three destroyers (two French and one British), and a U-boat sank one British destroyer. In view of the criticism leveled at the Luftwaffe in several of the essays by German admirals, they were less than generous in failing to acknowledge that, during May and June 1940 between the mouth of the Scheldt and the Pas de Calais, German aircraft had destroyed no fewer than twelve extremely valuable Allied destroyers (seven British, four French, and one Dutch), as well as smaller warships and many merchant vessels. As one port after another fell into the hands of the German army, the navy faced the enormous—but very welcome— challenge of ensuring that the essential port facilities could soon function again under German control.

Schulz: The wide extent of the newly acquired coasts produced such demands for personnel—for patrol, minesweeping, and harbor defense flotillas, port parties, harbor defense posts, and, above all, for coastal artillery detachments—which latter were entirely manned by the navy in Germany— that the available reserves of personnel were hopelessly inadequate and the shortage could only be met by new recruitment with short training. This again illustrates how little the war preparations begun in 1939 had progressed.

I would like to mention in this connection that the North Sea command provided powerful motorized commando units (each about two hundred strong), whose part in the western offensive was to move up immediately behind or actually with the advanced army formations in order to secure naval and merchant vessels, port installations, and building yards with warships under construction in the most important ports occupied. These commando units proved their value even though, for example, in Holland, in spite of the shortness of time, most of the new construction already afloat had been towed to England.

Schniewind and Schuster: The steps that had to be taken to guard the coastline, to take over and clear the ports, and to make them serviceable again were quite extensive and imposed a great strain on executive and technical naval establishments, and it seemed at times as though they would have to conjure up reinforcements by magic. By means of extensive stripping of the home coastline (from the central and eastern Baltic all the suitable L.A. [low angle] batteries and most of the ack-ack batteries were withdrawn), in the shortest possible time a defensive system of coastal artillery was established along the Dutch, Belgian, and French coasts, and minefields were laid west of the Dutch-Belgian coasts to protect the coastal sea routes. Patrol, escort, and minesweeping units had to be re-formed or transferred to the newly gained sea area at the expense of the North Sea and Norway. Ports had to be cleared and made serviceable again (docks and quay installations); shipyards had to be opened up again as repair bases or take part in the new construction program under the direction of the German Construction Directorate. Following step by step by step the advances of the army westward and later southward until the end of the campaign in the west, the navy established itself all along the coast of Holland, Belgium, and France right down to the Spanish border, and organized the shipping and the working of ports and shipyards.

At the same time suitable places were made ready and put into operation as naval bases for light units; these included Cherbourg, Brest, Saint-Nazaire, and La Pallice. It was planned to use Ymuiden, Rotterdam, Ostend, Boulogne, and Cherbourg as bases for E-boats and the ports of Brest, Lorient, Saint-Nazaire, and later Bordeaux as bases for U-boats; and in the course of the following months they were rebuilt for purposes of repair and rest (bunkering and dockyard installations).

Very soon after the conclusion of the campaign in the west, the greater part of the ports on the newly won coastline were ready to temporarily accommodate light naval forces and U-boats. Work on the port and dockyard installations was continued throughout the period of occupation, bringing them into a better state of efficiency and increasing their accommodation capacity. Furthermore, an important part was played by the provision and steady improvement of an adequate ARP system (air raid shelters and ack-ack batteries).

On 10 June, Italy entered the war as Germany's ally. By the end of June, France had been compelled to plead for an armistice; the German army seemed to be masters of Europe; and the Germans had begun to seize British territory with their occupation of the Channel Islands. Britain stood alone, guarded by a depleted navy and air force—and a defeated army that had lost most of its tanks, guns, and heavy equipment on the retreat to Dunkirk. Total victory seemed to be within Germany's grasp.

3

Operation Sea Lion

THE GERMAN ARMY'S offensive through Holland, Belgium, and France had been successful far beyond the expectations of the generals—and certainly far beyond those of the admirals.

Krancke: Free access to the Atlantic had been achieved. . . . We had not reckoned with such [a] rapid and complete victory.

Meyer: The German high command had not expected such a rapid and complete success in the west nor that the German army would reach the Channel and the Atlantic coast. Hitler was, perhaps, the only one who believed in the possibility of this, but even he did not exploit the opportunity.

The admirals acknowledge that, thanks to the army, the strategic possibilities open to the navy had, in the brief space of three months, been transformed.

Schulz: The situation at sea had altered during the short period April–July 1940 to a hitherto unimagined extent in Germany's favor.

Dönitz: With the conquest of Holland, Belgium, and France, Germany had gained a naval strategic position of first-class importance. All forces were immediately applied to build it up and profit by it as soon as possible.

If one discounts the tortuous exits from the Baltic into the Skagerrak at the beginning of April 1940, all German naval operations against Britain had to be launched from a coastal front of about 170 miles, running from the island of Sylt southward to Cuxhaven, at the mouth of the Elbe, and then westward to the island of Borkum on the Dutch frontier. Such a narrow front was vulnerable to enemy mining, aerial reconnaissance, and submarine operations. By the end of June, German victories had extended that front northward by more than 1,500 miles to Kirkenes in the far north of Norway, and then secured a further extension of more than 1,000 miles to include the whole southern shore of the North Sea, the southern shore of the English Channel as far west as Brest, and the French coast on the Bay of Biscay as far south as the Spanish frontier. The possibilities were enough to excite any naval strategist, especially if one took into account that Germany's new ally, Italy, brought to the Axis partnership a sizable fleet and not just the coastal facilities in Italy itself, but also Sardinia, the Dodecanese Islands and Libya in the Mediterranean, Eritrea in the Red Sea, and Somaliland in the Indian Ocean. In the summer of 1940, a neutral observer might have identified four promising ways in which Germany could win the war. The two quickest ways were either that Britain might recognize how hopeless her position was and sue for peace or that Germany might invade and conquer the enfeebled British Isles with the same ease as she had swept over her opponents on the European mainland. The two alternate—and slower ways—involved either starving Britain into submission by applying an increasingly ruthless and effective blockade to sever her supply lines across the Atlantic or making a wholehearted attempt to destroy Britain's imperial position by shutting her out from the Mediterranean and turning her out of the Middle East. Even a seemingly unstoppable Germany did not have the resources to pursue all those possibilities at the same time. For a short time, there were hopes that Britain would make peace, but Winston Churchill's defiance quickly convinced the German leaders that, to bring the British to their senses, an invasion might need to be launched after all.

Schulz: After Germany's renewed peace offer to England in 1940 had been rejected, all efforts were concentrated on preparations for an invasion of England. . . . The material and manpower difficulties were enormous.

Heye: The high command and many members of the public and armed forces had great hopes, after the cessation of hostilities, of a peaceful settlement. By suitable treatment of the French and by sparing their honor, it was hoped to pacify France. In particular, no humiliating measures and restrictions were imposed on the French navy. At the same time, however, preparations were of course made for the continuation of the war; an invasion of England from France was the only possibility. Furthermore, even with the

U-boats, the navy had not enough forces to blockade the British Isles without invading. In theory the possibility of invading England across the short stretch of Channel appeared to be not unfavorable. The military forces in England at this time were, without any doubt, smaller than those forces that were [available] for a landing by Germany. The RAF too was probably inferior in numbers to the German air force. At the same time the great losses sustained by the Luftwaffe in their attacks on London demonstrated the quick consumption of our own air force.

Dönitz: The situation that had developed—the destruction of the English expeditionary force and the weakness of the English land defenses—caused us to entertain the idea of deciding the war in our favor by a rapid invasion of England. On account of the circumstances . . . existing before the war and the—for us—surprisingly rapid development of the situation in the west, no preparations of any sort had been made. Since an invasion could only succeed if it took place quickly—in any case, before the autumn—it was necessary now, when the Führer gave orders for its preparation, to attempt to create the necessary conditions, both as regards material and training, with the greatest haste and with every means of improvisation.

Boehm: The Germans had arrived, as it were, suddenly on the Channel coast, had to improvise everything for an invasion, and they had but a small superiority in the air while they were completely inferior at sea.

Krancke: The apparent weakness of England on land led to the decision to attempt an invasion in any case, and thus end the war. But preparations for invasion had to be improvised in a few months.

Boehm and Krancke identify the crucial point. Invasion was the way to win the war, and it seems surprising that Germany, a nation renowned for its meticulous planning, does not appear to have given the matter much thought and was reduced to hasty improvisations. Schniewind and Schuster reveal that, as chief of staff to the naval war staff, Schniewind had been farsighted enough to consider the possibility in advance.

The main objective of German foreign policy, and the strategic planning and industrial production, did not include an invasion of England. No preparatory work or planning of any kind was done.

When, after the conclusion of the Polish campaign, the Führer's peace offer was rejected and the operational planning for the attack in the west begun, the naval war staff asked the general staff of the army whether, in the event of big successes on land and in the air, an invasion of England would follow. The army leaders rejected the idea. They looked with reserve on the prospect of success in the west. . . . In no way were the Führer nor the general staff certain that the offensive would even gain possession for us of those ports of the French Channel coast that were especially operationally important for the offensive against the enemy's sea communications (including Brest). All the less could the Führer at that time consider the invasion prospects.

As far as can be remembered, the naval war staff, to whom the magnitude of the operation was apparent and who foresaw approximately the extent and time necessary for the planning and practical preparation, had during the winter of 1939–40 accomplished the first theoretical initial work on a draft for their own use.

When, by the end of May 1940, the devastating success of the German western offensive was clearly apparent, the naval war staff . . . or the naval high command itself, again asked the high command of the Wehrmacht and/or the Führer whether preparations for a landing should be made. Again a negative reply was received.

After the complete collapse of France, the German war leaders hoped to be able to make a negotiated peace before making the decision to give the order for practical preparation for the invasion. The theoretical work (construction plans for vehicles, embarkation points in the harbors, organization, deployment, tide tables, etc.) had, however, already been put in hand by this time (end of June 1940). The authors cannot now remember exact dates of the commencement of the individual sections of the preparations. Cooperation began between the naval war staff and the army general staff at the beginning of July.

The first orders must have gone out to the local commanders at the end of the first week in July. On the Führer's instructions it gave a very short time for the completion of preparations (about 20 August). He had very soon to postpone it, for the setting up of embarkation points, the process of getting the landing craft ready, and their transfer from the construction dockyards (on the Rhine and the Frisian-Dutch coastal area) to the invasion ports could not be completed in a few weeks.

Schniewind and his colleagues, even without a directive from the Führer, appear to have done much of the preliminary paperwork, but the launching of a full-scale invasion calls for more than that—and first and foremost it must have adequate vessels to carry the troops and their equipment. It

must have been quite frustrating to feel that one has an army that would have an excellent chance of overrunning Britain quickly but to lack the means of getting that army ashore. In their advance across Europe they had fought their way across many substantial rivers—but the waters of the English Channel, though not very wide, were a wholly different type of obstacle.

Schulz: The most striking illustration that the German navy did not prepare in any way for war with England was the indisputable fact that not only the construction but even the design of any force of invasion craft was entirely neglected.

Krancke: We had no landing craft. We collected all our river barges and similar craft and fitted these provisionally with landing ramps. We had no naval ferry barges or similar special craft that were required. These slow and unseaworthy river barges would necessitate waiting for a fairly long period of calm weather, and, also, we needed absolute air superiority in order to protect our supply ships. The crews of these barges, gathered together from all quarters, were unschooled in military and maritime matters. Even if the shipping space could have been provided in these few weeks, and the naval and military personnel sufficiently trained, the danger from the British navy, whose full force had to be reckoned with if an invasion were attempted, was so great that, until we had achieved absolute air superiority and had built up sufficient coastal artillery cover for the landing fleet, operation *Seelöwe* [sea lion] seemed impossible.

Dönitz: To produce new landing craft in great numbers and in time was, from the point of view of material and construction, no longer possible, even though at this time the naval ferry barge had been designed and completed in the first series. It was thus necessary to fall back [to the greatest possible extent] on available tugs and barges of the coastal and inland water transport system. These were modified for landing purposes. Their greatest disadvantage lay in their very limited seaworthiness (up to sea three), and as most of them were not self-propelled, they required towing. Investigations were made into landing [places], currents, and weather conditions in the Channel. Training of the troops intended for the landing was extended as more of the necessary materials became available and all possible preparations of a tactical nature were made.

Schulz seems to have had little confidence in any of the invasion preparations.

Hitler's Admirals

All craft that appeared in any way suitable for landing purposes were collected together from the whole of Germany and the occupied territories of western Europe; and to this end recourse was had, to a considerable extent, to purely river craft, tugs, and barges, all of which now had to be converted.

All obtainable personnel in any way suitable for these numerous craft were collected together and given emergency training. A large number of landing exercises were carried out.

In spite of feverish activity in all dockyards in Germany and the occupied territories, these preparations could not be completed before the beginning of September, thus making the earliest possible date in question the middle of September.

An experienced naval officer could not but feel uneasy at all these preparations, since, apart from the many material and manpower difficulties, he could appreciate also the difficulties of seamanship, not to speak of the enemy's countermeasures.

The numerous proposed landing craft flotillas, with their neatly planned formations, indeed looked magnificent on paper—in the leading file always a tug towing two barges, the first of which had no motive power, the second an auxiliary motor; six or eight more of these trains of barges in relatively close line abreast were intended, with a line of motor boats and further trawlers towing barges, and so on.

How, in practice, this mass of loaded craft could be sailed in the evening on time from the ports, could take up their prescribed formation outside the harbor in the face of the prevailing Channel currents and in view of the low speed of the boats in tow, and how they could make the Channel crossing in this complicated formation, by night, across the current, was a problem to any seaman.

If one then took the enemy countermeasures into consideration—and it was obvious that the far-superior English fleet would be thrown in to the fullest extent against our covering forces, quite apart from the reaction of the Royal Air Force, which at that time might feasibly have been previously eliminated by our superior Luftwaffe—one can understand that a weight was lifted from the mind of every senior naval officer when *Seelöwe* (code name for the invasion) was called off.

Schniewind and Schuster, with all the inside knowledge from the former's job as chief of staff to the naval war staff, share the concerns expressed by Schulz about the quality of the landing craft, the problems of navigation and seamanship, and the anticipated reaction of the Royal Navy.

Much consideration had to be given from the first to the suitability of the landing craft (especially to their seaworthiness) and above all to the inland ships (barges), which had been built with landing ramps to transport the armored vehicles. They and all the other auxiliary transports (tugs, fishing boats, launches, yachts, etc.) made the convoys particularly unwieldy. Their prospects of reaching the landing places correctly, and to leave them again quickly, were slight.

The preparations and launching of [Operation] Sea Lion had to be made in the occupied enemy territory, with all the disadvantages entailed thereby —secrecy, sabotage, transport routes, and so on.

The English fleet was completely intact; one had to reckon with its opposition with all available forces at the moment of, or soon after, the beginning of the invasion. As far as the authors can remember the results of the air reconnaissance of these critical days, the German Luftwaffe did not succeed in keeping British cruiser and destroyer formations completely out of the western Channel ports, from where lay the first threat of enemy naval units to the invasion army. The German fleet was too weak (it had alone in Norway lost ten destroyers) to attack the English fleet in close battle and conceal the landing operations directly. It could only be used as a diversion, which was planned.

The English people and armed forces had recovered from the shock of Dunkirk by September 1940. The defenses of the coast of southern England had, by the end of July, substantially increased, and even more so by September.

Our second wave would have needed at least eight days for the crossing. The transport of the first wave would have had to return from the enemy coast to the invasion ports. Therefore it was difficult to estimate what percentage of losses would thereby be incurred; in particular, the safety of the supplies would have been of considerable importance so long as the English naval forces were not kept away.

Unwilling, perhaps, to see the navy take the full blame for the problems in mounting such a crucially important operation, Schniewind and Schuster claim that part of the problem lay with the army.

The army high command needed a wide bridgehead on the enemy coast to be able to start the operation in southern England and continue it; so automatically the limits of the invasion launching area and the sea area involved were extended, from which enemy naval units had to be screened off. The result of this divergence between the requirements of the army and the extent to which the navy could comply with such requirements was a compromise with obvious disadvantages.

The army could not practice embarking and disembarking exercises to the desired extent and in the necessary practical way, for the deployment of troops and transport fleets took time.

The admirals are also perfectly prepared to heap some of the blame on the Luftwaffe for failing to carry out its part of the invasion plans.

Meyer: There were no preparations for taking troops to England. It is probable that the German war machine could not, in any case, have undertaken such an operation with the short time at its disposal. There were neither enough parachute troops nor airborne troops available; neither were there enough suitable [aircraft] or crews for this purpose. As is known, we had to fall back on motor-driven and towed barges from the inland waterways. Preparations were, nevertheless, made in spite of all the difficulties and, as far as the navy was concerned, these were carried on almost to the end.

Heye: In the opinion of many naval officers, a landing at the time when it first seemed possible would, in practice, have been more than a risk. With numerous airborne divisions it would perhaps have been possible to form a bridgehead. These [airborne troops], however, were not available in sufficient numbers.

Schniewind and Schuster: A condition that was from the first laid down by the naval war staff and fully recognized by the Führer as a sine qua non was air supremacy over the operational area, and this had not been achieved.

Krancke: In the opinion of the German high command, air superiority was not achieved within the specified time. In my opinion the air attacks were too scattered; it was not the destruction of London docks but the annihilation of the English air force and the lines of communication that we should have aimed at.

Dönitz: From the beginning, it was clear to the leaders that the invasion could only succeed in certain particular conditions. The navy was certainly not in a position to protect the landing forces against the English fleet, whose full weight would have to be reckoned with in such a situation.

This task would have to be taken over by the air force. To this end it was necessary, not only to wipe out completely the Royal Air Force but also to attack beforehand the ports near the landing area with such effect that the English naval forces would have to be withdrawn to more distant bases;

otherwise they would be able to reach the landing forces at night by short approach routes without the air force being able to prevent them.

When, in September 1940, the preparations for invasion were complete, it also became apparent that complete defeat of the English air force had by no means been achieved. Thus one of the most important prerequisites for an invasion was lacking.

In their summary of an interview with Dönitz, British Naval Intelligence report his further criticism of the German air force, but for whose short-comings the German navy could have carried out its part of the plan:

If it had succeeded in defeating the RAF in the Battle of Britain [the German air force] would still have been incapable of keeping the Royal Navy off a seaborne landing force because it had not the necessary weapons; the bombs in use were of far too small a caliber to have been able to prevent main units from coming to grips with a landing force; the German main [naval] units were totally inadequate for this task. Granted that the GAF could have carried out its two tasks, the German navy would have had no difficulty in transporting the landing force in the vessels then available.

The longer the Germans hesitated about launching the invasion, the more problematic became the weather conditions they might expect to encounter.

Schniewind and Schuster: With the advancing days at that time of the year, the question of the weather became decisive. From the middle of September onward, sufficient long periods of calm (not over force two or three) could not be counted upon.

Krancke: When the autumn storms set in, the undertaking had to be given up immediately. At a later date it was no longer possible, after England had to a considerable extent consolidated her defense measures in the coastal area in question. . . . How helpless England was in 1940 was unknown to us.

Dönitz: There could be no question of a short postponement, for once October—and the beginning of the autumn gales—had set in, a long period of good weather such as would be required for success could no longer be expected. Postponement to the spring of 1941 could only render the military conditions less favorable.

With such limited prospects of success, the resolve to carry on with the invasion of England could not be justified unless it presented the only and final means of ending successfully the war with England. This was not the case, for the German leaders saw in the Mediterranean another possibility of striking a decisive blow against England, quite apart from the shipping war, which, as U-boat numbers increased and with the . . . forceful participation of the air force, should generally produce some result.

The Führer therefore decided to abandon the invasion, although the apparent threat of it was to be maintained.

In their overall judgment on the practicalities of Operation Sea Lion, the admirals' views are fairly consistent:

Weichold: [The] possibility of breaking British naval power by the seizure or destruction of her bases in the British Isles was planned but soon recognized as impracticable. Invasion and air offensive showed themselves as mirages in the face of hard reality.

Meyer: Personally, I am of the opinion that the invasion could have been possible in the autumn of 1940 had we had sufficient landing equipment of the modern type; [but] the position on the sea and in the air was such that, with the resources available, success was impossible. . . . One now hears much about the failure of Germany to invade in 1940 but she really had not the proper means at her disposal.

Krancke: A combined operation of such magnitude can hardly be improvised, especially when the enemy has control of the seas. On the other hand, the possession of the French coast provided the most valuable basis for the real sea war against merchant shipping.

Schulz: It is my firm conviction that the invasion operation of 1940 in its intended form would have led to a complete failure, if not even to a catastrophe.

Heye does not even accept that a successful invasion would have brought Germany the complete victory that would have been its triumphant justification.

Contrary to the opinion of many military leaders, the opinion was widespread in the navy that a complete or partial occupation of England would not mean the end of the war. Danger from the air to Germany would without doubt have been considerably lessened. But England, putting her trust in time and, in the last instance, in America and the empire, would probably have continued the war after the loss of Great Britain.

Finally, as a sailor, Schulz has no difficulty in identifying the decisive weapon in Britain's armory.

It should be said that, in the circumstances of 1940, the presence of the powerful British navy prevented an invasion, since at that time neither the Royal Air Force, the British army, nor the home guard was sufficiently powerful to stave it off. Even the fact that the German air force was unable in 1940 decisively to defeat the RAF could not have prevented the invasion had not the British navy stood in the background.

4

Ocean Warfare against Merchant Shipping, 1940–1941

DISAPPOINTED IN THEIR hope that an invasion would enable them to administer a speedy knockout blow in face of Britain's stubborn resolve to fight on alone, the Germans quickly transferred their energies into waging war against Britain's vital sea routes. That was the vulnerable target they had selected when the war began; that was the most appropriate target for Germany's available naval power; that was the target that had proved so rewarding in 1917; that was the target that must have seemed so attainable from the new bases won in 1940; and that was what many naval officers, like Krancke, regarded as "the real sea war." Dönitz had all along been convinced that his U-boats had the potential, over a longer time span, to establish a stranglehold on Britain's trade routes. He was eager to get on with the job, quick to establish new forward bases on the Biscay coast, and impatient to see coming into service the large number of additional boats ordered at the beginning of the war. In hardheaded calculations about waging a war of attrition—the "tonnage war" —against Britain, the new bases provided by the triumphs of the German army had to be measured against the boost to Britain's merchant tonnage by the addition of large numbers of ships from the considerable merchant fleets of conquered countries such as Norway and Holland. In his essay Dönitz gives an account of the way the U-boat campaign developed in 1940.

Conditions were particularly favorable for the U-boat war against shipping in the Atlantic, which was resumed at the conclusion of the Norwegian expedition. The possession of the Biscay ports eliminated the long journeys to and fro that had taken up almost the whole radius of action of the U-boats. The sea routes were now, so to speak, at the front door. The U-boat command took energetic steps to ensure that U-boats in the Atlantic were able, when their fighting resources were exhausted, to return to the Biscay ports for repairs and refitting as early as July 1940. The advantage of avoiding the long journey home was seen immediately in the doubling of the number of U-boats available in the actual operation area.

The shipping war was relatively successful until October 1940. English destroyers and escort vessels were either under repair as a result of the Norwegian campaign or else tied to the south coast of England by the threat of invasion. The protection of the shipping lanes in the summer of 1940 was, consequently, very limited. U-boats proceeding from the Biscay ports quickly contacted shipping, since they were able to operate close to the English approach channels, for example, the North and Bristol Channels. The U-boat losses were exceptionally small; technical difficulties were recognized and overcome. Torpedoes fitted only with impact fuses and of increased reliability were used. U-boats still operated singly, as up till then there was no difficulty in finding shipping near the coast.

From October 1940 the picture west of England began to change for the U-boat arm. For England the danger of invasion was over; the English defense vessels were apparently once more available for A/S [antisubmarine] defense. The Royal Air Force was being used on an increasing scale for guarding shipping routes and for A/S defense. The convoy system was apparently being most extensively used. In any case, it was becoming more difficult for U-boats to operate close in to the shore, and convoys were located less frequently. The U-boats were often at sea for lengthy periods without meeting any traffic, and the great successes of the summer came to an end. The U-boat command decided, therefore, from October 1940, on the controlled operation of U-boats at sea against convoys located by systematic search. These so-called pack tactics were developed in the clear knowledge that location [of targets] would be the main problem in the U-boat war, as through concentration of shipping in convoys, the empty spaces of the ocean would be extraordinarily increased. On the other hand, what mattered was to direct as many U-boats as possible to a convoy once found and thus set a concentration of U-boats against a concentration of shipping.

These tactics correspond to the principle held for thousands of years by every military command, of being as strong as possible in the right place at the right time. Organization and control of U-boats was carried out by radio on long- and shortwave from the command post in Paris and, after November 1940, Lorient.

The first convoy attacks at the end of October 1940 succeeded with very good results. In these the U-boats quickly exhausted their torpedoes. This resulted in quite short, but successful, operations. After the convoy battles there were no U-boats in the operational area, as owing to the ever present shortage of boats there were no replacements ready for sea. Thus, the operational area in November 1940 was empty and it was only filled at the beginning of December, which led immediately to another successful convoy battle. Tactically it was proved already with these first experiments that "pack" tactics had been developed correctly; that it was necessary to keep strict control of the boats having regard to their disposition for contacting the convoy, their keeping contact with a view to directing in other boats, and the issuing of the order to attack; that in the attack itself, however, the boats must have complete freedom. It was therefore a control in a tactical sense and not in attack.

It was further proved that night was by far the most successful time for attack, because the U-boats could get within firing range much quicker and more often. . . . Therefore the night was used basically for concentrated attacks by U-boats and day attacks [were] only undertaken in favorable conditions. The comparatively small and maneuverable type VIIC proved excellent for night attacks.

The great U-boat aces at that time, such as Kapitänleutnants Prien, Kretschmer, and Schepke, were all "VIIC drivers." They swore by this type of boat and, when changing boats, did not wish to take over any new large ones. Moreover, probably never have the front line fighters been so convinced of the quality of their technical material and their type of boat as the German U-boat men [were] in this war.

The German navy did not, however, intend that the U-boats should bear the entire burden of the naval offensive against Britain's trade routes. From bases close at hand, their fast and aggressive E-boats could be very effective in British coastal waters, as Schniewind and Schuster describe:

A very lively and spirited war of "little ships" developed in the autumn of 1940 from bases along the Dutch, Belgian, and French coasts, together with offensive and defensive minelaying operations. The area around the Hoofden, the Downs, and the English south coast were scenes of numerous operations by E-boats, torpedo boats, and destroyers that frequently came into contact with the enemy. Considerable damage and disorder was thereby caused to British coastal shipping. The losses among E-boats remained very small till the introduction of British countermeasures (MGBs and fighter aircraft). The losses in torpedo boats were more serious (enemy mines). The use of U-boats was discontinued in English coastal areas from the end of 1940 onward as the defenses were too effective and our knowledge of the minefields was insufficient. The naval war staff had the impression that merchant shipping along the coast of southern England (for instance that passing through the Dover Straits) had completely stopped for a time owing to the German air and sea fighting activities, and that the use of naval bases there had been considerably reduced.

For carrying the offensive to the more distant oceans, the naval war staff had devised a well-planned and well-executed plan to compensate for the acute shortage of surface warships by using former merchant vessels as armed auxiliary cruisers, as Schniewind and Schuster describe:

The warfare against merchant shipping by surface craft overseas, started by the pocket battleships *Graf Spee* and *Deutschland* at the outbreak of war, was continued from April 1940 onward by merchantmen converted to AMCs [armed merchant cruisers]. This kind of mercantile warfare had been the object of considerable and thoughtful preparation before the outbreak of war, when commanders were appointed, crews assembled, and steamers chosen. In the choice of steamers one had first to bear in mind:

> high speed (if possible not less than 14 knots);
> strong engine room installations;
> large radius of action; and . . .
> an unobtrusive appearance.

They were equipped with four to five 15-cm (6-in) guns, and surface and underwater torpedo tubes. They were sometimes fitted out to carry mines, sometimes as aircraft carriers, and sometimes to carry reinforcements (arms and material) for U-boats. Not every raider passed the test with regard to unobtrusiveness of appearance, robustness of engine room installation, and endurance. The arming and training of the raiders, originally estimated to take three to four months, lasted considerably longer than had been expected. The first batch was not ready to be dispatched till the beginning of spring 1940.

The direction of the raiders' operations in the war against merchant shipping overseas came immediately under the naval war staff. The commanders, however, in view of their experience, were allowed a great deal of freedom as regards the altering of, and sometimes withdrawal from, operational areas. Special security measures were taken for wireless communication with the homeland, which could not altogether be dispensed with.

The raiders' operations by the end of 1941 were considerably luckier and more successful than had been hoped for by the naval war staff. It was foreseen that this kind of mercantile warfare would in the course of time come to grief and that the raiders would probably fall victims to the enemy defense. The successful working of the raiders was practically limited to the years 1940–41. Later attempts to continue this form of naval warfare were less successful. . . . Most of the raiders obtained good results in the years 1940–41 (whaling boats, minelaying round Australia, the cruiser *Sydney*, engagements with enemy cruisers) and brought a series of valuable prizes back. A large part of these were successful in returning safely home.

> In this all-out assault on Britain's merchant shipping, the German air force might have been expected to make a significant—or possibly decisive—contribution. Meyer is outspoken in his criticism of the Luftwaffe's contribution, and he has no doubt about where the blame lay.

When the invasion did not take place in 1940, the aim of German policy at sea was to throw in everything we had in a strategical offensive against England. The navy was continually endeavoring to get the air force to follow suit, but with only partial success. It was impossible to get the air force to take adequate action against shipping harbors and dockyards, and the air mining effort never reached satisfactory proportions. That we did not succeed in starving England lay in the fact that the air force had so little understanding of the matter. The navy was continually pressing this forward, but we always ran up against the high command of the air force, and even Hitler would not make a decision, because neither of them could, according to the navy, realize the importance of a powerful sea power and mastery of the sea. One still retains this opinion, even if one remembers that the air force had to meet considerable demands on land because, when this situation became easier, there was still not sufficient understanding of these things.

> Other admirals are also less than satisfied with the air support received by the navy.

Schniewind and Schuster: The lack of appropriate, well-trained reconnaissance aircraft with a wide range made itself more and more felt. Assistance was only occasionally obtained from the C in C Luftwaffe through the insistence of the C in C U-boats and the naval war staff—and then it was not sufficient. [There was] a lack of understanding shown by the C in C Luftwaffe for the needs of the war at sea.

Krancke: Air squadrons schooled in overland fighting cannot be employed in naval warfare without further training, as the supreme command of the German air force believed. They had to be trained for this warfare and also given instruction on how to use their offensive weapons. The meager successes of the German air force against English sea power during the period of German air superiority are attributable to this state of affairs.

The advantage of an independent air force, its forces allocated according to strategic requirements at vital points, does not counterbalance the lack of experience in naval warfare. During this period, an attempt was made to employ the Luftwaffe as well as the [traditional] means used in naval warfare against merchant shipping.

Attacks on the great harbors and dockyards were to complete the strategic aim to starve England. But minelaying by the Luftwaffe, successful in theory, did not appear to produce the anticipated success, owing to lack of navigational knowledge. The reason why all these operations [did not achieve successes corresponding] to the superiority of the German air force at this time is beyond my comprehension. Perhaps the preparation and beginning of the eastern campaign, in the spring of 1941, for which the greater part of the German Luftwaffe had to be allocated, was a decisive factor.

With expert knowledge from the long period when he served as C in C U-boats, Dönitz is able to analyze the problems faced by the U-boats and why reconnaissance aircraft might have made a real difference to the success of the U-boat campaign.

The winter of 1940–41 showed even more that, with further concentration of English shipping into convoys and the forcing of the U-boat disposition into the open Atlantic, the main difficulty of the U-boat war would be the location of convoys. The more distant disposition of U-boats in the open sea was necessary for two reasons. First, owing to the growing English defense close in to the land, operating the [U-boat], which for the most part took place on the surface, was no longer possible. Second, time was necessary for a successful attack on a convoy by several U-boats, so that [they] could reach the convoy from their various reconnaissance positions, which were for the most part in distant areas. It was, therefore, no longer any use locating a convoy about twenty-four hours before it ran in under the English coast, as there was not sufficient time to direct the other U-boats to the target and carry out the attack.

The problem of location urgently required better reconnaissance. The U-boat itself with its extremely limited range of vision, was the worst possible medium of reconnaissance. The most vital and necessary complement to the U-boat, which was the main instrument of battle, was the aircraft. Here the flaw in the conduct of the war at sea was shown up with painful clarity. Fundamentally it was the fault of the direction of the armed forces that in peacetime had created a sea arm, which in wartime was incorporated into the Luftwaffe, and the construction of the Luftwaffe to be employed in a purely land battle did not meet the demands of the navy. This resulted in the navy's having to operate without air support. Pressure exerted by the German U-boat command and representation by the chief of the German general staff and the commander in chief U-boats to the Führer in September 1940 resulted in a squadron of aircraft with the widest range—[the] FW 200—being placed at their disposal and based [near] Bordeaux. Then there began very extensive experiments in air and sea cooperation between this squadron and the U-boat arm, which, however, produced at first completely negative results.

The lack of a corresponding cooperation carrying over from peacetime became painfully obvious. The primary essentials to be attained were a common terminology, a common medium of communication, and above all, experience of the pilots in flying over the sea, navigation, recognition of types of ships, and their clear and correct reporting, shadowing, directing U-boats by means of radio beacons, and other things. The first joint operations carried out proved unsuccessful. The lack of success was caused by one decisive factor—the U-boats being assembled in the wrong position, empty of shipping, through faulty navigation or else being split into two groups owing to two aircraft through faulty fixing having given two different positions (up to 120 miles apart) for the same convoy. Gradually these teething troubles were overcome and finally resulted in a profitable cooperation. Owing to the limited range of the aircraft, it was only practicable to operate on the England-Gibraltar convoy routes. The main shipping routes in the North Atlantic had to be reconnoitered by the U-boats alone.

In the judgment of Schniewind and Schuster, the achievements and endurance of the U-boat crews in 1940–41 are worthy of praise.

The attacking power of the U-boats in consequence of the small number of available U-boats was, on the average, very small in these years, but, in comparison, the results were completely satisfying. (Misfires of torpedoes had been reduced to a great extent by the end of 1940.) The author, owing to lack of more detailed information, is not in a position to name the number of boats at that time available. He estimates that in these years twelve to fifteen U-boats were in action against the enemy during the best periods, but for months sometimes considerably less. The average should lie between eight and ten boats. For weeks during the first half of 1941 there were only four or five boats in action. This is explained by the fact that considerable forces had to be withdrawn from the already limited number of U-boats for the training centers in the Baltic, in order to train commanders and crews for the larger number of newly built boats to be ready in 1942. The result was, nevertheless, as has been already said, very satisfactory. The tactic of attacking convoys by U-boat packs in particular proved itself both practical and successful.

The losses, even if considerable, remained within bearable bounds, and throughout were far less than the numbers reported by the enemy. All types of boats and crews stood the test well. The length of operations—especially when restocking at sea from a supply ship or auxiliary cruiser was possible —was considerably longer than had been expected before the war. At that time one had imagined that the physical powers of endurance of a U-boat crew would be exhausted after about four weeks of continuous operations. Operations lasting twice as long were soon no exception, and in the course of the war these performances increased considerably.

The achievements of the U-boats were impressive, but they were still a long way from starving Britain into surrender. Would they ever be able to choke off the supplies being brought across the Atlantic? Schniewind and Schuster answer:

In the U-boat arm itself, young commanders and crews believed implicitly in its effectiveness, even against British sea power. German naval officers in other branches viewed the prospect more soberly. The commander in chief U-boats (BdU) himself told the author in the course of a confidential conversation in Paris in the winter of 1940–41 that he knew that U-boat warfare alone could not end the war victoriously against the Anglo-Saxon sea powers; as far as the author knows he (Dönitz) had never let this doubt come out into the open. During the further course of the war . . . he never expressed himself as being other than hopeful, eager to attack, and full of energy.

The results achieved in 1941 are recalled by Dönitz with little satisfaction, and he once again voices his frustration at the lack of air reconnaissance.

The year 1941 presented the U-boats with almost insoluble tasks as far as the finding of merchant shipping was concerned; the number of U-boats was still limited; the building program, ordered at the beginning of the war, had as yet no effect on the fighting group. There was no longer any question of attacks near the coast; the disposition of forces had to take place in the open sea. Yet the number of U-boats was too small for the complete surveillance of the open sea. Its disposition could only succeed through surprise.

The enemy himself had recognized that the best protection for his convoys was in taking advantage of the wide spaces of the open sea by continually varying routing. So, for example, the U-boat successes were small in the months of July and August 1941 because of the failure to find convoys in the North Atlantic. Already, to some extent, long-range English aircraft began to locate and attack U-boat dispositions, so that, as far as possible, the U-boat patrols were detected by the enemy and then avoided by the convoys.

After an unsuccessful search for convoys in July and August, at last in the beginning of September 1941 a convoy was detected near the coast of Greenland and attacked with good results. This shows how very greatly the wide ocean spaces favored the enemy, the dispersal of his convoys from Greenland and Iceland down to the Azores, and the resulting difficulty on the part of the U-boats to find anything. Once contact was made with the convoy, the attack succeeded every time. The difficulty lay in the finding, not in the attacking. The limited sinkings for many a month resulted from the searching and waiting, lasting for weeks.

With its own extensive, long-range air reconnaissance the outcome of the U-boat war in the year 1941 would have been quite different. The lack of an extensive naval air arm proved to be a decisive disadvantage for the German conduct of the war at sea.

The U-boat arm knew that they could fight, that their limited success lay only in their failure to make contact with the enemy, and that this would improve as soon as greater numbers of boats were available for searching. They regarded future developments with confidence.

One way of increasing the effectiveness of the war on commerce might have been to establish forward bases even closer to the convoy routes.

Schniewind and Schuster explain why, after a preliminary study, the naval war staff decided that the plan should not go ahead.

Round about the winter of 1940–41 the naval war staff, both on its own account and at the direction of the high command, went into the matter of the possible success of an invasion of Iceland and the Azores. Apart from political obstructions, the possession of these areas or of single bases was certainly possible from a military point of view; and the creation of naval and air bases was extremely desirable, as these would form the pivot from which the war against English merchant shipping could be successfully carried out. But to keep these bases for any length of time was out of the question in view of the limited strength of the occupying forces that could at first be thrown in and the impossibility of keeping up a regular flow of reinforcements. This project, therefore, remained a theoretical investigation.

Among the "political obstructions" referred to by Schniewind and Schuster, the most influential was concern about the reaction of the United States. Although officially neutral, the United States provided increasing support for Britain during 1940 and 1941. On 3 September 1940 she had transferred fifty old destroyers to Britain in exchange for the lease of military bases in Newfoundland and the Caribbean. On 11 March 1941 President Roosevelt had signed the Lend-Lease Act by which America would supply food and arms to Britain despite her inability to pay for them. On 7 July 1941 U.S. troops took over the defense of Iceland from the British. From September 1941 U.S. Navy vessels became involved in escorting British convoys in the western Atlantic; on 17 October one of these escorts, the USS *Kearny* was torpedoed, but not sunk, by a U-boat; and a fortnight later U-526 sank the U.S. destroyer *Reuben James*. Whatever the niceties of international law, the Kriegsmarine and the U.S. Navy had become embroiled in open hostilities. While that situation was gradually evolving, the German navy's operations in the Atlantic had been seriously restricted.

Krancke: We knew that large amounts of ever-increasing supplies of war material were being—and had been—delivered from the U.S.A. to Great Britain since the beginning of the war. Beyond and above this, the extent of support given could be established by W/T [wireless telegraphy] interception. For instance, at the end of November 1940, when I contacted an English steamer off the Little Antilles and she made a short W/T message, which was however not picked up by any English station, the message was passed on by an American battleship.

The following example shows the extent of violation of neutrality. Firing pins and other machine parts of weapons were found in the first-aid chests on a Greek steamer when she was boarded, carrying alleged Red Cross supplies to Greece. In spite of these continual violations of neutrality, German ships were strictly forbidden [to engage in] any acts of war, even the challenging and searching for contraband of ships flying the American flag. The intention was to avoid giving President Roosevelt—whose policy was, in our opinion, purposely directed toward participation in the war against Germany —any excuse for entering the war.

Dönitz: The attitude of the United States of America was another stumbling block in the U-boat war. The U.S. had declared the Western Hemisphere to be their zone of protection and, although neutral, announced they would attack any German warships in the area. In fact German U-boats were actually depth charged by American destroyers. In spite of this contravention of international law, the German U-boat leaders had definite orders from the political leaders to avoid under any circumstances any incident with American warships and merchant ships. The result of this was that the U-boat leaders had to prohibit in this western area any attack on English destroyers, because by night or through periscopes it was quite possible to confuse [them] with American destroyers.

In addition to this, a situation most unfortunate for the captains, the political leaders forbade U-boats to proceed west of Newfoundland, because they wanted to prevent any incident in this area, with a view to avoiding war with the U.S.A. The U-boat leaders were unable, therefore, to search out the convoys proceeding to England near their point of departure and in the areas of strong concentration (e.g., near Halifax), but had to remain in the open spaces of the Atlantic where, after passing Cape Race, a very great dispersal of the convoys was possible.

Schniewind and Schuster: From the middle of 1941, when [Admiral Schniewind] took over the post as admiral of the fleet, [he] . . . still remembers that [the] zone (300 miles) round the American coast, safeguarded by the States, considerably injured the efficacy of U-boats as well as the attacking of merchant ships by surface craft. Attacks on shipping along the Canadian eastern coast and Newfoundland (Halifax), although so desirable and profitable, were forbidden, as it was necessary to avoid all possible friction with the U.S.A. When the U.S.A. relaxed her caution in 1941 and the "all-help-short-of-war" support to the western powers in the convoy and defense service south of Iceland was introduced, the naval war staff, following the orientation of high command policy, tried to prevent friction and incidents as far as possible.

Although the U-boats, with their ability to operate clandestinely, were likely to be the most effective weapon for attacking every aspect of Britain's sea power, the German naval war staff also showed little hesitation in committing the few major surface warships available to act as commerce raiders, but they were under no illusions about the grave risks to which their ships would be exposed.

Schniewind and Schuster: It was the fundamental decision of the naval war staff, with which the high command was in full agreement, that all suitable surface forces should be used for mercantile warfare against England and so give support to the U-boat campaign. This applied to the *Bismarck* also. . . . It was, moreover, foreseen that surface warfare on the high seas would eventually succumb to the strong enemy sea and air forces, [and] increasing effectiveness of enemy patrolling of the seas and straits.

Dönitz: After the conquest of Norway and western Europe there were no further tasks for the fighting units of the fleet in the waters of the North Sea and Arctic Ocean. The idea of maintaining it as a "fleet in being" was abandoned, for such a fleet with the ratio in strength would be as good as useless, and in addition there was the danger that they would, through the great range of modern weapons (bombs, airborne mines) be uselessly expended. In addition, just at this time the limited number of U-boats in 1941 demanded that the shipping war should be supported by all available means. The French Biscay ports, of which only Brest was suitable for battleships, were available as bases.

And so the decision was made to send the battleships and heavy cruisers as well as the pocket battleships into the Atlantic. Owing to their limited range it was not possible to send destroyers too on the trip round the north of England, as well as on the later far-reaching attacks from western France, where after their passage through the Channel they could only be used in the Biscay area. This lack of any protection for the heavy units was felt to be a great disadvantage, yet could not influence the decision that had been taken.

Krancke, who commanded the pocket battleship *Admiral Scheer* on a very successful commerce-raiding cruise in the winter of 1940–41, experienced

the exhilaration and anxiety of commanding a major warship far from a home port.

The naval war in the Atlantic was conducted at enormous risk, employing all the fighting means at the disposal of the navy. Besides the U-boats, which constituted the greatest factor in this warfare, and for which air-defended bases were created, auxiliary cruisers were ordered to every sea in the world. As a result of an attack against a convoy in the North Atlantic by the cruiser *Admiral Scheer,* the enemy was forced to protect its convoys with battleships. The arrival of the *Admiral Scheer* in the Atlantic and Indian Oceans tied down large enemy forces, and the battleships *Scharnhorst* and *Gneisenau* and the cruiser *Admiral Hipper* were sent to the North Atlantic to wage war against merchant shipping.

The winter of 1940–41 is remarkable on account of the wide use made of surface forces in the war against merchant shipping, a form of naval warfare that may be described as classical. Nearly a million tons of enemy shipping were captured or destroyed by surface craft. Countless prizes were taken to the Biscay ports; highly valuable raw materials were brought in from overseas. The English countermeasures were, for the most part, useless, as long as the stretches of ocean were not patrolled by their aircraft and electrical location gear was not as yet at their disposal. This period was the most successful for German naval warfare.

The end to this kind of warfare came with the incursion into the Atlantic of the new battleship *Bismarck*—Germany's most powerful warship— and the new cruiser *Prinz Eugen* in May 1941.

Schniewind and Schuster: When the *Hipper* and *Scheer* broke out and made their dash home, it was already evident that the [enemy's] supervision of the Denmark Strait had become more effective (? radar). The *Bismarck* had had to postpone her operation so long, waiting for the *Tirpitz* or even an aircraft carrier to join her, that the chances of a successful breakthrough with any worthwhile result became smaller and smaller in spite of the strengthening of her striking power. The departure of the *Bismarck* and *Prinz Eugen* finally came at the time of the Crete operation. The naval war staff deemed it most desirable that a diversion to this operation should take place in the Atlantic to draw off [the British] Force H from Gibraltar. Originally the *Scharnhorst* and *Gneisenau* were to work together for this purpose, but the plan came to nothing owing to the fact that they were still under repair in Brest.

These were the principal reasons that forced the naval war staff to risk the *Bismarck* operation. The diversion was indeed successful, but in spite of the success against the *Hood*, was dearly bought at the price of the sinking of the battleship *Bismarck*, together with the admiral of the fleet and naval staff. The *Prinz Eugen* managed to shake off the English cruisers and to contact the refueling steamer in the middle of the Atlantic. *Prinz Eugen* never again worked alone against merchant shipping owing to the unreliability of her engine room installation (teething troubles of the high pressure steam system). Thus this ship too was forced into Brest.

Dönitz: The difficulty of the Icelandic passage did not prevent the battleship *Bismarck* and the cruiser *Prinz Eugen* from being sent into the Atlantic as well in May 1941, after the completion of their working up and according to the strategic dispositions already mentioned. After the sinking of the battle cruiser *Hood*, which proved the outstanding fighting power of the new German battleship, the unit was able to shake off contact with the English once more, but on the next day was contacted again by an enemy aircraft. In a hard struggle the *Bismarck* fell victim to the English battleships and formations of aircraft, assembled together from the whole of the North Atlantic. Our own aircraft sent out from western France could not unfortunately bring her any effective help owing to the distance being too great.

The sinking of the *Bismarck* was a grave loss for the navy, even though the leaders, as already mentioned, in their bold and unusual methods of conducting the war had reckoned with such reverses. In this operation it seems that radio location from ships played a decisive part for the first time. It afterward became more and more apparent that the enemy had a definite superiority over us in this direction. This superiority was one of the reasons that caused the units of the German fleet, later the armed merchant cruisers too, to succumb outside home waters. On the other hand the strong reaction of English naval forces proved that the strategic objective had succeeded, that is, besides direct success in sinking, above all to keep the English fleet busy. At this time the English convoys were guarded partly by single battleships, partly covered by groups of battleships.

Krancke: The idea was to form a powerful group in the Atlantic, made up of the *Bismarck* and *Prinz Eugen*, with the *Scharnhorst* and *Gneisenau*, which would be in a position also to attack convoys escorted by battleships. Unfortunately, an aircraft carrier was lacking. The group was not to be scattered, but [operate as] a concentrated force. We did not wait for the *Tirpitz*, which was not yet ready for action, so that we could resume the Battle of the Atlantic with surface forces.

After the annihilation of the *Hood,* [the] *Bismarck* had to complete the action against the *Prince of Wales* and then start on her return journey, as it seemed unlikely that, after the brush with the enemy, the group would succeed in meeting in Brest without further action against a superior force. An attack by the entire English force of carrier-borne aircraft decided the fate of the ship by an unfortunate hit on her rudder. Our own lack of an aircraft carrier, as well as carrier-borne aircraft, was decisively evident.

Schniewind and Schuster: In the course of the *Bismarck* operation, after the battle with the *Hood,* discussions arose in the naval war staff as to whether it was not better to order the battleship to return to the Norwegian coast. This breakthrough appeared more feasible than continuing the operation or making for Brest. The same discussion was renewed when the report came to the naval war staff of the first aerial torpedo hit. The naval supreme commander [Grand Admiral Raeder] refused to commit himself to issuing definite instructions to the battleship or the group command directing the operation, because he was not sufficiently well informed as to the battleship's condition and radius of action and did not wish to hamper the free decisions of the commander in chief of the fleet and the group command.

The heavy surface craft warfare against English sea routes in the Atlantic came to an end with the sinking of the battleship *Bismarck.* In spite of many successes, it had not fulfilled the hopes of the naval war staff owing to the heavy enemy defenses. The plan to use this form of warfare again with the ships gathered in Brest was abandoned as, owing to the extensive repairs and new damage being continually caused by enemy air attacks, the ships were not ready for use till December 1941. The projected operation by destroyers, with the Gironde [River] as their base, against the enemy merchant routes west of the Spanish coast (15 to 20° W) was not carried out because of the weakness of the forces, the limited radius of action, and the lack of sufficiently reliable air reconnaissance.

The use of the Atlantic coast, striven for [and] attained by the naval war staff, for surface forces attacking merchant shipping had only been possible in a very incomplete manner.

From the outbreak of war to the end of 1941 more than 9 million gross registered tons of British, Allied, and neutral merchant shipping had been destroyed, while the shipyards of the British Empire and the United States had replaced about one-third of that figure in new tonnage. The Germans could be reasonably well pleased with that rate of attrition.

U-boats had been responsible for more than half the tonnage sunk, with air attacks accounting for more than 1.5 million tons, and surface raiders of all kinds and mines each claiming another million tons. Commerce raiding clearly waned following the loss of the *Bismarck:* losses to surface raiders, which totaled more than 325,000 tons in the first six months of 1941, declined to a mere 80,000 tons in the second half of the year.

5

War in the Mediterranean, 1940–1941

ITALY HAD FORMED, with Germany, the Rome-Berlin Axis in November 1936. A year later she had joined the German-Japanese Anti-Comintern Pact. The Italian dictator Benito Mussolini collaborated with Hitler in support of General Franco's nationalist forces in the Spanish civil war, and he also played a key role in brokering the Munich Agreement in 1938. Nevertheless, he had hesitated to enter the war as Germany's ally in 1939 but, eager to secure what looked like a very inexpensive seat at the anticipated peace conference, he finally committed his armed forces to an attack on Britain and France on 10 June 1940. In their postwar essays some German admirals express neither great enthusiasm nor gratitude for his intervention.

Heye: The entry of the Italians into the war was not everywhere considered correct in all circles of the armed forces. We heard that Italy's decision was made without German pressure, perhaps only because the Italians believed the war would last only a short time. For economic reasons too, for example with regard to coal, Italian participation in the war was bound to be a hindrance. A neutral Germanophile Italy would, in the view of many military circles, have been more useful to Germany than a belligerent Italy.

Schniewind and Schuster: The naval war staff regarded Italian neutrality as the solution most favorable to Germany. It was foreseen that, in the case of active participation in the war, Italy would soon be needing help. No help was necessary for a neutral Italy, whom the western powers treated cautiously but, politically, in an uncertain and threatening manner, and because of whom a certain body of forces had to be held in reserve in the Mediterranean although not actually taking part in the war. A way lay open through a friendly neutral into the whole world. There were no forces ready to protect the southern frontier of the Reich.

The course of the war, as I judge it today, has shown the correctness of the naval war staff's understanding of the situation. No opinion can be given on how far and for how long the western powers would have been satisfied with Italy's neutrality so favorable to Germany. That, however, could have been watched. It then soon became apparent that the naval war staff must give Italy help; at first, only in supplying material (arms, antitank guns, anti-aircraft guns, and fuel), but later also with military forces.

Krancke: After Italy had remained neutral in 1939, contrary to her treaties, her entry into the war just before the fall of France only acted as a political burden. . . . The Italian armed forces proved themselves to be of little fighting value. On sea, on land, and in the air the armed forces were inferior even to a weaker enemy, despite apparent numerical strength. Germany had to assist everywhere with considerable forces.

Other admirals emphasize that a strategy aimed at exploiting the strength of the Axis position in the Mediterranean would have had better prospects of winning the war against Britain than the Atlantic commerce war to which the German navy was committed. Rear Admiral Schulz sets out the case for a Mediterranean strategy.

Since . . . France as an opponent had ceased to exist, thus neutralizing the whole of French North Africa, and furthermore Italy, with her numerically appreciable fleet, had entered the war on the side of Germany, the situation at sea had altered during the short period April–July 1940 to a hitherto unimagined extent in Germany's favor.

It now required only the entry into our coalition of friendly Spain to close the Mediterranean in the west, thus making it to all intents and purposes an Axis sea.

The way to Egypt and the Near East oil fields would have lain open, and England would have had to accept the compromise peace for which the German political command was striving.

The naval command in Wilhelmshaven, on whose staff I was serving at that time, felt certain of the further development of the war in this direction and made the necessary preparations accordingly, including the allocation of guns' crews from the naval artillery to the straits of Gibraltar.

Why the political leaders of the Reich at that time were unable to secure Spain's adherence to the Axis, I do not know.

I have the feeling that the great naval strategic possibilities of such a development were not fully appreciated by them and that therefore this solution was not urged by them with sufficient vigor.

As I have been informed by colleagues, the German Admiralty's influence on consideration of important politicostrategic combinations of this nature was very slight, as a war council consisting of representatives of the various high commands did not exist, but the most important decisions were made by Adolf Hitler himself (by intuition) so that, in fact, only the translation of these plans into effect was entrusted to the high command.

In my view, therefore, a tremendous opportunity of rapidly bringing the war to a favorable conclusion for Germany was neglected.

Vice Admiral Weichold, who served as the German navy's liaison officer with the Italian navy, offers a fuller explanation of the case for adopting a Mediterranean strategy.

The entry of Italy into the war put an entirely new complexion on the military situation in the Anglo-German war. After the successful countering of the German air attack against the British Isles and when the German high command had renounced its plans for invasion, recognizing the sea as the only place where British power could be brought to battle, another very vulnerable point of the British Empire was now laid open to the Axis in the Mediterranean. The reason for the vulnerability lay in the dependence, even of a sea power, on the geographical situation. This was especially true of the Mediterranean, as British sea power relied on only a few bases. With the fall of these, the whole edifice of British power in the Mediterranean, above all in the Middle East, must needs crumble. England's Mediterranean possessions were, however, mostly of commercial value, which had increased considerably since the First World War. Through her obligation to territories in the eastern Mediterranean, England had now become vulnerable on land. A threat or struggle in these territories allowed the British Empire to be brought to battle on the land, which had hitherto only been possible on the sea.

The practical considerations governing the exclusion of Britain's sea power from the Mediterranean and the destruction of her imperial lifeline were the seizure of Malta, the blocking of the Sicilian Channel, and the conducting of operations from Libya against Egypt. Italy's situation in the central Mediterranean and her possession of Tripolitania secured French North Africa as a base for future land and air operations against the British on a grander scale.

It was quite clear that Italy's entry into the war afforded possibilities far greater than those that had hitherto been available to Germany, for the direction of the war against Great Britain. To profit from these new opportunities it was essential that the Axis high command should pool all their advantages both geographical and material so as to have but one aim. Following this plan, there should not have been any North Sea or Atlantic commands without also a German Mediterranean command on the Italian side.

Even if many of these possibilities had not been put into effect—as often occurs in coalition wars—and had not led to positive successes, at least they might have averted the misfortune that destroyed the southern flank of the Axis in the Mediterranean and later threatened the German southern position. The only presupposition for the execution of Axis Mediterranean operations was the recognition that in that sea and the bordering British territories lay the possibilities of concerted action with the Italian ally.

The German high command recognized in the new strategic German situation, the possibilities of a positive and decisive battle with Great Britain, but not the sources of danger. Moreover the German Admiralty was completely taken up with U-boat warfare as the means of forcing a decision with Great Britain. Thus after Italy's entry into the war the status quo was preserved as regards the direction of the war. The attack on British shipping was carried on principally by U-boats in spite of the shortage of surface craft, but the few surface craft available were subordinated to this aim.

For a variety of reasons some of the admirals would certainly have preferred to see an understanding—possibly an alliance—with France instead of Italy. The Vichy French collaborationist government of Marshal Pétain was not without encouragement to adopt anti-British policies. The British army's precipitate retreat via Dunkirk and the refusal to prejudice the air defense of Britain by committing more fighter squadrons to the defense of France could easily be interpreted as a betrayal of the Entente Cordiale. Most serious of all, at the beginning of July 1940, fearing that Germany might boost her sea power by gaining control of the French fleet, Britain had seized French naval vessels in British ports, interned the French squadron in Alexandria, and bombarded the French naval base of Mers el Kebir, near Oran in Algeria. Whatever the desperation that impelled Britain to take that action, German propagandists could argue that

Britain was no friend of France. The idea that the French might be prepared to take up arms against Britain seemed even more credible when they beat off a British and Free French force that attempted to seize the port of Dakar in West Africa on 27 September 1940.

Heye: The differences between France and Italy were . . . so strong that later collaboration with France must be considerably more difficult. On many sides a long-sighted view was held that collaboration with France and complete reconciliation with our western neighbors would be better than a narrow alliance with Italy.

Krancke: [Italy's involvement] hindered the conclusion of peace with France, as a result of Italy's [claims] on Nice, Corsica, and Tunis. In my opinion this peace might have been possible if Alsace-Lorraine had been returned to France. Germany had no further obligations in spite of the French declaration of war. We never demanded her fleet or her colonies. The armistice terms and the character of the treaty did away with all animosity and dishonor (as opposed to 1918).

Dönitz: Soon after the French [Biscay] ports were set working, owing to the great danger from the air, the navy wished for Atlantic ports farther to the south near French Morocco and Dakar.

Schniewind and Schuster: With regard to the policy toward France, the naval war staff insisted, just as was tried in Norway, that—apart from visionary ideals—the practical and actual war interests of Germany required an end to the war with France in a satisfactory manner, under which, naturally, occupational measures must remain for the duration. France had to be reassured, however, that in peace she would not undergo too hard a fate. By this the naval war staff hoped to gain in France a surer and more willing ally and her arms potential for the war.

For this reason the naval war staff allowed a strengthening of the French military forces in her North African possessions, so as to defend the area more effectively against enemy landings. Naturally these measures were two-edged and could have been turned against the Axis (African campaign). However, the naval war staff believed, after France had been brought even more over to the German side by the mild peace terms, that they would win the confidence of the political leaders of the country and, consequently, be able to place more confidence in her.

Considerable importance was attached by the naval war staff to the advantages of such a policy—the defense of North Africa, rear protection for Italian North Africa, facilities for sending reinforcements via Tunis, gaining of bases in the Mediterranean (Oran, Bizerta, etc.) and on the Atlantic coast (Dakar, Casablanca)—so that an experiment of this sort seemed to be practicable in every way. Moreover, France could perhaps, after adequate strengthening and training, be trusted with the carrying out of a large military expedition starting from Senegambia to recapture that part of equatorial Africa taken by De Gaulle.

Thus the danger, already realized by the naval war staff in 1940, could have been avoided—namely, that the western powers, by means of large scale measures in equatorial Africa and by the building of arterial roads to the Nile, could send reinforcements to the North African–Egyptian theater of war, while at the same time surrounding the Mediterranean theater of war, and thereby Europe in the south and southeast. This idea, coupled with the struggle to reach suitable conclusions regarding the high command's policy with France, could not be carried out by the naval war staff. It was conjectured at the time, and finally proved during the negotiations of the Armistice Commission, that Italy was also against such a treatment of France.

Even before Italy's entry into the war, Heye had no very high opinion of her capabilities as a potential ally.

The policy of alliances pursued by the government [before the war], as a substitute for the lack of British friendship, did not conform in many respects to the opinions of the armed forces. Italy was not considered as an especially valuable ally by the army, navy, and air force, in spite of her revival through Fascism. The Italian navy was considered by the German navy to be the most efficient part of Italy.

Certainly the Italian navy was, on paper, a force to be reckoned with. The six battleships (with two more building), more than thirty cruisers, more than fifty destroyers, and more than one hundred submarines of the Italian navy represented sea power far in excess of anything the German admirals had at their disposal and far in excess of anything the British navy could deploy in the Mediterranean. It is hardly surprising that the Germans were content, at first, to leave the Mediterranean war entirely in Italy's hands. Schniewind and Schuster explain how the Axis alliance functioned at the highest level.

Up till the autumn of 1940 no active aid was given by Germany through the sending of armed forces of the army, navy, or air force to the Mediterranean theater of war. German liaison staffs, however, were attached to the Italian army so as to keep in touch and give advice if required. The task of the German naval liaison staff with the Italian navy (Supermarina) in Rome was very difficult right up to the end of the war—probably because of the Italian sensitiveness.

Naturally Italian policy and direction of the war dominated the Mediterranean theater.

The actions—but above all, however, the omissions—in the political and military direction of the war in this area were determined by the interpretations and decisions that the heads of state of the two Axis powers—separately or together—developed, planned, and carried out, or tried to carry out. The personalities of the two directing statesmen had a great, and often decisive, influence upon events. Their deliberations were only written down in part and often were scarcely expressed verbally in front of those forming their nearest circle of advisers. The true and final motives of their actions at particular periods can, since they are both dead, no longer be determined by the historians or by military critics.

The influence of politics was naturally great upon the direction of the war in the confined area of the Mediterranean, with its multiple political interests of states within and without the area conflicting, interweaving, and seldom finding themselves in harmony. They did not only affect the relationship of the two Axis powers from the political and military standpoint and the Italian interests in their former territory and their efforts, with Germany's help, to enlarge it, which were disturbed, if not destroyed; above all, the formation of a political triangle—Germany-Italy-France—was hindered, which according to the navy's opinion, [could have] formed the basis for domination in the Mediterranean and for the defense of North and West Africa.

The Italian policy influenced the attitude of Spain—among other things—toward the acute problems of the Mediterranean war.

It should be mentioned in passing that not only the Führer's foreign policy, but also the OKW [*Oberkommando der Wehrmacht* (supreme command)] and the services in their plans and demands, thought they had to take into account, or really had to take into account, the internal political situation in Italy (strength of Fascism, Mussolini's personal attitude). The old saying, "That a coalition has nothing of the idyll in it" proved itself true again in this case.

The significance of the Mediterranean was clearly recognized by the German leaders, but above all by the SKL. It was, however, before Italy's entry into the war, the sphere in which Italy had a monopoly. Even after

June 1940 the German leaders strongly withheld their influence and military support in the Mediterranean. That this ally needed supporting forces was clear to the German military leaders, above all to the army and to the SKL. The German general staff were prevented from granting this aid by Italian sensitiveness, though it later became possible through decreasing resistance, but it was never at all easy.

From the detailed insights he acquired as senior liaison officer, Weichold is able to provide a blistering professional critique of both the serious inadequacies of the Italian navy's combat readiness and the working of the Axis alliance.

Before the war the Italian navy was judged favorably, but compared to other great navies an investigation of the technical and real value of its fighting units revealed discrepancies in many respects. These lay mainly in the following spheres:

> The mining department was obsolete and was therefore ineffective against the more highly developed British minesweeping devices. Minesweeping and mine protection were almost meaningless in the Italian navy.
>
> The Italian U-boats already suffered a serious weakness in the First World War from the well-known and dangerous track-revealing torpedoes. Moreover Italian antisubmarine technique had remained practically in the same state as in 1918.
>
> Their torpedoes lacked modern night-aiming and fire control devices, while improvements in the capital ships' optical instruments for torpedo-firing and range-taking on clear nights were also needed.
>
> MTBs, especially suited for the maintenance of sea power in the central Mediterranean, were, owing to their size and construction, quite useless in a slight sea and became purely show pieces or weapons of opportunity.
>
> The Italian navy also lacked a fleet of auxiliary vessels—an obvious necessity for any Admiralty—with the result that warships were given heavy commitments that lay outside their provinces.
>
> The fleet air arm, which owing to the characteristics of the Mediterranean and Italy's need of aircraft carriers became of special importance, was far behind the operational air force in equipment, numbers, and achievements.

Besides these technical deficiencies, the Italian navy suffered a want of modern tactics. The experience of the First World War, the consequent improvements in technique, and the coming of the air force as an important weapon at sea upset the strict conception of the Battle of Jutland and by the division of the fleet into groups at least for steaming and reconnaissance; opposition to the enemy became more mobile. This necessitated extensive independence for the senior officers, with common thought and action on the part of individual commanders responsible to them. In the Italian navy all this was not yet widely recognized, and independence of action had never been practiced. On the contrary, the strictest concentration of fleet units and flagships prevailed; similarly every decision resting on personal initiative had to be submitted to the officer in charge of the operations.

These technical and tactical discrepancies resulted in the inefficient fighting of ships. It is obvious that they all arise from the nonexistence of a long sea tradition and the lack of fighting experience with an equal enemy in the First World War. In contrast, the British navy, rich in tradition, was frequently constrained to face a newly built Italian fleet and was in many individual engagements inferior in equipment. It is understood that there were certain restrictions on the use of sea power. From a review of the historical development of the young Italian nation and its navy it may therefore be concluded that they cannot be blamed for these weaknesses.

When the German and Italian liaison staffs met at the end of June 1940, no common plan of sea operations existed for the war against England. The position of the German liaison staff in Rome was astonishing. German officers were not appointed as members of the Italian admiral's staff and could not gain the necessary insight into matters that might have resulted in a fruitful exchange of opinion between the operational staffs of both navies. They were excluded from the Italian operations rooms and were briefly informed of the results of operations by a liaison officer or by colorless, prejudiced situation reports. However, the Italian liaison admiral in Berlin was treated in a similar manner. This was the basis on which the cooperation of both navies was to be developed during the war. The reason for this reserve lay in the mutual conception that, as regards the war at sea, both navies were geographically separated and the collaboration of the two forces was therefore unnecessary, also that the responsibility for individual operations lay ultimately with the national direction of the war. Behind this attitude lay the mutual fear of interference in each other's direction of the war and the safeguarding of prestige arising from differences in national character and fighting qualities.

Such was the state of collaboration between the German and Italian navies in a world war that was basically a war at sea. An important difference between sea and land warfare was the universality of the sea: all oceans are but part of a world sea. They are directly connected with one another and all commands are in strategic relation with one another. The basic principle governing the Axis war direction was therefore not the geographical separation of their respective forces and surface vessels, but the freedom of action in both theaters of a common enemy, that is, England. The jealous theory of individual national responsibility for the direction of the war resulted in the nonsharing of commitments by the Axis partners and consequently lightened their opponent's task in two seas. [It would have been more sensible to agree to] a common strategy to coordinate simultaneously operations on both sides so that the enemy would have no opportunity to use resources against one then the other. These principles could not, however, be carried out in the joint German-Italian war. The ignoring of these during years of alliance was a canker that, to a certain extent, brought on the unfavorable course of the war. It was not until very late on that the enemy's pressure caused an improvement, but reason was helpless against the desire for national prestige.

In the second half of 1940, the Italian army attempted to take the offensive. In August, from Ethiopia they quickly overran British Somaliland, a small colony on the African side of the Gulf of Aden; in September they advanced from Libya and penetrated along the Egyptian coast as far as Sidi Barrani; and at the end of October they launched an attack into Greece from Albania. This last adventure was undertaken without consulting their German allies. Weichold was not impressed by the contrast between the contribution of the Italian navy as compared with the aggressive approach adopted by the Admiral Sir Andrew Cunningham, commanding the weaker British naval forces in the eastern Mediterranean.

The operational concern of the Italian navy was limited to a strong defense of the central Mediterranean and the keeping open of the sea routes to Libya. Neither was Malta, the thorn in the side of Italy's operational freedom, seized, mined-in, or blockaded, nor were the many opportunities offered by the enemy taken with the serious object of engaging his forces. The failure to utilize the favorable position in the Dodecanese must also be regarded as a further example of Italy's renunciation of offensive measures. In contrast, the British practically controlled the whole of the Mediterranean east of Crete, including Greek waters, and continually menaced even the central Mediterranean.

The reasons for the far-reaching caution of the Italian Admiralty in the conduct of the war [were]

> The Italian navy believed it could carry out its task of securing the sea communications with Libya merely on the basis of tactical defense. It did not think it could afford to accept the risk of losses in offensive operations.
>
> Aerial reconnaissance over the sea was insufficient. The weakness of the Italian fleet air arm became evident from the beginning of the war.
>
> The Italian navy's terror of using darkness as a cover for light forces and above all of the night attack of torpedo-carrying craft.
>
> An uncertainty in the direction of operations that in the first place was based on the silent admission of the enemy's superiority in war experience as well as in achievement in the battle of one ship against another.

By the end of 1940 the war had begun to look a good deal less attractive to Italy than it had looked in the summer. In Greece the offensive had ground to a halt, and the Italian army was being forced back into the mountains of southern Albania. On the night of 11–12 November British carrier-borne aircraft attacked the Italian naval base at Taranto, where they sank the battleship *Conte Di Cavour* and inflicted such severe damage on two more battleships, the *Caio Duilio* and the new *Littorio*, that they were disabled for months. Then on 9 December the British army went on the offensive in Egypt and quickly chased the Italians back into Libya. According to Weichold, the German high command had been expecting a reverse in that theater.

If the German high command for its own part did not recognize the distinct possibilities for the Axis in the Mediterranean and African theaters of war, it was at any rate not slow to realize that the progress of the Italian offensive in Egypt would one day be turned into a retreat. Accordingly, in the middle of October the help of a German panzer division was offered to make up for the Italian lack of armor. The Italian high command, however, refused the offer of German assistance. The German high command did not press the Italians to accept the help they deemed necessary, since they did not realize what could be the full effect on German interests of an Italian retreat in Africa. On the other hand, the British high command saw the situation with great clarity and, in spite of heavy commitments to meet the threat of German invasion, . . . did not hesitate for one minute to throw all available forces into the Mediterranean and Egypt. This shows clearly the importance the British attached to the Mediterranean and the Middle East and the danger of its loss.

Weichold is critical of Italy's decision to send aircraft to take part in the Battle of Britain and to send submarines to take part in the Battle of the Atlantic. He is also critical of the attack on Greece, which he describes as a "continental and prestige-seeking policy show[ing] clearly how distorted a view the Italian high command had of the main strategic issues of the war." He sums up the Mediterranean war in 1940 in these words:

It was carried on completely under Italian direction [and] exclusively by Italian forces with the intentional exclusion of German participation and influence to the extent that any deep insight into Italian intentions and operations was refused. Italy herself, and herself alone, therefore carries the full responsibility. At any rate, the German high command's underrating of the Mediterranean as an Axis theater of war, as well as their blindness regarding the many failures under Italian leadership with their resultant dangers, cannot exclude them from some blame. It is quite obvious that this first phase of the war laid the foundations for further failures in the Mediterranean that eventually had unfavorable effects on the whole war situation.

One should not overlook the fact that the Italian command held down strong British sea and air forces in the Mediterranean. In doing this, she had to take on a considerable part of the offensive power of Great Britain and her empire. This detraction of forces from British home waters and the Atlantic considerably facilitated German sea and air attacks. This fact should not be overlooked in criticism of Italy's part in the war.

The first quarter of 1941 was marked by a series of humiliating defeats for the Italians. The Greek army continued to push them back in Albania. British convoys continued to run supplies to Malta, and the Royal Navy subjected Genoa to bombardment from the sea in February. By the middle of that month British forces advancing from Egypt had swept right across Cyrenaica and beyond, taking large numbers of Italian prisoners. British forces were making good progress in conquering the distant Italian colonies in the Horn of Africa, culminating in early April with the capture of the Abyssinian capital Addis Ababa and the important Eritrean port of Massawa. Thus any possible Italian threat to sea routes through the Red Sea and the Gulf of Aden was removed. On 28 March Admiral Cunningham's fleet managed to intercept a foray by the Italian fleet in the

waters west of Crete. In what became known as the Battle of Matapan, British carrier-borne aircraft damaged the new Italian battleship *Vittorio Veneto*, and gunfire from the British fleet sank the heavy cruisers *Pola*, *Zara*, and *Fiume*, plus two destroyers. The Italians were in no condition to spurn any help or advice they could get from their allies, but in Weichold's opinion, Germany was reluctant to provide really effective support.

The German OKW only saw the necessity of assisting the army and the air force. Regarding help for the navy, the value of naval forces was underrated on the German side. The continental outlook of the German high command prevented their seeing the real implications of the setbacks in the Mediterranean. The German navy, which ought to have better recognized the importance of sea power in the Mediterranean and in Africa, denied assistance in the first place on the grounds that Germany's naval forces were barely strong enough for their own theaters of war, where they alone had to bear the brunt of the war against England. This side of the case seemed justified but it ignored the fact that sea warfare in a world war is indivisible and that the denial of help in one place would one day be felt by the German command itself in another. The German navy, concentrating entirely on U-boat warfare in the Atlantic, could not bring itself to give up any material that was essential for operational reasons. The many disasters suffered by the Italian navy might have been averted by German material help such as was given to the land and air forces. In any case, the fact remains that the Italian navy, the deciding factor in the Mediterranean war, never received any German reinforcements [in the first part of 1941], although it had shown itself to be in just as much need as the land and air forces. Therefore, the direction of the war at sea in the Mediterranean, as opposed to land and air warfare, remained a purely Italian affair without German influence or participation. The sum total of German armed forces assistance to the tottering Italian war effort was not very effective. This was the second basic strategic error in Germany's direction of the Mediterranean war. It ranks equal with the first error, namely, her lack of interest in Italy's entry into the war.

Weichold's description of German assistance to Italy as "not very effective" can hardly be justified in any assessment of the contribution of the air force and the army. The German forces sent to Libya under General Rommel seemed to put new heart into the Italian forces, which had been so precipitately turned out of Cyrenaica. Inspired by Rommel's drive and leadership, the combined Axis forces went on the offensive toward the end of March 1941, and within a month, they had advanced up to the Egyptian frontier and laid siege to a sizable British garrison shut up in Tobruk. Meanwhile the Germans were making their own incursion into the eastern Mediterranean. During the winter of 1940–41 they had, by threats and cajolery, extended their sphere of influence to take in Hungary, Rumania, and Bulgaria. In March 1941 the Yugoslav government agreed to align itself with the Axis, but was then deposed in a coup d'état. Determined to bring the whole of the Balkans under Axis control and to rescue the Italians from their ill-advised campaign against Greece, Hitler sent German forces into both Yugoslavia and Greece on 6 April. In less than three weeks, the Yugoslav and Greek forces had been battered into submission, the swastika flew over Athens, and the Royal Navy had been compelled to organize another desperate evacuation of some fifty thousand British troops from the inadequate harbors of the Peloponnese. Driven off the Greek mainland by the end of April, the British hoped to hold on to the strategically important island of Crete, where German airborne troops began landing on 20 May. German attempts to ship reinforcements by sea in locally requisitioned craft were thwarted by the Royal Navy.

Schniewind and Schuster: German warships did not at first operate in the Mediterranean. The German admiral commanding the Aegean put the first units into service during the conquest of Greece, spring 1941. They consisted of a few auxiliary transport vessels made ready for sea with some trouble and insufficiently armed, and of motor sailing vessels that had been left behind by the English in their evacuation of the Greek mainland and of the islands or that had evaded capture. In time a few vessels were raised and repaired: the most valuable addition of this kind was the English-built [Greek] destroyer renamed *Hermes*.

Weichold: [British] naval operations hindered the transport of further German reinforcements that had sailed in small ships. This made the German attack [on Crete] considerably difficult and for days the outcome of the battle lay in the balance. However, in the execution of their blockade the British naval forces had to lay themselves open to strong German air attacks. In the straight contest between sea and air forces, the German air force won control of the whole area, thereby exerting a decisive influence on the situation at sea.

Once again, as in Norway and off Dunkirk, the Luftwaffe had proved its ability to exercise sea power in restricted waters. By the end of May the last British troops had been evacuated from Crete. In a mere six weeks, the Luftwaffe had sunk four Greek destroyers, eight British destroyers, and three British cruisers. In addition, two battleships, an aircraft carrier, seven cruisers, and nine destroyers had been damaged in air attacks. British sea power in the eastern Mediterranean now seemed to be at the mercy of German air power or even, possibly, at the mercy of a resolutely handled Italian fleet. Weichold recalls the tempting strategic possibilities.

The seizure of Crete considerably improved the geographic and strategic position of the Axis in the Mediterranean. Every possible hope of the western powers' direct communication with Russia via the Black Sea was hindered. Moreover, a strong flank attack was made on the British sea-lanes between Alexandria and Malta and in the central Mediterranean, while a forward position for operations against the Middle East was reached. Egypt was now threatened from two sides. This situation could especially be used to advantage by the Luftwaffe, and in the further development of the war, opportunities for combined operations also presented themselves. The Axis war leaders had now only to continue to exploit their advantage in the war against Great Britain in the Mediterranean.

Would Turkey, in her own self-interest, accept the German embrace as other Balkan states had? Would airborne troops be able to repeat their success in Crete by seizing Cyprus? Would Vichy French Syria provide a stepping-stone to the Middle East? Could the recently suppressed revolt against Britain in Iraq be reignited? Could Rommel take Tobruk and roll on to Alexandria, Cairo, and Suez? Writing in 1945, some of the German admirals obviously regretted the missed opportunities of the summer of 1941.

Heye: The situation in the Mediterranean at that time seemed completely favorable for a continuation of our operations toward the eastern Mediterranean and the Suez Canal. Britain's fighting strength was then weak in this area. By a strong concentration of our own air forces, by throwing in the Italian fleet, and by the concentration of German U-boats in the eastern Mediterranean, it might well have been possible to attack England in this most vulnerable part of the empire. Here alone was it possible to bring Germany's strongest fighting force, her army, to bear on an area where British interests lay. The naval staff still held at this time that the focal point of the war at sea was in the area around England. No U-boats at all were therefore made available [for the Mediterranean]. The air force and the army had to turn toward the east [for the attack on Russia on 22 June 1941]; an opportunity of attacking England in a very sensitive spot, which would perhaps never occur again, had to be left unexploited.

Schniewind and Schuster: The German air force had been so effective in the occupation of Greece and, above all, in the capture of Crete, against enemy naval units that the departure of air force units for the Russian front was a serious matter. The 10th Flieger Corps, which alone remained behind, and the few squadrons of obsolete flying boats in the Aegean could not perform the continually increasing number of duties. Here, too, the lack of a systematic buildup of [a] trained naval air force was noticeable again and again.

Weichold: It was at this point that German leadership committed the greatest error of the whole war. It turned its attention from England, already sorely pressed, to attack a new and powerful adversary. Moreover strong German air squadrons were transferred from the Mediterranean for the Russian campaign. This decision characterizes the entire German participation in the Mediterranean war. It did not even arise from offensive strategic planning but from defensive supporting action for the Italian land warfare in the Balkans and in Africa. These points of view were continental, that is, concerned only with land tactics and were but the products of a universal strategic policy that was never put into practice. Through this dependence on a continental policy, German leadership missed one of the greatest opportunities for the Axis direction of the war from 1939–45.

After the failure to take advantage of the strategic situation, the chances of improvement in the Axis control of the Mediterranean became less and less.

The British, despite heavy losses, continued to fight their supply convoys through to Malta, and they used that island as a base from which to mount sea and air attacks on the Axis convoys carrying to Tripoli and Benghazi the supplies essential to sustaining Rommel's threat to Egypt. The results may be judged from figures supplied by Weichold. In August 1941, from Axis convoys to Libya, in round figures 36,000 tons of shipping were sunk; 13,000 tons were damaged; and 100,000 tons completed the voyage safely. In September 49,000 tons were sunk; 14,000 tons, damaged; and 100,000 tons arrived safely. In October about 19,000 tons were sunk; 13,000 tons, damaged; and only 18,000 tons arrived safely; while the figures for November were 26,000 tons sunk, 2,000 damaged, and only 8,000 tons reaching port safely. On 18 November the British forces in Egypt launched a new offensive to relieve the siege of Tobruk and reconquer Cyrenaica.

Starved of supplies, Rommel's army was forced to retreat, and by the early days of 1942 British forces were once more beyond Benghazi, reaching Mersa Brega on the Gulf of Sirte on 6 January. Weichold spells out the strategic consequences.

The slow but sure effects of British sea and air power in the Mediterranean were now being felt. The battle for Cyrenaica was not decided during a month of actual land fighting, but rather by these external factors. The battle had already been lost by the Axis months previously through the British mastery of the sea and air to which the German high command had refused to give sufficient attention in spite of all warnings.

Cyrenaica, next to Malta, was the key to sea and air supremacy in the Mediterranean. Whichever of the two powers occupied this territory was able both to protect its vital lifelines and attack those of its opponent. The British were able to ensure the safety of Egypt, the Suez Canal, the bases for their Mediterranean fleet, and the whole Middle East. While on the other hand, they could control the Italian sea routes to Libya and the gateway to the Italian mother country. It was quite the reverse for the Italians. The possession of Cyrenaica was, next to Malta, the keystone of the whole Mediterranean. It was therefore not a question of estimating the situation from a land-tactical or continental point of view, but rather from a maritime one, and our operations should have been planned accordingly.

The period of purely Italian direction of sea warfare in the Mediterranean, ending with the second loss of Cyrenaica toward the end of 1941, had been governed by a strategic defense. Rarely have the disadvantages of this operational policy been so clearly evinced as on the Italian side in this phase of the war. Thereby the Italians unknowingly played into the hands of the British, whose policy was strongly offensive. This does not alter the fact that valuable work was done by Italy's light naval forces in the protection of the African convoys. Her destroyers and escort vessels untiringly convoyed the transports to Africa. Credit must also be given to German and Italian merchant shipping, which was constantly at sea until enemy action reduced it to a minimum.

The British command had long been carefully preparing for a second offensive in Cyrenaica. Many months were required to create a new army and equip it with all the necessary technical weapons. To strike a decisive counterblow, military requirements must be sufficient for the task, which would make a great demand on British fighting potentiality and shipping space. This was done at the expense of other theaters of war. The defense of Malaya and Singapore had to bear the cost of the Cyrenaica offensive, a striking proof of the strategic connection between operations in a world war. The Axis powers thereby greatly facilitated Japanese successes in the Far East.

The German high command had not been completely deaf to the urgings of Weichold and those who, like him, were enthusiastic about the opportunities—and vocal about the dangers—in the Mediterranean theater. Even as they were preoccupied with planning and launching the Russian campaign, they had reluctantly come to realize that they must accept a bigger role in the Mediterranean, but changes of strategic emphasis take time, especially when influential voices are urging that priorities lie elsewhere. Weichold comments on the high command's lack of understanding.

Owing to the unfavorable course of the war, the German high command, after long hesitation, was obliged, at the end of August 1941, to bring in naval forces to assist. In the first place German U-boats were ordered to the Mediterranean. The OKW viewed this allocation of German naval forces . . . with displeasure, as they were completely concerned with the war against shipping in the Atlantic. Accordingly they at first succeeded in limiting the number of U-boats to twenty-one. Later the high command ordered an increase in the number of U-boats to thirty-six. However, after a time the C in C U-boats succeeded in obtaining a reduction to twenty-five U-boats.

Had the few German U-boats operating in the Mediterranean since the end of October immediately attacked British sea power, it would have been doubtful if their successes could have saved the Afrika Korps. A few months earlier the effects of their attacks on British supremacy at sea might have had far-reaching consequences in facilitating the supply of the African forces and saving Cyrenaica.

Besides the German U-boats, sweepers and landing barges for military transport purposes were also sent to the Mediterranean. In addition the Italian navy received important technical equipment (mines, minesweeping apparatus, Asdics, etc.).

German [air] squadrons were once more based on Sicily so that the battle for Malta could again be taken up and the central Mediterranean again be brought under control. For months the warning cry from [German representatives in] Rome had been ignored. Now at the last minute, as had already occurred in the case of the U-boats, German air power was to have saved the situation. The attitude of the German high command to this problem shows their complete lack of understanding of the basic principles of sea warfare, which, in contrast with land warfare, requires much more time for its effects to become apparent.

Reluctant though Dönitz was to lose them from what he saw as the decisive Battle of the Atlantic, German U-boats scored some impressive successes once they had become operational in the Mediterranean. On 13 November 1941, U-81 torpedoed the British aircraft carrier *Ark Royal* east of Gibraltar, and she sank under tow in the early hours of the following day. On the twenty-fifth the battleship *Barham* capsized and blew up off the Libyan coast after being torpedoed by U-331. On 14 December the cruiser *Galatea* was sunk by U-557 only thirty miles west of Alexandria. On the nineteenth the cruiser *Neptune* and destroyer *Kandahar* were sunk and two other cruisers damaged in a minefield laid by German E-boats north of Tripoli, while on the same day the battleships *Queen Elizabeth* and *Valiant* were damaged in Alexandria harbor by explosive charges planted by Italian swimmers sitting astride torpedo-like submersible craft. If the end of 1941 saw British arms triumphant in Cyrenaica, the British surface fleet in the central and eastern Mediterranean could muster no more than four light cruisers and a few destroyers.

6

Germany Marches Eastward, 1941

APART FROM A purely local conflict between Italy and Greece, the Second World War during the opening months of 1941 amounted to a war between Britain and the Axis powers. Writing of that time, Krancke claims:

The war against England was conducted almost exclusively by the German navy. The high command, consisting mainly of army officers, did not fully realize the overwhelming importance of sea power and naval warfare in this world war. They thought predominantly in terms of land fighting.

Having been forced to accept, in the years after Hitler's rise to power, that the rearmament of the army and air force would receive priority, the German navy had expected to receive a bigger share of resources after 1940. Schniewind and Schuster explain why that hope was doomed to disappointment.

[After the outbreak of war] it was intended to transfer to the navy forces from the army and also the arms potential that was set at the disposal of the army, as soon as the war on land had been brought to a satisfactory conclusion—which at that time it was hoped would take place in the summer of 1940. But this plan fell through in face of the war with Russia that was threatening.

The Russo-German Pact of 1939 might have looked like a masterstroke of diplomacy at the time, but the Germans had no real confidence that it would last. Within a few months Russia had swallowed broad swathes of eastern Europe. How far might her expansionist ambitions extend? Able strategists in Germany might argue the relative merits of launching an all-out invasion of the British Isles, putting everything into Dönitz's U-boat campaign, or making a massive effort to win total control of the Mediterranean and Middle East; but a huge question mark always hung over whether they could be confident that Russia would not then seize the opportunity to stab the preoccupied Reich in the back. With such a massive potential threat on land, it is hardly surprising that, much to the disappointment of the admirals, Germany's strategy continued to be dominated by continental, rather than maritime, considerations.

Schniewind and Schuster: The author has no knowledge of the final reasons of the Reich Party government that gave the decision for the declaration of war on Russia. As well as can be remembered, in the late autumn of 1940 there were signs that close relations again existed between the western powers and Russia. This finally gave rise to suspicion. It is furthermore to be assumed that the Führer was under the strong impression that Russia's policy of blackmail [Erpressungspolitik] against Germany, as he sometimes called it, which demanded greater and greater concessions in eastern and southeastern Europe, would never cease. Russia's behavior as regards Yugoslavia and her influence there was regarded as treacherous, and finally, in the spring of 1941, the Führer confessed his conviction, as he had often told the chiefs of the armed forces, that Russia was aiming at a war with Germany and that the advance in the east was already fully under way. The author does not know which of these reasons were genuinely believed by the Führer and which really fitted the facts. It is certain that his decisions were influenced by his fundamental attitude of shunning Bolshevism, which he regarded as Germany's greatest danger.

Dönitz: At the end of January [1941] the supreme commander of the navy was acquainted for the first time with the Führer's opinion that a campaign against Russia was unavoidable and that plans for this must be formed. Though at the beginning Russia abided loyally by the terms of the Russia-German treaty, she subsequently changed her tactics and exploited the position Germany had been forced into by withholding more and more of her supplies of wheat and oil to Germany and also flagrantly violated various conditions laid down in the treaty (Baltic States, Rumania). Besides this, intelligence had been received that Russian armament, which in the face of things could only be used against Germany, had been placed on a war footing and that violent anti-German propaganda was being carried on in the Russian army. Reliable intelligence was later received about the deployment of Russian troops on her western frontier.

In order that Germany should not risk the danger of being overrun by Russia while the bulk of her own forces were tied down elsewhere, it was decided to carry out a "preventive war" against Russia, as being vital to Germany's existence. For the naval command, whose strategic interests had been turned entirely toward the war against England and her sea communications, this new development was particularly painful, though they supported the Führer in his opinion that war with Russia was an urgent necessity and unavoidable. It was hoped, however, to bring the war with Russia to a successful conclusion within a few months, thereby releasing manpower and materials for the Mediterranean front, but we seriously underestimated the Russian war potential.

Krancke: A land war of such dimensions against Soviet Russia, who had been preparing for this war since 1919, and at the same time a battle in the west and south of the Reich, were beyond Germany's powers. The successes of 1939–40 no doubt confused the issue. Bolshevism stood threatening in the east and made demands that could not be agreed upon. I do not know whether the eastern campaign in 1941 was politically avoidable, but as far as I am able to judge Russian policy, the war had to come if Russia's unceasing armament program was to have any meaning. The supreme command was under pressure on account of this position.

Writing in 1945 the admirals make it perfectly clear that the decision to attack Russia was contrary to the considered advice of the German navy. Some of them even appear to imply that the perceived threat from Russia may not have been as serious as Hitler's personal animosity toward Bolshevism led him to believe.

Schniewind and Schuster: The naval war staff had viewed the preparations for war in the east and finally the declaration of war with great anxiety. This opinion was given to the Führer by the supreme command of the navy in the form of an urgent warning. The naval war staff represented the point of view that at all costs the war in the west—against England—that was taking up all the armed power of the Reich (the navy and air force especially bore the brunt) must first come to an end. It was obvious that the party government had allowed itself to be led to believe that the war in the west was as good as over. England's potentialities, supported by the U.S.A., and the danger of a warlike intervention on the part of the United States and her military efficiency were not fully appreciated.

At that time, in the naval war staff's opinion, it would have been strategically better to have sent large land forces to fortify the position in North Africa and to strike against Egypt and the Suez [Canal]. This should have been done at the latest after the conquest of Greece and Crete. (It was certainly necessary to strike here after the collapse of the negotiations with Yugoslavia, to avoid a similar situation to that in 1914–18—Salonika). If this was carried out, England would receive a blow in a most sensitive spot. It would also be necessary to see whether later, with the help of Russia perhaps or by Russia herself with German support, a thrust from the Caspian Sea in the direction of the Persian Gulf or over Turkey and Syria or to the Suez Canal could or should be made. It is known to the authors that the first discussions by the German armed forces took place with this aim in view. To the best of the authors' knowledge, there was no close collaboration with Russia—in fact the matter was never broached to her.

Schulz: I know only that in the navy, as in the army, the war against Russia met with little sympathy. It was a purely political decision.

Just as the army had correctly estimated the difficulties of a campaign against Russia, with its great population and land spaces, and—as I have heard from well-informed army colleagues—advised earnestly against this war, so on the other hand the navy had no illusions regarding the potentialities of the [British] Empire and the toughness of our English opponents; at the same time they gave full weight to the possible throwing in on the side of the English of the mighty armament potential of America.

The navy, therefore, was unable to understand why, in these circumstances, Germany should burden herself with a two-front war, which so far had been avoided, and we considered it—on the contrary—of the first importance for German policy further to develop cooperation with Russia, thereby avoiding entanglement with the Russians and securing the considerable Russian supplies of raw material and foodstuffs for the future.

I have definite knowledge that Grossadmiral Raeder represented this view both at the German Admiralty and to Adolf Hitler on many occasions, but without success, since "an unalterable decision" by Adolf Hitler was in question.

Meyer: One thing is perfectly clear; Grossadmiral Raeder, commander in chief of the navy, had warned Hitler against attacking Russia. I have myself read a document on the matter at the German Admiralty. I assume that this attitude of Raeder's was strongly influenced by reports received from the naval attaché at Moscow, who was always said to have stressed his opinion that Russia should not be underestimated and to have referred at the same time to the strength of British sea power. The commander in chief of the navy—and, generally speaking, the whole of the officer corps—fully appreciated what it would mean to go to war against the British Empire, behind which stood the United States. Such a war, if continued to its conclusion, would become more and more extensive and would demand all the strength of the nation. No sooner had the offensive against Russia started than this became clear to all. Air attacks on England practically ceased; support from the air force for the navy assumed the smallest proportions; the stoppage of supplies to Britain was no longer to be expected; and we no longer had sufficient forces to carry on the operations in the Mediterranean that were so important in the war against England. All our schemes with regard to Malta, Egypt, and Gibraltar were sunk.

I think it possible that, in his judgment in regard to Russia, Hitler fell a victim to his own propaganda. For years it had been spread about that Russia was a rotten structure, and the constant dinning-in of this idea proved stronger than the factual reports that must have come in in considerable numbers. In any case, in dealing with this question, one must point out that during the winter of 1940–41 there was a general anxiety, based on the unaccommodating attitude of the Russians, that Russia would hit Germany in the back while she was engaged in the west. It seems to me that Hitler realized that war with Russia was unavoidable and that he therefore started it at the earliest possible moment. If he had any idea of Russia's real strength, he would certainly not have sought to make war himself but would have used every possible means to avoid it.

Heye points out that a study of history would have taught the dangers of invading a huge country such as Russia.

After the costly conquest of Crete there followed the unexpected outbreak of war with Russia. Even the supreme commands of the three sections of the armed forces in the southeast became aware of this possibility only a very short time before the outbreak of war. Many senior officers of the armed forces saw a particular danger in this decision. Such an extension of the war into the depths of the Russian continent was bound to be too much for Germany's strength, unless she could find a political solution to the war. Napoleon's Russian campaign and Japan's operations in mighty China pointed out the lesson. Finally, this brought about the war on several fronts, which in the end [had] created a military superiority against Germany in the 1914–18 war. It was clear [however] that Russia, as the only European state so far unweakened by war and rearming herself strongly, would always constitute a danger, even for a "friendly" nation, as Germany was. This [had been] made clear by the Russian attack on Finland, the Baltic States, and Rumania.

Code-named Operation Barbarossa, the German assault on Russia was launched on 22 June 1941. Scything through the Russian defenses, the German armored spearheads with close support from the Luftwaffe were able to execute sweeping encircling movements that trapped hundreds of thousands of Russian prisoners. It soon began to look as though the techniques of blitzkrieg would achieve a stunning triumph that would be even more remarkable than the earlier victories in Poland and France. Within three months the German northern group of armies had overrun the former Baltic States and reached the gates of Leningrad, which was laid under siege. The center group of armies had stormed through eastern Poland, taken the great Russian cities of Minsk and Smolensk, and were moving up to attack Moscow itself. In the south, supported by their Rumanian and Hungarian allies, they had driven deep into the Ukraine to the capital, Kiev. In a campaign such as this there could only be, for the German navy, a number of minor roles—demanding roles, no doubt; locally important, no doubt; requiring great professional competence, no doubt; but the kind of sideshows that were a far cry from the maritime control of the Mediterranean or mastery of the Atlantic trade routes that the sailors felt might have been achievable. Dönitz describes the navy's role in the Baltic during the opening stages of the Russian campaign:

At the beginning of the Russian campaign the navy only took part in the Baltic. It saw that its task consisted of preventing the Russian fleet from taking any action from the very beginning by energetic measures and of bottling it up even tighter in the Gulf of Finland with the advance of land operations. As the initiative of the Russian fleet and its ability were estimated as slight, the strength of our forces placed in readiness for this purpose was kept within modest limits. A cruiser squadron, the so-called Baltic fleet, was for a time held in readiness in the waters of the Aaland Islands. It participated by coastal bombardment in the conquest of the Baltic islands and provided security against the possible breaking out of Russian surface forces.

The conduct of the naval war in the Gulf of Finland was left to our own light forces from torpedo boats downward in collaboration with the allied Finnish navy. On [the] night the war began, mine barrages were begun in the central and western Gulf of Finland, which in course of time were developed into strong minefields, pushed out as far as possible to the east. As it was unfortunately not possible to take Leningrad and Kronstadt, and with them to eliminate the Russian Baltic fleet once and for all, the mines had to be maintained till the end of the war. In the first days of our own advance, especially at the time of the evacuation of Talinn and Hangoe, they inflicted heavy losses on the Russians and prevented any Russian surface craft from breaking out of the Gulf of Finland until the loss of Estonia in 1944. A few submarines that broke out in the first year caused only slight damage.

Other admirals also refer to the onerous role of the German navy in the Baltic.

Schulz: The manner in which the campaign in Russia developed in 1941 was a particular disappointment to the navy in as much as the whole Russian Baltic coast had not been brought under German control, an event that would have brought peace to the whole Baltic and secured the port and dock installations of Kronstadt and Leningrad, together with the whole Russian Baltic fleet. On the other hand, the occupation of the greater part of the Russian Baltic coast as well as our campaign in the Black Sea, together with the conduct of naval operations in both seas, made further demands on the already very extended German naval forces.

Schniewind and Schuster: The Baltic was again drawn right into the foreground of the war by the outbreak of war in the east. The security measures of 1939 were reintensified against submarines and other surface forces, which were worthy of serious consideration in comparison with the forces at Germany's disposal (about one hundred U-boats). The central Baltic coastline had to be almost completely refortified. The threatening danger of interference with sea and exercise operations did not materialize. This was chiefly owing to the rapid advance of the army eastward at that time, and also to the effectiveness of the naval blockade measures (minefields at the exit to the Gulf of Finland and between Juminda and the Finnish coastline opposite). The Baltic, including the Gulfs of Bothnia and Finland but with the exception of the innermost point of the Gulf of Finland (Kronstadt, Oranienbaum pocket) was as good as free from the enemy by the end of 1941.

The navy's cooperation with the army in its campaigns was much in evidence, especially on the occasion of the occupying of the islands in the Baltic and in the transport of reinforcements. Here, for the first time, the naval ferry barges and the LCAs that were still being built in large numbers proved their worth. These had been intended for the invasion of England. The barges were also indispensable as means of transport along all the coasts, especially in Norway and the Black Sea.

In the far north German and Finnish forces failed to reach the strategic objective specified by the German navy.

Dönitz: In northern waters the objective demanded by the navy, the conquest of Murmansk, Poliarno, and the Ribachi Peninsula, was never attained, as a result in particular of insurmountable difficulties of terrain. There developed consequently in this sphere a protracted struggle for sea communications in which we succeeded in maintaining permanently and without serious encroachment the important maritime traffic with Petsamo and Kirkenes.

Boehm: I considered it as important for the whole German war effort to extend the Norwegian base and to occupy the strategically important harbor of Murmansk immediately after the commencement of the Russian campaign, for I foresaw that Murmansk and the connecting railway would be a support line for the oversea supply of the Russian army. The naval high command agreed with me in this, but practical steps were not taken by the higher authorities to increase the land forces correspondingly.

The advance of the German armies along the northern shores of the Black Sea required the German navy to expend some of its limited resources even farther afield.

Dönitz: In the third naval theater against Russia—the Black Sea—the Russian Black Sea fleet possessed an overwhelming superiority over the few units of the Rumanian navy, which were still badly trained and without sea experience. These were strengthened in the end by six type-II German U-boats and an E-boat flotilla, which were transported to the Black Sea via the Elbe, Reichsautobahnen, and Danube, and by a number of landing craft, armed trawlers, and auxiliary vessels that were fitted out there. The Russian superiority however was, as a result of the almost incomprehensible inactivity of their Black Sea fleet, . . . ineffectual, so that we were in a position to carry out very much better the tasks that had fallen to the lot of the navy in the Black Sea than could [have been] expected with such a strength ratio.

Heye: [When] the Black Sea also became a theater of war, the available forces were likewise improvised with the exception of the Rumanian fleet, which however had great limitations. Marshal Antonescu had no intention of risking his ships. He feared that, in the event of the loss of his fleet, he would experience postwar difficulties with nonbelligerent Bulgaria.

Russian activities were confined to U-boat warfare, which in part was very successful. The Russian failure to use strong striking forces made possible a considerable support of the army by seaborne supplies. Few means of defense against the Russian U-boats existed, which explains their successes.

Cooperation with [the Balkan] states was not simple: Bulgaria, in particular, remained completely out of the war. Only a war against Turkey, in the same way as the war against Greece, would have had the sympathy of the Bulgarian people. It was in Germany's interests to avoid such a war with Turkey at all costs. Between Rumania and Hungary there were differences as between enemy states.

> In the closing months of 1941 the German advance into Russia rolled on, except in the north, where the defense of Leningrad could not be overcome. In the south, before the end of November they had taken Rostov-on-Don, at the entrance to the Caucasus, only to be promptly driven out again by a Russian counterattack. In the center, despite the fact that their clothing and equipment were ill suited to the rapidly deteriorating weather conditions, the German spearheads had advanced to within sight of Moscow, where they were checked and then forced into a difficult retreat, which infuriated Hitler. Heye analyzes the opening stage of the war in Russia from the point of view of a naval strategist.

The campaign in Russia achieved great successes at first. Because of the great distances involved and of strengthening resistance one had, however, to expect that the war would be prolonged here too. I cannot imagine that the high command reckoned with a blitzkrieg—[the decision to attack] must have been made for political considerations. Opinions differed regarding the aims of the operation. The navy believed that strategic and political considerations called for a concentration on the northern flank, that is, Leningrad, as the main theater. This appeared also in order that the Russian naval forces might be wiped out once and for all and the Baltic, with its vital sea communications, [be] safeguarded.

The second most important operation, in the opinion of the navy, was a thrust toward the Caucasus in order to capture the oil fields. The only possible route by which pressure could be exercised on the British war effort by land forces, in the direction of the Persian Gulf and the Indian Ocean and so on, would be from the Caucasus. Despite these appreciations, the main thrust was in the center of the front, that is, toward Moscow.

At the end of 1941, it was clear that the rapid advance had come to an end and that the front had become stabilized without any one of the three important objectives—Leningrad, Moscow, or the Caucasus—having been reached. Since Leningrad had not been reached and the Russian fleet had not been eliminated, what was in effect a new defensive front in the war at sea was formed: the Russians had to be prevented from breaking out of Kronstadt and threatening German sea communications and the most important U-boat training bases in the Baltic. The attack planned from the extreme north of Norway against Murmansk was also not carried out owing to the difficulties of terrain and the insufficient number of German troops available.

The Russians were thus able to use Archangel and Murmansk as bases for their fleet and as ports of entry for British and American supplies. In this way the commitments of the German navy, which was already too weak, were increased. An advantage was therefore seen in the occupation of large tracts of Russian territory because it would strengthen Germany's own economic resources with grain and raw materials. Many of the factories and mines remained in ruins, however, for a long time. The large dockyards in Nikolaiev [were] comparatively slightly damaged but could not yet be used for the equipping of our own ships.

The stalling of the German advance in the ice and snow of a severe Russian winter had repercussions on the shipbuilding program, which was regarded as crucial by those who, far away from the Russian steppes, were still planning to bring about a crushing naval triumph in the Battle of the Atlantic.

Krancke: Owing to an unexpectedly heavy frost setting in as early as October 1941 . . . the majority of our heavy war equipment was lost in Russia. Consequently, industrial capacity had to be switched over to the benefit of the army at a cost to the navy and the air force. The effect on the navy was a smaller output of U-boats and light forces.

Schniewind and Schuster: The war against Russia had not made as much progress in 1941 as had been hoped. A serious crisis on land arose through the early setting in of a very severe winter. The certainty persisted, however, that the Russian forces were so badly hit that the enemy in the east would be successfully overpowered in the following year.

The naval hopes of the shifting of priorities in armaments to the building of U-boats and aircraft had to be postponed for the sake of strengthening and reviving the army. This again caused a delay in increasing U-boat forces.

7

Ocean Warfare against Merchant Shipping, 1942–1943

WHILE THE GERMAN armies were grinding to a halt at the very gates of Moscow in December 1941, the whole scope of the conflict was suddenly altered by events on the opposite side of the world where, on the morning of 7 December, Japanese carrier-borne aircraft launched their attack on the United States' Pacific fleet at Pearl Harbor, Hawaii. Now the world was truly embroiled in a conflict that could accurately be called a "world war." Up to that point, Japan had remained neutral so far as the mainly European war was concerned. She was, in any case, prosecuting her own private war with China. She had, however, been a friend of Nazi Germany since signing the Anti-Comintern Pact in 1936. Heye gives his assessment of Japan as a potential ally.

The change of policy toward Japan too came as a surprise after the earlier preference for China shown by former officers and by our economic support for her. The German army had a lower opinion of the efficiency of the Japanese army than did the German government, especially in comparison with modern armies. The Japanese navy had a good reputation, even though it was assumed that it would be conventional in its leadership and tactics. At first there was no exchange of inventions with Italy or Japan.

Reflecting on Schniewind's experience of trying to foster relations with Japan, as a neutral power friendly toward the Axis, Schniewind and Schuster obviously found Japanese officials rather unforthcoming.

After the arrival of a large Japanese commission led by Admiral Nomura at about the beginning of 1941, a closer alliance was made with the Japanese navy. This led to large-scale exchanges of ideas between the two navies about armament and war experiences. As long as the author, as chief of staff of the naval war staff, took part in the frequent discussions and personally kept in touch with the leading Japanese personalities, he could not divine the final Japanese intentions and preparations. He was under the impression that, in the course of the discussions, the German navy gave far more information and that the Japanese did not reciprocate. No opinion can be given as to whether this was the Japanese intention or whether the members of the commission themselves had not the knowledge.

Japan's friendly relations with Germany do not seem to have extended to confidences about the projected assault on Pearl Harbor. Many of the admirals state that the attack came as a complete surprise to them, even though, according to Meyer, they had been hoping for some development of that kind.

The war in East Asia came as a surprise to Germany and, to my knowledge, also to Hitler (in any case, I was told so by one of his headquarters officers). From 1939 to 1941 the German navy had endeavored so to influence the Japanese navy that Japan should expand her power in a southerly and southeasterly direction rather than to the west. This was still true after the outbreak of war with Russia. It was hoped thus to tie the great sea powers down on an extensive scale; the navy considered their defeat to be decisive for the whole war, while the Russian campaign was looked on as a purely continental matter that, even if important, took second place.

At least in theory, Germany could have declined to become involved in the war in the Far East, just as for a time she had remained neutral in the Italo-Greek War in 1940. Indeed, Japan remained neutral in the Russo-German War, so Germany would have had some justification for remaining neutral in the war between Japan and the United States. Perhaps Hitler and Mussolini considered that option, but four days after the attack on Pearl Harbor, Germany and Italy declared war on the United States. The admirals express little dissent from that decision, although they do not all offer the same justification for it.

Heye: Germany . . . declared war on the U.S.A., in my opinion as a consequence of the political ties and agreements with Japan.

Meyer: During 1941, the opposition of the United States was more and more noticeable. Measures against Germany became so acute as to be almost acts of war. The U-boat war was considerably handicapped. As the months passed, it became ever clearer that a war with the United States had become unavoidable. Matters had developed so far that, when Japan declared war against the United States in 1941, the German declaration was almost a relief.

Schniewind and Schuster: That Germany was soon drawn into this war was viewed by both authors as the necessary consequence of her alliance with Japan although, in the long run, war between Germany and the U.S.A. would have become inevitable since many measures taken by the United States against Germany in the Atlantic could only be regarded as war measures. It might even be said that a state of war had already existed de facto between the U.S.A. and the Axis, and that the declaration of war only represented a formal confirmation of this situation.

Krancke: The German declaration of war on America, I presume on the grounds of political treaties, was only induced by the outbreak of war between Japan and the U.S.A. At this point the one-sided, war, which the U.S.A. had been fighting up till now, came to an end, and U-boat warfare had the greatest opportunity for success so far offered to them in American coastal waters.

The . . . changeover of American industry to war production and the extent of the actual output had unquestionably been underestimated by the high command. Many statistics, later proved to have been correct, were considered bluff. The increasing strength of British air and sea patrols, and the addition of the American continent as an enemy power, were responsible for the diminishing attacks against merchant shipping by surface vessels. It was no longer possible to escape observation [in] the Atlantic.

Schulz: Since the U.S.A. was departing further and further from her neutrality status, had even adopted armed escort of her merchant shipping to England, and had, moreover, given her naval forces freedom to attack German U-boats, it appeared more and more certain that the U.S.A. would at the first suitable opportunity enter the war against Germany.

The intervention of Japan, which incidentally came as a complete surprise to us, was regarded in our navy predominantly—or in any case in the operational command to which I belonged—as a considerable alleviation of the German position and on that account was welcomed. Practically no opposition was raised against the subsequent German declaration of war on the U.S.A. as it was generally assumed that we had given the Japanese corresponding assurances in the case of her intervention. Apart from this, the severe restrictions that American neutrality, though hardly worth the name, had imposed on our conduct of the war at sea, particularly on the U-boat war, were hereby removed.

Later, it is true, I remember hearing isolated expressions of the view that it would have been wiser to refrain from declaring war on the U.S.A. as it would have been impossible, or at least very difficult, for President Roosevelt, immediately after Pearl Harbor and the consequent sharp reaction of American public opinion, to find an excuse for making war in Europe against us and for concentrating the main strength of America against Germany. Seen in retrospect, this conception may have been the correct one, provided that we were not under treaty obligations to Japan to declare war, a possibility that I do not overlook.

Schniewind and Schuster suggest that Germany may have seriously underestimated the strength of the U.S. military-industrial complex.

The entry of a nation like the U.S.A. into the war, as may be concluded in the light of subsequent knowledge, but that was definitely not recognized at the end of 1941, really meant the final overthrow of Germany's prospects of victory. Tests were indeed made—partly at the instigation of the naval war staff and based upon research carried out during the 1914–18 war—to determine the arms potential of the U.S.A., how much her steel production could be increased under war conditions, and how her achievements in the construction of warships and merchant ships, in the production of arms and ammunition, her potentiality for building up an army and obtaining the necessary manpower could be estimated.

In making these appreciations and researches everything that was unfavorable for Germany was purposely taken into account. In spite of this, however, the immediate and unfavorable result of the research was far below the actual achievements of the U.S.A., which came to light later in the war. It is the opinion of the authors that in the 1939–45 war, as in the war of 1914–18, the entry of America into the war with her enormous arms potential was *the* decisive factor that brought about Germany's defeat.

Heye makes a similar point and draws the conclusion that the involvement of the United States meant that, in the long run, Germany could only hope for a drawn war of attrition.

The navy reckoned from now on with a considerable strengthening of the enemy's naval forces. The experience of the [First World War] showed that industrial capacity and manpower must have their effect in the course of time. It was hoped that the war in East Asia would ease the situation in Europe, and especially in the Mediterranean, because of the withdrawal of British naval forces.

In my opinion, the entry of America into the war finally destroyed all hopes of a successful military conclusion of the war in the sense of a victory and a short war. I and many other officers of all three services believed that it was, from now on, a case of holding out in a military sense until such time as a political solution of the war presented itself. We believed, too, that the Anglo-Saxons would not be in favor of a long war. If the war lasted a long time England would be at a disadvantage vis-à-vis Russia and America and she, at least, had no reason for dragging the war out to immeasurable lengths. The situation as a whole made it clear that for Germany it was now a question of holding firmly onto the conquered territory and turning from an offensive to a defensive strategy. If this aim could be successfully achieved and Europe could be turned into a self-sufficient fortress, so to speak, it was to be hoped that the enemy would also be ready to come to terms: this must happen when the enemy recognized that the war around the fortress of Europe would last for an unforeseeable length of time and that the results of victory would never be commensurate with the costs of war

Although Japan's declaration of war on the United States came as a surprise, we considered a war between the United States and Japan inevitable. German naval and military circles were worried as to Japan's capacity to maintain a war of any length against the United States. It was to be assumed that Japan's strength was already weakened by the war with China, that her merchant fleet was not very large, and that her industrial capacity was not comparable to that of the United States. We could not judge how long Japan, despite her willingness to make sacrifices and her initial successes, could carry on the lengthy war we foresaw.

For Dönitz and his team of staff officers, directing the daily—and nightly —U-boat war against commerce in the Atlantic, the German declaration of war against the United States meant that their whole campaign for 1942 could be planned on the basis of wider boundaries, fewer restrictions, more targets, and greater opportunities for their growing U-boat fleet. The C in C U-boats sums up the transformation:

The Japanese attack on Pearl Harbor on 7 December 1941, was a complete surprise for Germany's political and military leaders. It also resulted in a state of war between U.S.A. and Germany. Conditions for U-boat warfare in the North Atlantic were once again clarified. Limiting factors vis-à-vis North America ceased to operate. The bar against German U-boats entering American waters was raised by the political leaders.

Because of the great distance separating the European and the Far Eastern theaters of war, cooperation between the German naval staff and the Japanese Admiralty, which was carried out by the formation of naval liaison staffs, was limited mainly to the mutual reporting of events, the exchange of experiences, and dealing with general strategic questions. With the rapid and successful advance of the Japanese to the edge of the Indian Ocean, the possibility of a limited measure of direct cooperation presented itself. In order to avoid interfering with one another's naval operations, longitude 70° E was fixed as the limit of operational areas. It was incumbent upon each to obtain the other partner's approval before crossing the line, this approval being granted in principle, and to conform to his wishes regarding the waters navigated and the sea routes used.

German armed merchant cruisers . . . could henceforth run into Japanese bases for repair and to replenish supplies. This often happened and was the more valuable as the passage through the North Atlantic and Bay of Biscay became steadily more dangerous owing to strengthened enemy reconnaissance and warship patrols; and a breakthrough via the narrows of Iceland could only succeed in especially favorable and rare cases. Nevertheless the raider war was continued successfully. For the purpose of exchanging valuable military and commercial goods (rubber, metals, fuel oils) a blockade-runner traffic using fast German merchant ships was instituted between western France and Japan; this blockade running worked very well to begin with and provided us with an important quantity of supplies.

Dönitz lost no time in exploiting the new opportunities he and his staff identified. Their deployment of U-boats to American waters, code-named Operation Drumbeat, produced an impressive number of sinkings, and the pattern of success was repeated in other theaters of operation.

Heye: In 1942 the successes of the U-boat war increased. The growing number of boats made it possible to gain considerable successes even against convoys on the high seas. Off the United States and Central America we found at first a favorable operational area owing to the absence of defensive forces there. It was clear that in time, just as happened off the English coast, the defenses would become so strong that it would no longer be worthwhile to operate U-boats there. It was our guiding principle then from time to time to change the focal point of the U-boats' operational areas.

Dönitz outlines some of the operational factors that affected the successes of his U-boats. He was, obviously, frustrated by what he regarded as a shortage of U-boats created by lack of foresight by the government.

[In 1942] compared with 1941 each U-boat was economically valuable even if, as already stated, its value had sunk, despite the great successes, to one-tenth of the 1940 figure. The large U-boat program ordered at the outbreak of war was, in 1942, implemented only to the extent of 10 percent of the expected figure. Had the political leaders of the navy before the war recognized England as a probable opponent and in 1937 prepared for a war with England and constructed a large U-boat fleet, the number of U-boats available in 1942 would have been available in 1940, but with ten times greater results. The political desire of Germany's leaders not to make war against England and the corresponding armament policy of the navy led, when the war with England nevertheless broke out, to its not having the requisite U-boats available at the right time or in the right numbers.

In order to increase sinkings wherever possible, the U-boat command used the long approach route and sailed in company with the boats that were to operate in North American waters, roughly on a great circle course in a wide rakelike formation. In this way convoy traffic was often unexpectedly encountered. Apparently the English convoy command [western approaches command] had had to abandon the dispersal procedure usual in 1941. This great circle procedure continued throughout the whole summer and autumn of 1942, convoys being attacked again and again and dispersed by U-boat packs lying in wait. The 1939 building program developed in such a way that, by late autumn 1942 boats were available for American waters, for operations against Cape Town, for three convoy-attacking groups in northern waters, and in the North and Central Atlantic, and often also a group to attack the Gibraltar-England traffic.

Losses were small. The main enemy, particularly in relation to the tactical maneuverability of the U-boat on the surface, was the aircraft. As these had, however, apparently not yet been fitted with long-range location devices, they were only able to spot U-boats close to. In a rough sea, and particularly at night, aircraft were not dangerous.

Depth charge attacks by destroyers against U-boats were not much feared. They were dangerous only when the U-boat was not protected by a sufficient depth of water. In general, depth charges dropped by sight over the diving position were more accurate than the patterns dropped later on the basis of Asdic bearings.

A U-boat that lay low and left no oil traces was generally lost by its pursuer after a certain time and could surface under cover of night and escape. The U-boat crews had in the meantime received an excellent training on the basis of experience gained in repairing failures and in combating leaks. Damage and failures that, in the early war years, would have forced the boat to surface and led to its destruction were now overcome underwater and the boat consequently saved. Proof was also given of the excellent construction of the boat, which was extraordinarily elastic by reason of the pressure hull sections having been welded, in contradistinction to the usual riveting process used in the First World War. Thus when depth charged the boat shook, but did not break. Provided the valves held, nothing could happen to the boat unless a depth charge exploded close by and caused the pressure hull to burst.

Generally speaking, therefore, the U-boat attack in 1942 was superior to the defense. The finding of convoys was facilitated by the large number of boats. The U-boats' greatest possession, the element of surprise, was still effective. The U-boats, when on the surface, were not spotted soon enough for the enemy to be able to avoid them, and when attacking, they could not be detected early enough by surface or submerged means of location.

At first glance one might have expected that the German navy would see 1942 as offering tempting opportunities to continue its policy of using its few major surface ships in support of the U-boat war against the enemy's maritime trade routes. Five American battleships had been sunk or crippled at Pearl Harbor. Britain had lost the battleship *Prince of Wales* and the battle cruiser *Repulse* to Japanese air attack in the South China Sea on 10 December 1941, and the *Barham* had been sunk and two other British battleships crippled toward the end of that year. Fresh incursions into the Atlantic by major German warships would have found the enemy hard-pressed to reinstate the policy of adding a capital ship to the escort of every major convoy. And whenever they did provide protection of that kind, the capital ship would have been exposed to torpedo attack by the U-boats. The Germans had the new battleship *Tirpitz*, plus the pocket battleships *Lützow* and *Admiral Scheer* available in Norwegian or home waters, and, ideally placed for operations in the Atlantic, the *Scharnhorst, Gneisenau* and *Prinz Eugen* in Brest. Instead of being sent in search of enemy convoys, the ships in Brest were sent back to Germany. By that time Schniewind had been transferred to the post of C in C fleet, and he and Schuster provide an authoritative explanation of why a strategic retreat of that kind was ordered when the U-boats were mounting their own highly effective strategic offensive.

[In] 1941 the air force suffered a heavy reduction in their operations over England as the squadrons had to be withdrawn in large numbers and rested for the coming eastern campaign. These steps taken by the German air force were especially felt by the navy about the middle and end of 1941. The naval position was particularly weakened by the heavy reduction of extensive reconnaissance (U-boat warfare) for which only ineffectual types (FW 200, HE 111) were available, which in spite of possessing a good radius of action had insufficient powers of endurance, and by the decrease in fighter forces along the French coast and for the bases there. The ships lying in Brest received a great deal of punishment from the enemy air force, which repeatedly held up their readiness for operations. By order of the high command, a specially strong air defense that included fighters was provided for Brest, which made it possible to have all the ships simultaneously ready for action in January 1942.

At the end of December 1941, when the repairs to the large ships that were lying in Brest were almost completed and the question of their future employment had been raised, the Führer decided that they should return to home waters. Naturally the navy wanted to leave these ships on the Atlantic coast for use in further attacks against merchant ships. The Führer's decision was put into effect, therefore, against the navy's wishes (since they could not foresee any tasks for these ships in home waters) because

> [the Führer] did not think that the future prospects for these ships in the war against merchant shipping were good enough;
>
> he foresaw that they were always liable to be heavily bombed in their bases in western France;
>
> in face of the tension in the east, he could not at that time provide a sufficiently strong air defense (fighter aircraft) for the protection of Brest; and
>
> he considered the attacks of these ships from the Norwegian coast against the Murmansk convoys to be an important and promising task for surface vessels.

Meyer also mentions Hitler's personal involvement, and he emphasizes the inability of the Luftwaffe to protect the ships in Brest. Nevertheless, Meyer questions the wisdom of the decision:

The spur to the withdrawal of [the] *Scharnhorst* and *Gneisenau* from Brest through the Channel to the east was given by the air force, which was responsible for their protection from the air but no longer had sufficient strength for the task. It is interesting to note that Hitler gave the navy one of two alternatives: either to dismantle the ships in Brest or to withdraw them to Germany or Norway.

Would it not have been better to have held back our surface units for some later operation (for example, during the invasion of Normandy in 1944)? I can only say that the German fleet was too small and too ill balanced to be used as a whole against such powerful superiority as was possessed by the enemy.

The German navy's implementation of the decision to withdraw the ships involved considerable risks.

Dönitz: The operation of naval forces in the North Atlantic was no longer possible in 1942 on account of the serious danger of air attack on the Biscay ports and the increasing enemy watchfulness in the North Atlantic. When this was fully recognized, a decision had to be made whether to leave the *Scharnhorst, Gneisenau,* and *Prinz Eugen* where they were in Brest or to bring them back to Germany via the Icelandic route or through the Channel. Taking into consideration the well-equipped locating installations on the English coast, the far superior British fleet, and the very strong British air forces in this area, this operation represented an unusually hazardous venture, which could only succeed by its surprise element. The preparations were accordingly made in secret.

Schniewind and Schuster: The navy had to decide how the journey should be made. They decided in favor of a dash up the Channel in spite of the greater danger from the enemy air force and from mines, since this route, being the most dangerous, would also be the one the enemy would least expect them to take. It was thought that the danger from mines could be dealt with by massing large numbers of minesweepers, and it was only on this route that the necessary fighter protection could be given by our own fighter units.

Under the command of Vice Admiral Ciliax, the three heavy ships, escorted by six destroyers and many smaller vessels such as minesweepers,

sailed from Brest at 2245 on 11 February 1942. Fortune favored them. The RAF, guarding against some move of this kind, were keeping the exit to Brest under surveillance but radar failure in two reconnaissance aircraft enabled the ships to escape detection in the darkness. They were, in fact, approaching Boulogne before an RAF aircraft made a sighting report, and they had passed through the straits of Dover before, shortly after noon on 12 February, they encountered the first attempts to stop them. First an attack by British motor torpedo boats was beaten off by the escorts; then six slow Fairey Swordfish torpedo-bombers of 825 Squadron, fleet air arm, were all shot down before they could score a single hit. Six old British destroyers from Harwich and heavy bombers of the RAF also failed to inflict any damage as the Germans passed up the Dutch coast and turned toward their home ports. British sea power had been humiliated, but the Germans did not escape unscathed, as Schniewind and Schuster acknowledge:

With good security measures and fairly favorable weather conditions it was thought that the operation could be regarded with confidence. This expectation was fulfilled. The breakthrough itself was considered by the navy to be a tactical success, but the withdrawal from the Atlantic was regarded as a strategic defeat. The breakout was much more successful than had been expected, but *Scharnhorst* was damaged by a mine west, and again northwest, of Holland, which kept her in dry dock until the autumn of 1942. The battleship *Gneisenau* suffered slight underwater damage through contact with a wreck in the Elbe, and shortly afterward, while in dock in Kiel, she was hit by a heavy bomb during an air attack. Since the repair of this ship would have been a long and difficult task, the attempt to make her seaworthy was abandoned for the duration of the war. The cruiser *Prinz Eugen* was sent to Norway, together with the pocket battleship *Admiral Scheer*, to join the battleship *Tirpitz*. The *Prinz Eugen* was damaged by a torpedo from a submarine near Trondheim, which first kept her in Trondheim for temporary repairs until May, and later, after bringing her home, delayed her there until autumn 1942. The . . . forces [in Norway] were continually strengthened by the addition of other ships—*Lützow* [ex-*Deutschland*], *Hipper*, *Nürnberg*, *Köln*—as well as destroyers, torpedo boats, U-boats, and minesweepers.

The strategic purpose in basing the German navy's heavy ships in Norway, instead of joining the main battle in the Atlantic, is spelled out by Dönitz.

The main sphere of activity of the remaining heavy units of the fleet had now moved to northern Norway, where new tasks awaited them. From the general strategic point of view our main interest lay in further immobilizing as large a part of the English fleet as possible in English home waters, thereby relieving both the Mediterranean and the Far Eastern theaters of war. The Anglo-American convoys to Murmansk and Archangel that had meanwhile come into operation represented an objective of equal strategic importance, which was attacked by our naval forces at different times with varying success, while U-boats and aircraft operating jointly frequently achieved considerable successes.

Schniewind and Schuster once more accuse the German air force of making an inadequate contribution to the battle against the Arctic convoys.

Naval operations from Norwegian bases, including those undertaken by U-boats, were very much hampered by the weakness of our own air force, which could place few aircraft at our disposal for naval operations. In this area the air force's insufficient support of the navy was particularly in evidence. Not only for the operations themselves was there no satisfactory reconnaissance or fighter support, but at the bases and in the inshore routes no really strong fighter protection was assured or it was given only for special operations of limited duration in a designated area. In spite of this, however, no severe losses occurred in the course of 1942. Cooperation with the reconnaissance units (FW 200, BV 138) improved through practice in the course of the year, but their strength never rose to a satisfactory figure.

The first Allied convoy to north Russia had arrived at the end of August 1941, and by the end of the year six convoys had made the passage without losing any merchant ships to enemy action. In the first six months of 1942, 28 Allied merchantmen were sunk, either on the outward or homeward leg of voyages to Russia. Of those, 17 were accounted for by the Luftwaffe, 7 by U-boats, 3 by destroyers in surface actions, and 1 by mine. In the next three months another 46 Allied merchant ships were lost on the north Russia run. Again, the Luftwaffe played a major role, sinking 21; U-boats sank 20; and 5 were lost to mines. More than half the merchantmen lost were from Convoy PQ 17, which received a direct order from London to scatter on the mistaken assumption that it was about to be attacked by the German heavy ships. In the final quarter of 1942, another 8 merchant ships were sunk (6 by U-boats, 1 by aircraft, and 1 by a German destroyer). In these operations the Royal Navy also lost 2 cruisers, 2 destroyers, and 2 minesweepers. Although the Royal Navy made dispositions to meet the potential threat posed by the German heavy ships, that threat never materialized. The apparently undistinguished contribution of those ships to the war effort led to a sharp difference of opinion among senior German naval officers, as Heye describes:

The increase in the number of U-boats made itself very noticeably felt in the navy by reason of the large-scale transfer of officers and men from all other units. The idea then occurred, and was advocated by C in C U-boats, of abandoning the surviving large units of the fleet and using the personnel in U-boats, and the working capacity thus released in the yards for U-boat construction. These plans were rejected by Grossadmiral Raeder since, in the opinion of the experts consulted, such an abandonment of the larger ships would bring about no real increase in [the number of] U-boats. Moreover, Grossadmiral Raeder, on the advice of Admiral Carls and other senior officers, supported the retention of the larger ships. A certain number of the ships were in any case necessary to train new entries. The lack of officers at that time did not permit a general training in the naval officers branches. One had to be content with training the young officers for only one branch, for example, U-boats.

On the last day of 1942 the German heavy ships at last had an opportunity to show what they could achieve. Convoy JW 51B was intercepted in the Barents Sea by Admiral Kummetz with the heavy cruiser *Admiral Hipper*, the pocket battleship *Lützow*, and six big German destroyers. In a series of confused encounters, the German ships were fought off by the convoy's destroyer escort and finally driven off altogether by the arrival of two British cruisers. The convoy escort lost a destroyer and a minesweeper, and three other destroyers were damaged. The Germans lost one destroyer and suffered damage to the *Hipper*, and they failed to sink a single merchant ship. This failure infuriated Hitler.

Schniewind and Schuster: A skirmish occurred off the north coast of Norway between German ships (*Hipper, Lützow*), that were attacking a convoy, and British destroyers and convoy escort vessels; the latter's escape again raised the question with the high command as to whether large surface vessels could still be usefully employed or whether it would not be better to bring them home, in view of the dangers they would encounter in north Norway, and either hold them in a state of readiness there or lay them up and use their crews, weapons, and engines for other purposes. The Führer ordered their return against the pressing advice of the C in C of the navy, who wanted to continue the threat to the convoy routes with heavy ships for military-political reasons (Pacific, Mediterranean) so that the enemy would also be forced to retain heavy surface vessels in home waters. This difference of opinion contributed to the change in the command of the navy and, in consequence, [changes] in a number of other high positions. The new C in C of the navy succeeded in having the surface forces left in north Norway and in having *Scharnhorst* sent there as a reinforcement in the spring of 1943.

Meyer: It was only occasionally that Hitler interfered; he did so in January 1943, for example, when, after the disappointing engagement in the Arctic of two cruisers and six destroyers with a Russia-bound convoy on 30 December 1942, he demanded the paying-off of all battleships and cruisers. This was the occasion of Dönitz replacing Raeder. The curious thing was, however, that Dönitz, who as C in C U-boats had favored a different policy, saw things from a higher plane when he became C in C [of the German navy] and kept the big ships in commission.

Although he was now commander in chief of the whole German navy, Dönitz continued to direct the operations of his U-boat fleet with considerable success during the first quarter of 1943. Certain matters were, however, causing him anxiety.

In 1942 the German Cipher Office was fortunate enough to read various convoy ciphers. The German U-boat command thus had at its disposal the place and time of convoy meetings and also gathering points for convoy stragglers. This valuable assistance to attacking U-boats ceased in the early months of 1943. It was, of course, possible, granted a sufficiently large number of W/T messages, to break down the code, but advantage could no longer be derived from this, as the enemy was now changing the code at shorter intervals than formerly so that the wearying labor of breaking it down had to be recommenced each time.

The secondary reason for this reduction in the tracking of convoys during the winter of 1942–43 may be that, at this time, the enemy grasped the U-boat reconnaissance patrol tactics and took avoiding action. This possibility had already [posed problems for] the *surface* warfare, that is, mobile operations employing the so-called wolf pack system, in order to achieve the desired concentration on one convoy. If this principle were given up, no great results could be achieved. In this respect the same conditions apply to sea warfare as to land warfare. Here also no decisive results can be obtained by static trench warfare, but only by mobile operations.

The U-boat command therefore had to concentrate before the war on what means the enemy might employ to hinder U-boat movement on the surface, and what could be done by us against his A/S measures. The enemy air force was at that time the greatest problem for the U-boat command, and it was therefore surprising that it was only later that the enemy recognized and used this weapon as being the most effective means against the U-boat.

Dönitz writes of his U-boat campaign with great enthusiasm and commitment, and with real affection for the U-boat commanders who had the task of putting his orders into effect. It is obvious that, in the opening months of 1943 his belief in the "wolf pack" tactics of U-boats operating mainly on the surface remained undiminished.

Although fewer convoys were encountered in January–February 1943, due not only to the weather but also to the two aforesaid causes, nevertheless the danger that the surface warfare against convoys might come to an end did not appear to be immediate. On the contrary, new well-equipped U-boats were coming out from home and their numbers were rising monthly. The number of boats in the Atlantic rose continuously in spite of continued deliveries to the Mediterranean and to northern waters to attack Russia-bound convoys. In March 1943, conditions on the main battleground, the North Atlantic, were again very favorable. Many convoys were met and attacked with great success. The most successful convoy battles of the whole war were fought. The U-boat leadership in these battles and also the attacks on the convoys by the commanding officers reached their peak.

It had now been proved unmistakably by years of war experience that the directing of the U-boats from another boat away at sea or in the neighborhood of the convoy was impossible. The whole operation had to be conducted by a U-boat commander ashore and often a thousand miles away. Between such a commander and the commanding officers under his orders at sea such an understanding had gradually developed that the conduct of operations in view of general conditions at the convoy position, air protection, close and remote screening, and the state of the weather was so effective that it could successfully control the tactical direction of the distant action and was also felt by those under orders to be correct and practical. In this the higher command made unrestricted use of wireless and obtained the necessary information from the boats concerning conditions at the convoy position. If radio communications were inadequate, the commander of the U-boats communicated by R/T [sic] from his command post with the most experienced commanding officer at the convoy position.

No case is known to me in which agreement was not established by this method between the higher command and these veteran fighters. The battle at the convoy position itself was waged by the U-boats in tactical cooperation and with a high standard of individual performance in attack. With regard to reconnaissance, shadowing in spite of air and sea escort, clear reporting procedures, diving at the correct time to escape aircraft and destroyers, surfacing again as soon as possible and pressing home the attack, breaking through the escort to attack, and carrying out the attack itself, the conduct of commanding officers was excellent. They were men who, through years of seafaring in wartime, felt at home in the Atlantic in both summer and winter—a group of bold seamen of outstanding fighting ability. Consequently there were convoy battles in which more than half, and in some cases two-thirds, of the convoy were wiped out.

Looking back over this period, it can be said that U-boat successes were at their peak. The number of U-boats was continually increasing; losses were slight; and the reinforcement by boats from home considerable. The radius of action of all the boats was considerably extended by the use of supply U-boats from each of which about ten U-boats could each draw forty tons of oil and additional provisions, thus obviating the voyage to and from even the Biscay ports, which according to German conceptions were not far distant. The U-boats were also fueled by surface tankers when such were available. These could also supply torpedoes. Operations in the South American area, in the area around Cape Town, and in the Indian Ocean were thus made possible.

Through the construction, under timely orders from the Führer, of the U-boat shelters in the Biscay ports, the repairing and fitting out of the boats could be fully maintained without losses due to bombing attacks.

The torpedo branch had gained an extraordinary amount of technical experience from its failures at the beginning of the war and had reached a high stage of development. In the acoustic torpedo, now ready for action, the U-boat also possessed . . . a weapon against the depth charge–throwing escort vessels. By means of various kinds of looping torpedoes, the probability of scoring hits, especially with the concentration of targets in a convoy, was considerably increased. Even though anxiety over the development of enemy air support over the Atlantic and the improvement of surface location had a depressing influence on the U-boat war, the advantages mentioned above could be set against such anxiety, so that the U-boat arm in its pride in the very great successes gained up to March 1943, hoped to be able to meet even a strengthened A/S defense with an increase in the number of U-boats and thus maintain its successes at the same high standard.

Grand Admiral Dönitz had solid evidence on which to base his optimism. In 1942 German U-boats and Italian submarines had been responsible for sinking 1,555 Allied and neutral vessels, amounting to almost 6.15 million gross registered tons of shipping. In the first quarter of 1943 they sank a further 221 vessels totaling more than 1.3 million gross tons. That meant a total of about 7.45 million tons in fifteen months; and if one added vessels sunk by aircraft, surface actions, and mines, plus those sunk by the Japanese, more than 9 million gross registered tons of Allied and neutral shipping had fallen victim to the "tonnage war" in that period. The strain on the capacity of the Allies' worldwide shipping requirements was even greater than the figures for sinkings suggest, for they also had to face the problems caused by the slow speed of convoys, delays through evasive routing, and the temporary loss of damaged ships while they were undergoing repair. Over that same period, 308 new U-boats had been commissioned into the German navy, more than making up for the 127 U-boats lost in that time. Dönitz's conviction that with sufficient U-boats he could find the convoys and overwhelm the escorts had been confirmed by the sinking of 13 ships from convoy SC 121 between 7 and 11 March 1943, during which one U-boat was lost after being rammed by one of the merchant vessels. Then, in a battle from 16–20 March 1943, 2 Atlantic convoys from New York to Britain—SC 122 and HX 229, totaling 100 merchant ships—were assailed by 40 U-boats, which sank 21 ships amounting to 140,000 gross registered tons. On the German side, only one U-boat was lost during the battle around these two convoys. If results on that scale could be maintained, Dönitz may well have hoped for a complete victory in the Battle of the Atlantic or, at the very least, to make continuing the battle so costly that the British and Americans might be forced into agreeing to a compromise peace for which Hitler had been hoping since 1940.

8

Decision in the Mediterranean, 1942–1943

AS 1941 DREW to a close, with the German and Italian forces once again being driven out of Cyrenaica by the British, the German high command realized at last that they needed to give greater attention to the war in the Mediterranean. Their first step was to send air force reinforcements to Sicily and to appoint Field Marshal Albert Kesselring of the Luftwaffe to be commander in chief south, a post he took up toward the end of December 1941. He had not been given an easy job. Schniewind and Schuster outline the difficulties of the command structure.

It must be briefly stated how great the difficulties were that in practice obstructed the unity of command that was to be effected in the spring of 1942 by the appointment of Field Marshal Kesselring to the supreme command of the whole southern theater of operations. Not only could branches of the armed forces of each Axis partner not free themselves satisfactorily from personal and internal sensibilities, or from the other menaces of special interest in relation to their own supreme commands (OKW and commando supremo), but even the different types of units only saw things from their own angle in their relations to each other and to the commander in chief south (Ob-Süd). This constantly recurring friction in the Axis command, however, could be still less supported without more serious consequences than would have been the case among approximately equal opponents with less important war aims, and in a theater of operations where great strategic aims had to be achieved with very limited, weak forces and the fewest possible reserves against an experienced, tough, and strong enemy.

Rommel, commanding the German forces in Libya, but nominally under the command of an Italian general, was quite ruthless in exploiting the loopholes in command organization on the spot, in Rome between Kesselring and the Italian high command, and in his own direct channels to the German high command and the Führer. As a result, he became something of a law unto himself in the deserts of Libya. With characteristic boldness and energy, he quickly regrouped his forces, and on 21 January 1942 launched a counterstroke against the British in Cyrenaica. After quickly regaining the port of Benghazi his progress toward Egypt was halted in February by a British defense line at Ain el Gazala, to the west of Tobruk. Weichold is inclined to claim that the preconditions for such an advance were created by the Luftwaffe and the navy.

The attacks of the new German air force in the Mediterranean . . . were directed against Malta. The attacks of the stukas and bombers on the aerodromes on the island soon reduced the enemy air attacks on the sea transport to Africa. Furthermore, the harbors increasingly lost their value as bases for the British ships and submarines. Thus it was that this key British position in the central Mediterranean—which only a few weeks before had been the chief cause of the losses in Libya—was eliminated.

A singular effect . . . was that during January not a single ship and not one ton of material on its way to the armored corps in Africa were lost. Furthermore, in spite of the bad weather, extraordinarily large quantities of stores were moved from Tripoli to . . . harbors near the front. . . . This was particularly important at a time when about 50 percent of the transport belonging to the armored corps was in need of repair following on the retreat from Cyrenaica. It was for this reason that it became possible to reform the armored corps in good fighting order . . . an astonishing fact considering the difficult retreat and the considerable losses in both men and material. It is clear that this was due in the first place to the energy and steadfastness of both leaders and men but also to the endeavors made to bring in supplies by sea, and this latter factor was solely dependent on the newly won mastery of air and sea.

The military effects of the Axis dominance in the central Mediterranean on the African campaign were astonishing.

Kesselring and other German officers could see that the capture of Malta was the only way of guaranteeing that supplies would continue to flow steadily to the Axis forces in Libya.

Schniewind and Schuster: On the instigation of Field Marshal Kesselring the conquest of Malta was planned for the summer of 1942 and preparations were begun—for example, landing barges were brought to Sicily from the Black Sea. The operation was to be carried out before General Rommel's new eastward drive. Misgivings in the highest circles [and] lack of accord on the German side as to the amount of German support that would be necessary . . . contributed at least to the abandoning of the plan, although in the spring of 1942 an unusually favorable situation existed for this extremely important and decisive operation.

Heye: Throughout the African campaign the navy had the impression that too great a reliance was being placed on the supposition that the supply routes by sea could always be maintained. The position would have been appreciably altered if we had succeeded in taking Malta. Such an operation was planned but, to the best of my knowledge, was to have been undertaken primarily by the Italians. I believe that Malta might have been captured by a surprise attack shortly after Italy's entry into the war. I consider it doubtful whether success could have been gained later; it was certainly impossible without considerable support from German troops and aircraft.

Weichold: Malta, the British sea and air base, was in a bad way owing to the blockade that had been going on for several months. If [a supply convoy from Alexandria, sighted on 21 March] could be prevented from reaching Malta, this would be the best preparation for the occupation of the island. The fall of Malta, however, would, for the Italian Mediterranean command, be like the healing of a creeping disease, and it would mean the final security of the supply routes to Libya and success for the operations in Africa. In addition to this, however, the occupation of Malta would secure the Italian motherland from invasion by the enemy, and furthermore, it was fundamental to all further large Axis operations in the Mediterranean and the Middle East, because it would remove the possibility of a stab in the back. The fall of Malta, therefore, could have very far-reaching results on the strategic plans of the whole war. The success of any operation against the island, however, depended on her position as regards supplies.

With so much at stake, it is easy to understand Weichold's professional frustration when, in what British historians call the Second Battle of Sirte, an Italian force consisting of a modern battleship, three cruisers, and a large number of destroyers, which intercepted the convoy on 22 March, allowed themselves to be outmaneuvered and beaten off in a confusing series of encounters with the British light cruisers escorting the convoy.

The Italians never closed with their primary target, the four fast merchant ships.

The worst effect of this failure was, however, that the German air force lost all confidence in the ability of the Italian navy and their faith in sea power was even more greatly shaken than it had already been by past events and by their own attitude toward the navy. The German air force had never been very eager to operate with the Italian navy, and after this event they were even less prepared to cooperate, as any possibility of their own success was very small. It was only when backed by German aircraft, however, that the Italian fleet could be got to operate at sea at all. From this moment, the German command of the air force went more and more its own way, and in this, they certainly achieved some considerable success, but alone they could never be a decisive factor. In the light of these events, the Italian defeat on 22 March had, as a consequence, a far worse effect than its previous defeats at Taranto and Matapan. To this depressing fact can be added the regret that the German-Italian cooperation was not practical enough to instill any strength of leadership into the Italian navy. The German command is as much to blame in this as the Italian, as the actual position at the time and the consequences were clear to them both. The German high command had, however, not the foresight to realize that the fight in the Mediterranean would one day have a tremendous effect on the whole war situation. For this reason, the high command could not absolve itself from the happenings in the Mediterranean and their disastrous consequences.

No doubt the failure of the Italian navy to destroy the convoy on 22 March contrasted starkly with the success of the German air force in sinking two of the merchant ships before they reached Malta and destroying the other two while they were in harbor there. Thus, of the 26,000 tons of supplies carried, only 5,000 tons were safely discharged at Valetta. The British fully understood the value of Malta and were prepared to accept heavy casualties in both warships and merchant vessels in operations to keep the island supplied. At times they were reduced to desperate expedients such as flying fighter aircraft in from aircraft carriers, conveying urgent stores on board fast warships such as minelayers, or trying to sneak in supplies with individual unescorted merchantmen disguised as Vichy French vessels. In the summer of 1942, however, Malta was desperately short of supplies and under almost daily aerial bombardment, which prevented the British forces based there from interfering effectively with the

Axis supply convoys to Libya. With a steady flow of ammunition, equipment, food, fuel, and reinforcements, Rommel was eager to take the offensive against the British defense line at Ain el Gazala. He attacked at the end of May, fought his way through to take Tobruk, and by the end of June had pursued the British far into Egypt, where they occupied a defense line at El Alamein, only about sixty miles short of the main British naval base at Alexandria. Weichold shared Rommel's eagerness to see the strategic opportunities seized and exploited, but he was anxious to see properly coordinated measures to win firm control over the whole central and eastern Mediterranean.

To support the land operations progressing in Cyrenaica against the enemy, dependent upon his bases in the eastern Mediterranean, it was worth the struggle to divert the main weight of Axis sea power to the east. The Italian Admiralty were not fundamentally opposed to the possibilities of offensive activity in the eastern Mediterranean from the bases in Crete and the Dodecanese proposed by the German naval commander in chief [i.e., Weichold himself]. They only requested German assistance for the joint fuel oil requirements. The German high command refused an increase in the amount of fuel allotted to the Italian navy for the protection of transports to Africa. This resulted in the refusal of the Italian navy to divert their naval forces to eastern bases. The efforts of the German Admiralty to switch Italian sea power from the defensive protection of Africa convoys to the participation in offensive operations in the eastern Mediterranean, were, therefore, finally wrecked. Therefore the cooperation of the Axis sea power was limited, in the conquest of Cyrenaica, to the carrying out of coastal supply in Cyrenaica by German transport and naval forces. The Italian high command entrusted this operation to the German naval commander in chief.

With the joint planning and carrying through of the preparations for the Malta operation, a complete joint staff work was achieved in the Mediterranean for the first time, proof of how the collaboration of the Axis partners could have functioned by the use of German materials and experience for the strengthening of the Italian forces.

[He implies that Rommel was tempted to advance too far into Egypt. In previous campaigns] it had been learnt at the cost of blood that the planning of a front without nearby harbors and without a secured sea supply route would not result in safe positions and would lead to a heavy defeat.

[The British responded by stepping up air activity in the central Mediterranean.] The weakening of the German Luftwaffe in the Mediterranean in early '42 was very favorable for [the enemy]. Considerable units of the Luftwaffe had to be withdrawn at this time, for the new German Russian offensive. On account of this the British were in a position to win back air supremacy over Malta. . . . Once again the threatening monster of reduced supplies for Africa loomed on the horizon. While at the front the soldiers of the Afrika Korps fought and conquered, far from the decisive areas of the land fighting, the British were systematically throttling the supplies of the German-Italian Panzer army. We were threatened with losing the fruits of the Cyrenaican victory. Only a quick solution of the Malta problem, by the occupation of the island, as had already been provided for in the great operational plan of 1942, could finally remove the again impending danger.

In this situation the supreme German command, in agreement with the Italian command, decided to postpone the execution of the Malta operation. This far-reaching decision was made under the impression of the Panzer army's success in the area of the Egyptian frontier. The commanders of the Luftwaffe and the Kriegsmarine in the Mediterranean were not party to this alteration in the plans, while the influence of Field Marshal Rommel turned the scales.

Field Marshal Kesselring and the naval C in C pointed out to Rommel the difficulties that would be encountered in a further advance. The enemy would be able to fall back on his reserves, supplies, and good communications, while our own lines of communication would continue to be lengthened. We could in no way continue to rely upon a supply route as well maintained as before or upon the support of the Italian navy in the eastern Mediterranean. Above all the newly gained supremacy of the enemy in the central Mediterranean caused a constant weakening in seaborne supplies from Italy to North Africa. Field Marshal Rommel considered the military situation on land so favorable and promising that he believed himself able to advance right into the Nile delta in spite of all the difficulties. There the supply difficulties could be met from British supplies.

The new plan of campaign was a terrific gamble; everything was staked on one card. Everything depended upon the lightning execution of the land operation. If this expectation was not fulfilled, heavy defeat would ensue. The German naval command raised no objection to the postponement of the Malta plan.

With the expansion of the theater of war to the Egyptian area, the transfer of the great power of the Italian sea forces to the east was an unconditional necessity. The naval commander resubmitted to the Italian Admiralty his earlier proposals on 25 June 1943, in a form modified by the development of the war.

The Italian navy agreed with these points in all respects and carried out the suggested preparations. Nevertheless, they again pointed out that the carrying out and timing of the planned switch over depended in the first instance on solving the fuel problem. Because the German high command and also the naval command were deaf to all the German admirals' efforts to increase the delivery of fuel to the Italians, the necessary removal of Italian sea power to the east again fell through. That the German headquarters watched this with indifference again proved their underestimation of sea power in the general military conduct of the war and the significance of the Mediterranean to the total conduct of the war.

In this period, critical for the supply of the Panzer army, the protection of the ships of coastal traffic, of the coastal waters, and of the ports of discharge should more than ever have been carried out by air cover. The Luftwaffe could, however, meet no great demands for these purposes, and it increasingly scaled down its previous efforts for protection of sea transport, since its aircraft were completely occupied in the land fighting. Owing to these difficulties and losses the traffic in the coastal waters was unable to continue to play the role of main supply route, and the supplying of the Panzer armies fell once again mainly on the long land supply route.

With Rommel's forces so far forward in Egypt, amateur strategists could let their imaginations have free rein in speculating about where his next advance might be, once he had driven the British out of Alexandria, Suez, and Cairo. Would he pursue the British up the Nile valley into the interior of Africa? Would he drive on eastward to effect a junction in the oil fields of Iraq and Iran with another German army driving south through the Caucasus? Would he emulate Alexander the Great by leading an army into the Ganges plain to meet the Japanese advancing westward from Burma? In fact, his advance turned out to have been permanently checked at El Alamein. Here was a position that, with the sea to the north and the Qattara Depression to the south, could not be outflanked; and Rommel's attempt to effect a breakthrough was defeated at the end of August and beginning of September. To save Malta from starvation and resume offensive operations based on the island the British were prepared to engage in a major battle to fight through the famous Operation Pedestal convoy of August 1942, when 2 battleships, 3 aircraft carriers, 7 cruisers, and 25 destroyers were used to escort 14 merchant ships from Gibraltar. Nine of the merchantmen were sunk, and of the 5 that reached Valetta, 2 were barely afloat. The operation cost the Royal Navy the aircraft carrier *Eagle*, the cruisers *Manchester* and *Cairo*, and the destroyer *Foresight*, with many other ships taking damage and casualties. The convoy had paid a heavy price, but from a strategic perspective it was a price worth paying. British attacks on the convoys carrying supplies for Rommel slowly began to deprive him of the resources he needed to continue his offensive. Weichold gives figures showing that, in August, September, and October 1942, the Axis dispatched 318,000 tons of shipping in convoys to Libya and lost 85,000 tons, more than 25 percent. Most crucial of all, of 10,000 tons of vehicle fuel sent in October, only 3,300 tons arrived safely. Weichold had already drawn his own conclusions:

[I] was of the opinion that very serious setbacks could be expected for the African war if nothing definite was decided for the provision of a larger defensive unit in the Mediterranean. If a reinforcement of the German forces should be impossible it would be better to choose the lesser evil and voluntarily to withdraw from the endangered El Alamein positions. All the official and personal efforts of the naval commander in this matter came to nothing, as it was the opinion of those in command not to give up any territory that had already been occupied. This was a one-sided attitude emanating from the War Office, which, for sea warfare or for operations to be carried out across the sea, was not applicable. At every step the continental viewpoint of the supreme German command could be seen.

Writing in 1945, Weichold gives vent to all the frustrations he must have felt when serving as German naval commander in chief in the Mediterranean in the summer of 1942.

Fate had again . . . offered the Axis command the chance to start again from the beginning, and to attain the mastery of the Mediterranean area with all the future advantages for the final victory. The military situation was extraordinarily good. . . . Everything appeared to be ripe for the harvest. There was only one condition for the carrying through of the decisive operation of the Axis. This was the consideration of the lesson learnt in 1941: that an African operation could only be carried out if solid foundations could be created by the position at sea. And again in 1942 the astonishing thing happened: the German high command, in sight of a probable victory, became fatally blind and threw all the lessons of the past away. The maintaining of that foundation of combined warfare—mastery of the sea—was again endangered. The generally favorable overall situation misled them into over-emphasizing the importance of land operations, while neglecting the necessities of sea warfare. The Egyptian offensive of the Axis amounted to overstretching the possibilities of land warfare across the sea, without the cooperation of naval units.

The warnings of those who appreciated the gravity of the situation were completely ignored. The refusal of the German high command to give any further German aid was a death blow to the Mediterranean campaign. . . . It needed only the necessary preparations and a thrust on the part of the enemy to tip the scales once and for all against the Axis in the Mediterranean.

Schniewind and Schuster also identify the crucial importance of Rommel's supply difficulties, but they also doubt whether the idea of overrunning Egypt was realistic.

Supply for Rommel's Panzer army had to suffer from the obvious disadvantages of lengthened communications from the progress of the attack eastward. The conquest of new ports, lying near the enemy, and auxiliary landing grounds (Derna, Tobruk, Sollum, Mersa Matruh) could not even out the shortages of all types of supplies: hundreds of kilometers of desert sands remained to be covered.

In relation to these difficulties on land, the serious interference with seaborne supplies was decisive. The lack of shipping space, the weakness of the convoy vessels, and the sinking of fighting ships by air force and fleet units—which tactically or operationally ought to have formed a cover for the transports against English cruisers, destroyers, and air force—led to the attempt to get the vital supplies through to the army and Luftwaffe in Africa by a series of "stopgaps" and by emergency measures, which very early went beyond the bounds of what appeared right to a healthy, strategic judgment. And, toward the end of 1942, they even further exceeded these bounds. The demands of the fighting front at Alamein grew more frequent and more pressing—and shipping space got shorter. In the end it frequently came to the point where one tanker, at least, was brought to an African port as far east as possible because, without its cargo, tanks and planes would have had to lie idle through lack of fuel after one or two sorties.

With such supply difficulties, no attack could be fed from the advanced bases or the homeland. It was forced—apart from the failure of the Italian troops in the front line—to come to a halt, and retreat was unavoidable.

Independent of this, the fact remains—as far as is known to the authors—that Rommel's troops, who had to push forward to Alamein in autumn 1942, would have been too weak to gain permanent control of the area Alexandria, Port Said, Cairo, Suez. If Rommel had not evacuated his positions —operationally far too late—[and] if he had succeeded in breaking into northern Egypt (against the will of OKW, he had pressed on too far eastward after Mersa Matruh), he would have come up against massed British reserves . . . for whose defeat he would have needed far stronger forces. Such [German or Italian] reserves were simply not there and, in view of the endangered sea communications and the lack of shipping space, they could not have been brought up in time or collected in the right place.

So failed the last attack against the eastern bastion of the British position in the Mediterranean and the whole attempt to cut off this decisive sea. The Axis powers had not succeeded in completely interrupting the enemy's sea communications, nor had they been able to effectively protect their own sea communications.

For the various reasons mentioned above, the Axis powers failed to obtain the necessary control of the sea, even if it were only for a short time or over a limited area. In spite of favorable geographical conditions, the shortage of manpower and weakness in military training and, above all, the limitations and lack of unity among the leaders led to a failure that not only influenced the further course of events in this theater of operations but also was decisive for the whole future course of the war.

By 23 October the British forces at El Alamein were ready to take the offensive against Rommel, and after a very hard fought battle the Axis forces were in full retreat by 4 November, leaving behind large numbers of Italian infantry to surrender because there was neither transport nor petrol to carry them away from the El Alamein position. By 13 November the British had retaken Tobruk, and by 21 December they were back in Benghazi. Effectively the two armies were back in the area where Rommel had begun his offensive twelve months earlier, but this time he lacked the resources to mount one of his characteristic counterstrokes. This time he could only fight brief delaying actions before retreating farther into Tripolitania. By 23 January 1943 the British had taken Tripoli, and the whole of Libya was effectively in their hands by 10 February. Meanwhile there had been important developments at the western end of the Mediterranean. On 8 November 1942, only four days after Rommel had been forced to begin his long retreat from El Alamein, American and British forces had landed in both Morocco and Algeria, then included in French North Africa and controlled by the Vichy government. Within a few days French resistance had been overcome and Allied forces were advancing eastward toward Tunisia, another French possession. The German admirals are by no means unanimous about whether the invasion of French North Africa had been expected.

Krancke: The most important event in the western theater was the Allied landing in North Africa. Neither the preparations nor the transit of the landing barges was known to the German naval staff. Consequently, U-boats were not put into operation off the African coast.

Meyer: It is my opinion that the German high command had, strangely enough, not anticipated such a landing—in any case there were no written or oral instructions to cover such an event—in spite of the fact that North Africa was the weakest point on the [fringes] of Europe. (Did they believe that the enemy would not take such a step for political reasons? If so, this was another big fallacy.) In any case, Germany could have done nothing against the landing; the only effective measure would have been to have occupied North Africa, but Germany had not sufficient manpower for this purpose. It can be seen that the political leadership of the armed forces was faced with an impossible task.

Schniewind and Schuster: [The American and British landings] brought about a state of affairs that had been considered for a long time by the naval war staff as a serious menace to the war in North Africa and in the Mediterranean; a definite threat to the position of the Axis, that is, the Italians in North Africa, the complete isolation of the Mediterranean and with it the whole of southern Europe, and the gain by the western Allies of positions for further attacks on the European coastal areas of Greece, Italy, and southern France. It was hoped for some time that the French forces in North Africa were willing and in a position to offer effective resistance.

It was not altogether unreasonable for the Germans to hope that the invasion would embroil the Allies in prolonged hostilities with France, where there was still much resentment at the British attack on the French fleet at Mers el Kebir in 1940 and subsequent operations against Vichy French forces in Dakar, Syria, and Madagascar. On the first day of the landings, the French lost a cruiser and ten destroyers, either sunk by the British and Americans or so badly damaged that they had to be beached. However, as Krancke explains, any hope that France might be encouraged to join the Axis and throw her still very substantial fleet into the struggle for dominance in the Mediterranean soon faded.

The political effects were at first stronger than the military effects. Admiral Darlan, who until then had always emphasized cooperation with Germany, went over to the enemy. With him went many French generals. Germany, therefore, had to consider unoccupied France as a military danger, with the possibility of an unhindered Allied landing in the south of France. Circumstances demanded the disarmament of the French army and the occupation of the whole country, including the south coast of France. Further, the Führer did not think he could trust the French fleet in Toulon any longer, which had been considered reliably neutral (understandable after the occurrences at Oran).

When the danger of occupation became imminent, the French fleet scuttled itself. It was for political reasons that the Italians, who were hated by the French navy, were vested with the task of occupying the zone up to Toulon, although in actual fact the Italians hardly participated in the occupation itself. All these measures had changed the attitude of the French considerably and aided the rising of the Maquis and other resistance and sabotage organizations. The collaboration aimed at by numerous Frenchmen and by various German circles had come to an end.

The analysis by Schniewind and Schuster of the attitude of Admiral Darlan, the high commissioner and commander in chief for French North Africa, can probably be taken as applying to a far wider section of French public opinion at that time.

In connection with his attitude during these events, the question arises whether the French Admiral Darlan, who during the war had always shown himself to the German authorities (e.g., Grossadmiral Raeder) to be a convinced supporter of "collaboration" and an opponent of England, was playing a double game. The authors are of the opinion that he pursued an opportunist policy, in which his advocacy of collaboration and his enmity toward England at that time really represented his true feelings. Then, after the Allied landings in North Africa, his attitude was conditioned by his opinion of the general situation, that is, that it was impossible for the Axis to win the war.

In all, the French scuttled 1 battleship, 2 battle cruisers, 1 seaplane carrier, 7 cruisers, 26 destroyers and flotilla leaders, and many smaller warships.

Dönitz regrets that diplomatic measures could not have averted this destruction.

The incursion into North Africa of the Anglo-Americans left no alternative but the occupation of southern France by German troops. In spite of the loyalty of the French navy in North Africa it was unfortunately impossible, on account of the secrecy of the whole operation, to come to any agreement beforehand with the French Admiralty regarding the fate of the Toulon fleet, with the result that, when the surprise German invasion took place, orders were issued to scuttle all warships. In spite of this the German government abided by the German-French armistice agreement by which the Toulon fleet remained in French hands even in respect of undamaged or only slightly damaged units. Only a few torpedo boats and auxiliaries, which did not come under the armistice terms, were taken over for coastal defense. The defense of the French Mediterranean coast west of the Rhone was taken over by the German forces, with the navy taking its appropriate share, while the defense of the eastern coastal sector was left to the Italians.

At sea the Germans reacted to the Allied landings in North Africa by ordering U-boats to concentrate in that area. The order was not really welcomed by Dönitz, who saw it as a diversion of U-boats away from what he had all along regarded as the potentially war-winning attacks on merchant shipping in the Atlantic.

Heye: The major landing operations in North Africa were at any rate a very successful surprise. It was made possible by our own lack of aircraft reconnaissance over the sea. The situation could not be altered by the unrestricted U-boat warfare that was immediately ordered against Anglo-American troop transports going to Africa, especially since the U-boats had to fight without reconnaissance and against stronger defenses. As far as I know, these U-boat operations went contrary to the ideas of the C in C U-boats.

Dönitz: The surprise Anglo-American landings in North Africa called for a concentration of U-boats on both sides of Gibraltar. Every U-boat that could reach these waters within ten days was mustered. This resulted in a considerable reduction of tonnage sunk, which was not made up by sinkings off Gibraltar. Defense in these African waters was quite effective particularly in the air. U-boat losses were correspondingly high. Through this withdrawal of forces to the Mediterranean, the Atlantic command suffered during the following months from a shortage of boats; this led to a reduction in the number of convoys sighted and consequently in the number of sinkings. Other grounds existed, however, for the renewed decrease during the winter of 1942–43 in the number of convoys sighted.

As the German naval commander in chief in the Mediterranean, Weichold obviously resented the fact that sending more U-boats was now a case of "too few and too late," whereas a few months earlier they might have tipped the balance to give Germany total control of the Mediterranean.

The Italian fleet, apart from U-boats, E-boats, and a few light craft, was without fuel. This was a fateful reduction of fighting strength at a moment when the final decision in the Mediterranean strategy was at stake. The German U-boat service in the Mediterranean had at first only nine boats at their disposal, a very good percentage of the total force, having regard to the difficult conditions imposed by the repair problems, but quite insufficient for an even partly efficacious defense against a large-scale enemy operation. It was only now that the German high command decided on the reinforcement of the Mediterranean U-boats, so often and urgently requested by the naval commander in chief.

The U-boats destined for this purpose were routed to the Mediterranean in all haste, without special equipment or instructions for the job, partly taken off tasks in the Atlantic. They had to carry out their first patrols against large-scale enemy operations then in progress in the immediate neighborhood of the difficult Gibraltar passage, and because of this and the long approach trip, were soon at the end of their tether. It was clear how very much the effectiveness of the total U-boat arm suffered under these limitations. The U-boats had to be thrown into battle one after the other.

Neglecting to reinforce the U-boat arm in the Mediterranean brought a bitter revenge in the hour of decision. The German supreme command, however, believed it had done its duty completely by dispatching a few U-boats to the Mediterranean and expected to be able to harvest the fruits of this decision immediately. It was evident that these few U-boats on their own could never have a decisive effect.

British and U.S. convoys were attacked and damaged by U-boats and aircraft. The main point, however, was that the German-Italian defense did not succeed in seriously hindering the Anglo-American landing operation and its reinforcement according to plan. From the operational point of view, success lay unquestionably with the enemy. All French North Africa up to the Tunisian frontier was in enemy hands within a short time.

In addition to sending U-boats, the Axis command reacted to the Allied

landings by rushing in troops by air and sea to occupy Tunisia, the French possession lying between Algeria and Libya. Krancke describes how dramatically the Axis position had deteriorated within three months of the Battle of El Alamein and the North African landings.

In Africa the landing of Allied forces necessitated the speedy occupation of unoccupied Tunis and the concentration of all [the Axis] African troops in this, the most important African country that is nearest to Sicily. The western Mediterranean was suddenly conquered by the enemy; the entire south coast of the eastern Mediterranean too was in the enemy's grip. The English navy had regained its freedom of movement in the Mediterranean. The numerous aerodromes along the African coast, now at the disposal of the enemy, as well as their increasing air superiority in this area, and the inability of the Italian navy to guard the reinforcements for Tunis again necessitated the movement of German naval forces for this task (transport of naval ferry barges, E-boats, and minesweepers from the north of France on [canal] and land routes to the Mediterranean; the placing of all escort and antiaircraft vessels from the southern French area under the German naval command Italy as well as the best-trained personnel). At the same time a weakening of the defensive forces in the [English] Channel occurred.

The position in the Mediterranean, shown earlier on, did not permit [the Axis powers], despite German efforts, to get a sufficient supply through to Tunis. The enemy, however, was able to approach unhindered. Whenever our air forces attacked, they attacked the transport columns instead of the tankers in the harbors. Despite numerous orders by the Führer, it could not be made clear to them that this was uneconomic. Thus the German Afrika Korps, except for the few [remnants] that could be evacuated, was smashed in Tunis by enemy air force operations.

Weichold is outspoken in his criticism of the strategic judgment of those who, without providing adequate resources to the commanders on the spot, took the decision to try to hold Tunisia as a bridgehead on the south shore of the Mediterranean.

This operation was of the highest strategic importance, because it had to prevent the hostile forces already landed from reaching the straits of Sicily and thereby the central Mediterranean. It was obvious that the enemy's operation was directed at this area, it being the nerve center of the Mediterranean. On the successful buildup of the Tunisian bridgehead and the adequate supplying of it, which could on the whole only be accomplished by sea transport, depended the future course of the Mediterranean war. Our position was characterized by the complete inadequacy of the available means.

On 8 December 1942 the naval commander in chief made a renewed request for the German U-boat arm that, a year before, had played a decisive part in the wresting of sea superiority. The naval high command, however, declined this request. They had a unilateral point of view in favor of the Battle of the Atlantic—viewed by the C in C U-boats as a decisive factor in the war —and therefore rejected any withdrawal of forces in another direction.

If the necessary sea and air forces could not be procured, it was clear that we would have to face the loss of the Panzer army, the Africa position, and all the ensuing consequences for the conduct of the Mediterranean war, and the war as a whole, would have to search for the best possible way to retreat from the lost position to the most advantageous defensive position, with regard to maximum economy in expending valuable blood.

This remained true not only for Rommel's army and the Tripolitanian position but also for the position in Tunisia. The only explanation of the dispatch—undertaken in spite of this—of a further army to the new African theater of war can only be seen in the psychological orientation of the German command responsible. They would not confess to themselves that their own means were at an end and the enemy powerfully on the upgrade. If they still believed that it was possible to carry and supply an army more easily over the shorter connecting routes south (Italy–Tunisia) then the last month of the year 1942 again showed the error of this hope, one of the last of a series of illusions under which the Mediterranean command of the Axis lived and from which it died.

The continuation of the piecemeal buildup of a German army in Tunisia was, in comparison with the broad and unimpeded flow of enemy supplies, an undertaking that had been divorced from calculation, understanding, or war experience. There came a time when it had to be paid for with hundreds of thousands of men.

After Admiral Dönitz had been appointed to replace Admiral Raeder as commander in chief of the German navy on 30 January 1943, Weichold was summoned to Berlin to report on the situation. On 9 February he gave his review of the situation in the Mediterranean, but he does not seem to have been tactful or diplomatic in his assessments, either then or in his 1945 essay. The essay was written in the formal, third-person style, but is here edited to the first-person to show clearly that he is writing about himself.

[I] sketched the course of German participation from the complete lack of interest at the outbreak of war to the now imminent collapse of the Africa command. . . . [I] pointed out that this catastrophe was not ascribable to an unpredictable Higher Power, but represented a clearly visible, logical development. It had been accompanied by current appreciations of the situation as well as by timely warnings and advice without the necessary heed being given to these proposals. Thus it was the Germans' fault, who could be excused neither by lack of knowledge nor by shortage of the means to help. Finally [I] emphasized clearly that a very heavy burden would result from the loss of the Mediterranean for the German high command affecting the whole outcome of the war. In the eyes of the German people the main guilt would not be Italian, but German.

In his previous post as C in C U-boats Admiral Dönitz had hardly come into contact with the problems of the Mediterranean war. . . . With his strong personal ties to Hitler and his fundamentally high opinion of the German high command, he considered such sharing of responsibility and guilt on the German side of the Mediterranean command to be impossible. He therefore did not recognize [my] appreciation of the situation to be right but considered it a pessimistic interpretation lacking the necessary simple steadfastness in the face of temporary setbacks. As in addition he considered that the U-boats' Battle of the Atlantic was decisive, he saw no fundamental necessity to alter the German attitude to the Mediterranean problem and to bring corresponding influence to bear on the German high command. With this difference of opinions Admiral Dönitz did not consider [me] as suitable at that time for working in the spirit of the high command and ordered [my] dismissal. This dismissal and [my] subsequent treatment by the new supreme commander placed on [me], the former naval commander in chief Italy, the responsibility for the loss of the Mediterranean war. Thereby our own high command was relieved of this responsibility, as they had wished. It can be left to history to verify this judgment.

The Tunisian bridgehead did not survive for long. On 8 April 1943 British forces advancing from Libya effected a junction with U.S. forces advancing from Algeria, and Rommel was evacuated to take up a new post in Europe. In the final battles Allied forces took Tunis and the naval base of Bizerta on 7 May, and the remaining Axis troops surrendered on the thirteenth when further resistance could serve no useful purpose. The Allies took almost a quarter of a million prisoners of war. Further defeats for the Axis followed in quick succession. On 11 June the Italian forces on the island of Pantelleria surrendered; Sicily was invaded and overrun between 10 July and 17 August; and on 3 September British and Canadian troops crossed the straits of Messina to land on the Italian mainland. Meanwhile the Italian dictator Benito Mussolini, having lost the support of his own Fascist Grand Council, was dismissed by King Victor Emmanuel on 25 July, and the new government headed by Marshal Badoglio lost no time in negotiating an unconditional surrender to the Allies. The surrender came into force on 3 September, but the formal announcement was delayed for five days. Some Italian naval vessels were scuttled or sabotaged in harbor, but most of the Italian fleet put to sea and, with the exception of the new battleship *Roma*, which was sunk by German air attack, surrendered at Malta. The Germans reacted quickly and ruthlessly by rushing in troops to disarm their former allies in Italy itself and in the Balkans, occupy most of their country, and settle down to conduct a long fighting retreat up the length of the Italian peninsula. Looking back to those critical times, some of the German admirals are scornful of the Italians.

Krancke: [The loss of Tunisia] meant that the Italian islands as well as the Italian "motherland" were threatened by invasion. The fighting spirit of the Italians fell; Pantelleria surrendered practically without fighting. The Italian forces hardly resisted the Allied landing on Sicily. Again the German soldiers remained practically alone to fight, too few in number to hold the island and to prevent the landing on the Italian mainland.

The loss of their colonial empire, their inferiority complex as soldiers, and the danger of war in their own country, as well as the "underground" political intrigues of the Italian Royal family and their circle, led to the treasonable act on Italy's part with the aim of handing over the former [ally], who had sacrificed lives and material for the Italian cause, to the enemy. Quick counteractions averted disaster.

Schniewind and Schuster: The enemy landed in Sicily. The attempts at defense there were unsuccessful—not a little because of the failure of the Italian units.

Dönitz: The situation in the Mediterranean became worse. The loss of the Tunis bridgehead was due chiefly to the fact that the enemy, because of his superior naval forces and more especially because of his use of strong air formations, succeeded in crippling our sea supply routes. Also the morale and fighting spirit of the Italians diminished considerably. The capitulation without serious resistance of the Italian island fortress of Pantelleria was an undeniable symptom of this. The swift success of the Anglo-Saxon landing on strongly occupied Sicily was due entirely to the fact that right from the first the Italians put up no resistance at vital points on the island. The evacuation of Sicily and later of Sardinia and Corsica, which were carried out almost without loss, was a splendid feat in which the German navy played a decisive part.

The betrayal by the king of Italy and his forces in September 1943, which had been anticipated by the Germans for some time, was adequately made up for in a surprisingly short time, as the feared landing in northern Italy, which would have unhinged the whole German position in Italy, did not take place but was substituted by the less dangerous landing at Salerno. Unfortunately it was not possible to seize the Italian fleet, as it had, for the most part, previously withdrawn and was out of reach. The greater part of Italy remained in German hands; the important economic and industrial sources in the north Italian plain could be used for our own war effort till the end of the war. The defense of the coasts of southern France, Croatia-Yugoslavia, and Greece had now to be taken over by the German navy with, however, only a very small and improvised force. In the Aegean the Dodecanese were occupied with very little Italian resistance and taken as our own defenses.

Weichold, who in his time had suffered plenty of irritation and frustration in working with the Italians, shows considerable sympathy and understanding in assessing their final collapse.

[Claims were made, by Hitler and the high command, that the Tunisian campaign had served a useful purpose.] All these were pure propaganda contentions that were confirmed neither by the situation at that time nor by the subsequent course of the war. It is not conclusive that the time taken by the battle in Tunisia gave the Axis command the possibility of building up a new defensive front on Italian soil, in the same way, perhaps, that the German Atlantic wall in France represented a defensive front.

On the contrary the defense of Tunisia used up the last Italian strength in weapons, equipment, personnel, and fighting power, with the result that after the loss of this great, active Italian position, there were insufficient Italian forces for defense in the home country. By this time it had finally grown too late for any sort of help for Italy. The hourglass of the Mediterranean had run out. The remainder of the war meant only the gathering of the ripened harvest by the enemy.

After the loss of Tunis, Italian resistance collapsed like a house of cards. Only in one respect was this the result of military action: in other more important respects the occurrences of this period were most heavily influenced by psychological motives and, therefore, only intelligible from this angle. It is in any case incorrect to ascribe malicious motives to the Italian collapse. This reasoning, if not in itself actually malicious, leads to error. The present appraisal of the war shows clearly how and why Italy was finished both morally and materially, that the German partner could not or would not give decisive help, and that until the loss of Tunisia the Italian forces did their duty with devotion and suffered heavy losses. Only a one-sided attitude, therefore, can deny that for Italy the war was really lost and every further sacrifice useless.

The Italians have made heavy sacrifices in a hard and bloody war, and have thereby proved that it is not weakness or fear in themselves that have been the mainsprings of their manner of acting, but rather a clear insight into the situation as it exists and prevision of the situation to be expected, an easy adaptability, and on the part of the authorities, a strong feeling of responsibility for the future of the people. For the individual Italian, who possesses a special, often an exaggerated, feeling of honor, the defection from his ally was doubtless extremely painful.

9

Seeking Victory on the Russian Steppes,
1942–1943

HAVING BEEN COMPELLED, by the severity of the Russian winter
of 1941–42 and by Russian counterattacks, to retreat some distance from
the most advanced positions they had reached in 1941, Hitler and the
German high command were still confident they could secure a decisive
victory that would knock Russia out of the war when the weather conditions for campaigning improved in the summer of 1942. That was also
the year when Dönitz's U-boats were scoring their most impressive successes in the Battle of the Atlantic, and when Rommel and Weichold were
striving, in their different ways, to break Britain's power in the Mediterranean and the whole Middle East. In both those theaters of operations
the commanders on the spot cried out for the resources that might enable
them to transform encouraging success into complete triumph, but Hitler
and his senior generals chose to pour men, steel, ammunition, fuel, and
aircraft—and their own energy and total commitment—into a renewed
offensive across the Russian steppes. The Battle of the Atlantic and the
Battle for the Mediterranean came lower in their list of priorities. The
1942 summer offensive in Russia was launched at the end of June under
Hitler's personal direction. Instead of an attempt, as in 1941, to advance
on all sectors of the eastern front, the main effort was concentrated in
the Ukraine, driving the Russians out of the basin of the River Donets
and pressing them back in the great bend of the River Don until the
whole west bank from Voronezh to the Sea of Azov was in German hands.
By the end of July the German army Group A had taken Rostov-on-Don

and was thrusting deep into the northern Caucasus, with the twin objectives of clearing the eastern shore of the Black Sea (to deprive the Russian navy of its last bases) and to seize the major Russian oil fields around Baku on the Caspian Sea. By 25 August they had reached Mozdok (about halfway from Rostov to Baku), and on 10 September they captured the Russian naval base of Novorossisk. The amateur strategists could begin speculating about a drive ultimately directed at the Persian Gulf or India itself. Farther north the German army Group B had forced a crossing of the River Don and, in mid-September, mounted an assault on the industrial city of Stalingrad on the River Volga. This initiated a tremendous battle of attrition against stubborn Russian resistance. Dönitz shows that if the campaign had achieved all that was hoped, the German plans were undoubtedly very ambitious.

The beginning of the German major offensive in southern Russia toward the lower Volga, the Caspian Sea, and the Caucasus on 5 July 1942, and its first successful phases, raised the hope that the reverses suffered in Russia during the previous winter would be made up for and the Russian campaign brought to a successful conclusion. Strategic objectives of the first order could be attained here: the total control of the Black Sea, the Caucasus oil, and the threat to British positions in the Near East, which, together with the ensuing favorable development of the situation in the Mediterranean (the breakthrough of Rommel's army toward Egypt) gave promise of influencing this sphere too. The conquest of the Crimea and Sebastopol and the advance of the German armies as far as the western Caucasus, along with the capture of Novorossisk, gave the weak German naval forces in the Black Sea numerous opportunities for operations and forced the Russian fleet into the extreme southeast corner of the Black Sea. The German advance to the Caspian had already led to preparations for setting up auxiliary formations of small craft there for coastal defense and for the struggle against the weak Russian naval forces in this sea.

The reasons why those very ambitious objectives were never reached are analyzed by Schniewind and Schuster.

The . . . attempted offensive in order to finish the eastern campaign by completely destroying at least the Russian armies and to press forward into the important oil fields of the Caucasus, to the Caspian Sea, and to the Volga, did not turn out as expected. Sebastopol, the Russians' last stronghold in the Crimea, the foothills of the Caucasus, and the Maikop oil fields were indeed taken, and the attack reached Stalingrad, but the real aims—the destruction of the Red Army and the drive toward the Caspian Sea, to Baku and Batum and to the River Volga on a broad front—were not realized. The military forces engaged were not strong enough to reach these . . . widely separated and distant objectives, and in the following year they were not even strong enough to hold the positions they had won. The authors, who do not know the details and are not military experts, consider that the causes of these disappointments were as follows:

> definite underestimation of the Russian defense and arms potential
>
> underestimation of the British/U.S. aid to Russia, hence the objectives were too far ahead and/or too numerous (One objective—the Volga *or* the Caucasus—could perhaps have been reached. The attacks against *both* were ordered by the Führer, and as far as is known to the authors, against the advice of the general staff.)
>
> too small attacking forces (Stronger forces could not be used because of the claims of other theaters of operations.)
>
> too long and too weak lines of communications, which at the time were often broken by partisans
>
> insufficient support from our allies and their unsatisfactory attacking and defensive powers (north flank of the Stalingrad salient)

The navy had to cooperate in the framework of these operations in the taking of Sebastopol, in the bringing up of supplies, and above all in the crossing of the Kerch Straits, and in the guarding of supplies for the army in the Caucasus. It carried out most of its tasks, often in the face of tenacious enemy resistance, during which time the naval landing barges and other craft rendered valuable service. Besides the Rumanian forces, the navy was supported by E-boats and minesweepers, which had been brought up during the summer, and by light Italian forces. From the late autumn onward, it also had at its disposal small type U-boats that had been brought down the Danube. There were no large-scale actions on the open sea with the Russian forces based on Poti and Batum, and very few against the light forces near the coast, for example near Kerch. No decisive setbacks to the navy's task were caused by this means, although the few losses suffered by the Germans appeared more serious through the initial lack of tonnage.

With their front overextended, their flanks inadequately protected by Hungarian, Rumanian, and Italian units, and unable to break down the Russian defenders of the city, the German forces at Stalingrad were caught

by a great Russian encircling counterattack in late November 1942. The German 6th Army, trapped in a pocket between the Don and the Volga, was forbidden by Hitler to attempt a breakout to the west. Instead they were promised relief by armored columns and supply from the air. The promises were unfulfilled, and the men of the encircled army fought their hopeless battle against the Russians and the winter weather, while the main battlefront moved farther and farther to the west, and the German forces in the Caucasus, apart from retaining a bridgehead in the valley of the Kuban River and the Taman Peninsula, withdrew at top speed to avoid being trapped themselves. On the last day of January 1943 Field Marshal von Paulus surrendered the remnants of his encircled 6th Army to the Russians outside Stalingrad, but some determined units fought on for another day or two. The defeat there lost the Germans more than 200,000 men dead or captured. A number of the German admirals comment on the significance of the defeat, both for the whole campaign in Russia and for the subsidiary involvement of the German navy.

Schniewind and Schuster: The German leaders were disappointed in their expectations of the end of the war in the east in 1942. The Russian armament strength had been badly underestimated, just as it had been before the outbreak of war, and also the possibilities of English-American support for Russia had not been appreciated.

Krancke: The [1942] summer campaign on the eastern front, as well as on the African front, began successfully, but it was impossible to hold the main force of the Russian army. They avoided contact, leaving their equipment behind, and moved toward the east. On the Volga and in the Caucasus our offensive campaign came to a standstill. The supply routes became endless; the Caucasian oil (Maikop), which was essential for the maintenance of the supply system, had not reached us. The fronts were so long that Rumanian, Hungarian, and Italian armies had to take over large sections of the front. These collapsed during the first Russian counteroffensive in the autumn of 1942 [and] tore the front apart [over] a width of several hundred kilometers.

Schulz: The failure of the German operation against the Caucasus is attributable to two causes: first and principally, because, as was the case with all German military operations in Russia, it had to be undertaken with insufficient forces, and second, because the supply service was unable to satisfy requirements in the later stages owing to the failure to occupy . . . harbors farther east and enable supplies to be carried by sea on the last stretch.

Dönitz: The successful Russian counteroffensive on the Don, with the encirclement of Stalingrad in November 1942, the retreat of our own Caucasus armies to the Kuban bridgehead that this compelled, and finally the defeat at Stalingrad on 3 February 1943 brought about a fundamental reversal of the situation. In the Black Sea a stubborn, static war between naval forces developed now in the vicinity of the military fronts, in which the supply of the Kuban bridgehead across the Kerch Strait played a special role. In these engagements the Russians did not succeed in taking decisive advantage of the overwhelming superiority of their larger units. Only the Russian submarines east of the Bosporus were successful here and there in their attacks on the German supply traffic coming from the Black Sea to the Aegean.

Meyer is particularly outspoken in analyzing the wider implications of the defeat.

Nineteen forty-two was the first year of German reverses, which henceforth increased continually until the end of the war. It became clearer and clearer that the high command had made a big mistake in underestimating the power of Russia and [in that year] already one often heard it said in the navy: "The eastern campaign is devouring us."

Stalingrad and the Caucasian oil were never reached for the simple reason that Germany had insufficient strength. These campaigns were continuously directed by people who underestimated enemy resources and overestimated our own.

One continually heard it said that nearly all the plans for the eastern campaign were fundamentally and authoritatively influenced by Hitler, that again and again the views of the general staff were opposed, and its good name would soon have been squandered away. The general opinion was that, had there been the right kind of military command in Germany, she could have won the war in spite of the very unfavorable conditions in which she was placed.

Heye also writes quite frankly about the failure at Stalingrad and its effect on the morale of the German army.

The allied troops in Russia caused repeated disappointments. The best were a few Rumanian corps, especially their cavalry; Hungarian and Italian troops could not be used without German support, and then only at the less important points.

The withdrawal from the Caucasus also meant giving up the Caucasian oil, for which preparations to obtain it had already been made. It also meant the final abandonment of offensive operations toward Persia and Arabia. The loss of the oil alone could have been borne at first by a possible increase in other European supplies; the decisive factor in my opinion was that this oil aided further Russian operations.

As a result of the fall of Stalingrad, the conduct of the war in the east was changed. Many Germans realized this. Opinions of the inevitability of the defeat at Stalingrad were even then very varied. It was known how few forces were available in the area between the Caucasus and Stalingrad. Many army officers were of the opinion that withdrawal to prepared lines would have been better tactics. Adolf Hitler's contention that a voluntary surrender of territory costs more than a withdrawal, now, for the first time, made itself felt in the crudest form, and the troops were ordered at all costs to hold lines that had once been established. It cannot be doubted that strong criticisms by the high command began at this time. They concerned the capability of Adolf Hitler and the commanders appointed by him to lead experienced armies. This apprehension also found expression in the transfer of countless senior army officers.

Perhaps Stalingrad is also the point at which the German soldier's frame of mind underwent a psychological change. Right up to the end of the war he held himself man for man to be superior to the Russians. At Stalingrad, however, he realized the enormous size of Russia and its inexhaustible manpower, supported by the deliveries of the Anglo-Americans. He must have felt that it was like the labor of Sisyphus. The Russian industries, moreover, were as far out of the reach of the German air force as were the American and, by this time, the greater part of British industries too. On the other hand one could not fail to recognize that the position in the air over Germany was becoming worse.

At this time the question might have been discussed as to whether it would have been more profitable in the interests of a strong defensive policy to abandon untenable territory. Such proposals were made on countless occasions. If I remember rightly, the army proposed a voluntary withdrawal to the Dnieper line, and the navy a withdrawal from the Greek islands and Greece itself. Such proposals were not sanctioned either then or later, partly for reasons of economic and political disadvantages.

By the spring of 1943 the German front in Russia was back more or less on the line where the 1942 offensive had begun, but the Germans were no longer capable of mounting another summer offensive comparable with those of 1941 and 1942. True, in March they drove the Russians back out

of Kharkov, and in July they initiated the greatest tank battles in history by an assault on the Russians in the Kursk salient. But the Kursk offensive quickly stalled with heavy losses, and in August the Russians once more occupied Kharkov. In September–October the Germans evacuated by sea their troops from the last bridgehead in the Caucasus. The triumphant Russians pressed forward on most sectors of the eastern front. By the end of 1943, in the center the Russians had driven the Germans back beyond Smolensk, while in the south they had forced their way across the River Dnieper on a very wide front, retaken Kiev (capital of the Ukraine), and isolated the German forces in the Crimea by advancing to the mouth of the Dnieper. Schulz had good reason to remember those difficult days.

As sea defense commandant, Crimea, I had under my command for all purposes all naval units ashore in the Crimea, including four naval artillery units, one naval M.T. division, and the harbor defense flotillas, for tactical purposes the entire army coastal artillery, and for general service two light flotillas each of thirty naval landing craft stationed in Sebastopol and Feodosia, one minesweeping and one escort flotilla, the naval dockyard, arsenals, and so on.

At the head of all German naval units at sea and on land was the admiral commanding Black Sea with HQ first in Bucharest, later in Simferopol (Crimea), and from the beginning of 1944 in Constanza. He was at that time, subordinated to Group South in Sofia. The latter also controlled the admirals commanding Aegean and Adriatic.

[He goes on to write of "excellent cooperation" with the Royal Rumanian Navy, and also pays a tribute to the Italians.] I would . . . like to stress that the Italian E-boat flotillas commanded by the able and skillful Captain Mimbelli enjoyed an excellent reputation with the German navy in the Black Sea, and their return to Italy . . . , before the change of regime, was generally regretted.

Other points worth mentioning in my Crimean service are the evacuation in October 1943 of the Caucasus army from the Kuban bridgehead to the Crimea across the Kerch Straits, carried out almost without loss; [and] the uninterrupted supply by sea, despite all difficulties, of this army cut off from all land communications.

As 1943 drew to a close, the whole German campaign in Russia was beginning to look more and more like a fatal error, and it was becoming more and more difficult to see where or how a strong defensible line could be established as the eastern boundary of Hitler's concept of an impregnable Fortress Europe.

10

Ocean Warfare against Merchant Shipping, 1943–1944

DURING 1943 THE German high command could have found very little cause for satisfaction or optimism. The army in Russia was driven back inexorably as one Russian offensive followed another. In the Mediterranean, they had been driven out of Africa completely; their Italian ally had deserted them; and they became committed to a stubborn defensive battle in Italy. It could only be a matter of time before the Americans and British mounted an invasion of western Europe at some point of their own choosing. The Germany of 1939–42, capable of exploiting her central position to launch breathtaking blitzkrieg attacks in any direction selected by the Führer's strategic intuition, became in 1943 a Germany forced onto the defensive and beset by enemies on all sides. In the spring of 1943 Germany could, however, still view with some confidence the prospects for developing the campaign against enemy merchant shipping. Much would depend on whether the destruction of enemy ships and cargoes could continue at the rate achieved in 1942 and the first quarter of 1943, when a grand total of more than 9 million tons of British, Allied, and neutral shipping had been sunk in the course of fifteen months, almost 7.5 million tons by German and Italian submarines. If that rate could be maintained —or even bettered now that new German U-boats were being commissioned at the rate of twenty-four each month—it might be possible to make the shipping war too costly for the Allied powers. Then the Mediterranean theater might be starved of reinforcements, fuel, and munitions; the convoys taking equipment to Russia might be massacred; and Britain's food supply might yet be drastically curtailed. Perhaps even more important than those objectives, the buildup of Britain as a base for the air assault on Germany and an invasion of the continent might become impossible. If the threat from the west could be contained, Germany might yet be able to stave off the threat of Bolshevism from the east and win time until some new development in diplomacy or weapons technology might enable her to force a compromise peace on her enemies. Dönitz was acutely aware of how much depended on the commerce war, and after the highly successful convoy battles of March 1943 he must have been disappointed at how quickly the Allies were able to counter the U-boat threat.

After the winter of 1942–43 had produced changes in the situation in Russia and the Mediterranean unfavorable to us, there appeared in the spring of 1943 a similar change in the U-boat warfare that was, however, quite independent from these former [developments], and due to completely different causes.

Though in March [1943] the major attacks on convoys could still be carried out, by May it was quite clear that the enemy's air strength in the Atlantic, consisting of long-distance machines and of carrier-borne aircraft, had increased enormously. Of even greater consequence, however, was the fact that the U-boats could be located at a greater distance by the enemy's radar, apparently on shortwave, without previous warning on their own receivers, and were then heavily attacked by destroyers and aircraft carriers without even seeing the convoy, which was obviously diverted. If, however, in spite of this a convoy was contacted, it was discovered that the problem of finding it was no longer the only difficulty, but that the U-boats could not now attack the convoy itself whose firepower forced them to submerge.

From this new situation it was evident that the enemy's aircraft and destroyers must be fitted with new radar. The U-boat losses, which previously had been 13 percent of all the boats at sea, rose rapidly to 30–50 percent. In May 1943 alone, forty-three U-boats were lost. These losses were not only suffered in convoy attacks, but everywhere at sea. There was no part of the Atlantic where the boats were safe from being located day and night by aircraft. All the U-boat entrance and exit channels in the Bay of Biscay were particularly carefully watched. Losses here were especially high.

The full extent to which the advantage in the commerce war shifted away from Germany during 1943 can be judged by the quarterly figures for the

number of Allied and neutral merchant vessels that fell victim, most of
them to German U-boats and a few to Italian submarines.

Period	No. of Ships Destroyed	Gross Registered Tons	No. of German U-Boats Lost
1942			
3d quarter	309	1,516,090	31
4th quarter	279	1,723,468	34
1943			
1st quarter	221	1,303,008	41
2d quarter	112	600,409	72
3d quarter	82	429,072	72
4th quarter	37	177,815	52
1944			
1st quarter	41	235,580	61
2d quarter	25	143,978	72

In other words, by the end of 1943 every merchant ship sunk was cost-
ing the German navy in excess of one U-boat, and by mid-1944 about
2½ U-boats were being lost for every merchant ship sunk. The crucial
importance of radar, especially airborne radar, which Dönitz identifies
as the most significant development in antisubmarine warfare, is also
emphasized by Krancke, although he also speculates on whether the evasive routing of convoys might have been influenced by the British gaining
information about where the U-boats were concentrating. That supposition was, of course, absolutely correct, but at the time when he wrote his
essay the success of the British in breaking the German codes was a closely
guarded secret.

Already at the beginning of the year [1943] an obviously maneuvered evasion
on the part of the convoys was recognized by our U-boat "packs." Was it interception of our code methods, treason, or new direction-finding methods
on aircraft? From April onward the number of sinkings decreased rapidly; the
loss of U-boats rose. The enemy air force had come to master the electric
direction finding gear of the U-boats formerly in use. Thus the naval war
threatened to be a failure unless it was possible to find countermeasures.

During the decisive period (summer 1943–44) the U-boats were practically useless as support to the naval war. The invasion fleets were able to get
troops and material across the sea with hardly any loss at all. I regard this

factor as the turning point of the war. This was particularly tragic for Gross-admiral Dönitz who had directed the U-boats so successfully up to now. That all possible action was taken to meet this catastrophe goes without saying.

It was impossible to catch up to the technical advance of the enemy's centimeter direction-finding gear that was based on lengthy research in the U.S.A.—and that, as far as I know, despite the fact that we alone had electrical direction-finding gear at our disposal from 1939 to the spring of 1941. We succeeded too late with the changeover from the decimeter gear to the far superior centimeter gear. These types of enemy direction-finding gear not only overcame the U-boat warfare but also brought success to the battles of surface vessels, to coastal batteries, to direction finding in the Channel, and above all, to the enemy air force. The night, invisibility, and vast areas had lost their significance. Although we could make out that we were being located, we ourselves were blind.

The future impact of aircraft and radar on submarine warfare had not come as a complete surprise to the German navy. Dönitz reveals that they had begun thinking about the problem even before the war.

The U-boat command . . . had to concentrate before the war on what means the enemy might employ to hinder U-boat movement on the surface, and what could be done by us against his A/S measures. The enemy air force was at that time the greatest problem for the U-boat command, and it was therefore surprising that it was only later that the enemy recognized and used this weapon as being the most effective means against the U-boat.

The second anxiety at that time was already the possibility of the development of surface location. Two possibilities appeared to be available to counter this:

> Surface countermeasures—protection for U-boats on the surface against radar beams, that is, the absorption of such beams so that the transmitter, in the absence of echoes, was unable to obtain a bearing [and/or] the development of a search receiver for enemy radar beams of all wave lengths, with a view to warning the U-boat in good time. [In the] development of our own location apparatus, the U-boat command expected only small advantages . . . since the low altitude of the apparatus on the bridge would allow only a restricted range. The important point about this group of possibilities was that the U-boat was enabled as it were to assume a cloak of invisibility. During the following years the most varied experiments were carried out in this

direction. They led to a clear recognition that, at the most, a reduction, but not a total absorption, of radar beams could be achieved.

The fast submerged U-boat . . . to completely change our tactics, that is, to abandon surface tactics and to submerge the U-boats. This required, however, a high underwater speed and a great underwater radius of action. Without these properties the U-boat would have sunk in underwater warfare to a purely static instrument, and it would have meant a renunciation of the great results achieved by concentrating forces at the right place at the right time. However, in the years just before the war the development of a *fast* underwater U-boat took place. Very high underwater speeds were reached by means of the hydrogen peroxide drive. Already before the war the U-boat command demanded the most energetic development of such a propulsion and such boats, but unfortunately it was found that much time was required and many setbacks were experienced. In the most successful months of the U-boat warfare in 1942, the U-boat command continually called for a speedup of this development and for the building of faster U-boats; they had many meetings with the technicians to try to achieve this.

A general criticism of the inadequacy of technical innovation in the German navy and air force is expressed by Meyer.

Radar was the chief trouble: the enemy had made great advances that had not been caught up with when the war ended. Both the navy and the air force had, in my opinion, committed the great mistake of trying to get along with small technical staffs, instead of using the great national scientific potentials. When this was tried toward the end of the war, it was too late.

Schniewind and Schuster recognize the superiority of the enemy's radar and blame the limitations imposed on Germany by the Treaty of Versailles and the oppressive nature of the Nazi regime.

The absolutely catastrophic effects the new Anglo-Saxon radar devices had on the conduct of the German U-boat war were not known to the authors to start with. Even today, however, like many older naval officers, they are still of the opinion that the fatal setback in the whole conduct of the war—if real causes are being sought—did not spring from the personal failure of any particular people (physicists, constructors, building officials, technical officers, military leaders) but that this was one of the numerous fields of German work, organization, research, and leadership in which—even if no one or only a few people had noticed or considered it—the results of the loss of World War I, and particularly the terms of the Treaty of Versailles and the financial extortions of the postwar period, were still coming to light.

The disarming of the German people and state, the limitations imposed on almost all branches of scientific research and development, on military organization, on ordinary industry as well as on the armaments industry, and the closely related small capacity or very limited means in almost all fields of technical development, stood out in sharp contrast to the plentiful means, the superfluity of raw materials, the huge industrial capacity, the armaments industry that was not bound by any political fetters, which our Anglo-Saxon opponents could use unopposed between 1918 and 1939 for the evaluation of wartime experiences and, following out new ideas, for the buildup of their armed forces.

In contrast to the main theme, a minor role was played by [a] fact that, in view of the technical problem under discussion, cannot be overlooked entirely, though it is less important. The author considers that, in the field of high frequency technical research (even VHF) in Germany, unnecessary obstacles were placed in the way of further development at the instigation of various ministries (principally the post office): the work of a large number of amateurs was definitely limited in the postwar years by means of decrees concerning the construction and use of shortwave sets. The writer does not know if this was caused by financial reasons, or because of the striving for monopolies authorized by the state, or through overzealousness in the province of political and police supervision. The fact remains, however, that the possibilities for development were even more limited through the loss of the cooperation of a wide circle of amateurs who—as history teaches us—often produce people who, without or in opposition to the attempts of the expert thinkers and workers, often discovered new lines of development or reopened old ones.

When the admirals wrote the essays in 1945, they identified radar as the most important adverse development from their point of view and were clearly unaware that the British intelligence establishment at Bletchley Park had broken their Enigma codes. But a number of other developments contributed to the destruction of the U-boats. Among the most important were very long-range aircraft capable of reaching the farthest corners of the Atlantic, small escort carriers and merchant aircraft carriers to accompany convoys, more escort vessels and support groups equipped with high-frequency direction-finding equipment to get a bearing on the U-boats' numerous radio signals, forward-firing depth-bomb throwers,

and Leigh lights for aircraft to illuminate U-boats in the last stages of an attack. The mounting U-boat losses forced Dönitz to scale down the "tonnage war."

Under these circumstances, the previous surface war on convoys could not be continued. As in the meantime the favorable conditions of the American sphere of activity had also changed, the U-boat successes diminished considerably. The enemy air force with its modern methods of location had produced this change in the U-boat warfare. As countermeasures the ideas already started had to be followed up with all speed:

> First to produce as quickly as possible a new U-boat with as much maneuverability when submerged as U-boats had, up till now, possessed on the surface.
>
> Second, until production of these new boats, to make all possible alterations to the existing U-boats so that in spite of the enemy's radar and superior air power they might be as effective as possible.

On 30 January 1943 the commander in chief U-boats [i.e., Dönitz himself] was appointed supreme commander of the navy. He was, therefore, in a position to deal personally and energetically with these important problems of naval warfare. In the meantime the whole of German industry had been united under the armaments minister Speer. He was, therefore, also given the order to produce the new U-boat. The well-known electro-U-boat types XXI and XXIII were worked out with great speed and put into construction. By means of very large batteries and an external design specially constructed for underwater cruising, they attained a high speed when submerged and could remain submerged over a great length of time. The development of the Walter boats with hydrogen peroxide propulsion was also greatly hastened.

In the meantime the defensive armament of the available old type U-boats was improved by an increase in the number of A/A guns against aerial attacks. This succeeded in reducing the number of losses as compared with the month of May 1943. The fundamental realization that the final solution was to be found in the U-boat did not, however, change.

In September 1943 another surface attack on convoys in the old manner was tried out in the North Atlantic with these more heavily armed boats. The boats were ordered to remain on the surface when attacked by aircraft and cooperate in fighting off the attack. Then they were to attack and break up the destroyer screen with acoustic torpedoes and, in the third phase of the battle, attack the convoy, now deprived of its protection. It was a bold attempt that demanded a great deal of pluck and a high standard of capability from the U-boat. The vulnerable U-boats had to combat the enemy's overpowering defenses in the air and on the water before they could fulfill their main task of sinking the ships. This succeeded in so far that they managed to remain on the surface in spite of aerial attacks and in the second phase of the battle sank a number of destroyers. The third phase of the battle, the sinking of the [merchant] ships was, however, not so successful as a smoke screen was put out in which the ships were not visible. In this action the U-boat losses were small. The success of the experiment encouraged repetition.

The convoy battle that Dönitz describes, in which the *Zaunkönig* homing torpedo was used for the first time resulted in the sinking of six merchant ships and three escorts (plus one more escort so severely crippled as to be not worth repairing). The Germans lost three U-boats. Dönitz goes on:

It appeared however that in the first attempt the smoke had also impeded the enemy's air activities. In further attempts the air force was so powerful that had the U-boats remained on the surface they would in all probability have been completely destroyed. It was, therefore, finally clear that surface warfare for U-boats had come to an end. It was now a matter of filling in time till the new type should be ready for action. At the same time there was being developed for all types the *schnorkel,* which was to enable the boat to recharge [its batteries] underwater. This also was as yet not quite ready, as it necessitated alterations to the diesel and extensive trials so that its use at sea should not endanger the crew.

In these difficult months of 1943 and 1944, when the U-boat warfare was achieving only minor successes with high losses, the tough fighting spirit of the U-boat crews showed itself as never before. It was plain that the U-boats must continue to operate. Through the mere presence of the U-boats, the enemy was forced to sail in convoy, which tied up a large part of his tonnage most uneconomically. The presence of the U-boats also forced the enemy to maintain constant reconnaissance in the air and on the sea, which tied up a large amount of men, materials, and industrial and dockyard capacity. The U-boats survived the difficult period.

Dönitz's comment on the qualities of the U-boat crews is an understandable tribute by the admiral who directed them in the Atlantic battles. Schniewind and Schuster, however, express some reservations:

The making up of U-boat crews from a numerical point of view never presented any difficulties. Even the physical endurance and the morale of the submariners, who were always taken from the younger age groups, never suffered. The only thing that did become noticeable—the authors do not know how far—was the falling off in the results of training because this could not be extended to cover all the operational needs; often it even had to be curtailed and definitely suffered from the effects of the air war.

The thing most felt was the falling off in the efficiency of the commanders. Their age and seniority became lower; after a comparatively short operational period as officer of the watch they had to be promoted commander, often at the age of only twenty-two. Thus, with the best will in the world and a high sense of responsibility, they could not master the technical, nautical, and tactical details and qualities of leadership that a commander must have if he wants to operate successfully against the enemy in the difficult conditions of the last phases of the war.

Despite these many problems, Germany still clung to the hope that a new offensive against merchant shipping could be mounted with improved U-boats in 1944.

Heye: The most decisive event in 1943 was the practical cessation of the U-boat war. . . . After considerable losses, Admiral Dönitz, meanwhile appointed C in C of the navy, decided on a pause in the U-boat war until the necessary improvements and defensive weapons could be developed. Experiments, which were carried out with all our resources, extended not only to the countering of enemy radar but also to the creation of a new type of U-boat, a real submarine. New means of propulsion were also explored that would give increased speed and longer submerged endurance. Experiments of this nature had, it is true, already been made, but [they] were now pressed forward by a concentration of all necessary scientific and material resources. It should be noted that, in this situation, when every man was needed for the war on land, even Hitler adhered to the policy of maintaining and resuming the U-boat war. The U-boat was the only remaining offensive weapon left to Germany.

Krancke: The necessity to develop new U-boat types later, on account of electric direction finding, naturally made for delays. The number of U-boats, E-boats, minesweepers, and torpedo boats planned was not reached completely as the events of 1944 and the bombing interfered.

Schniewind and Schuster: The distinct raising of the speed when submerged and the underwater radius of action . . . were sought and found in different ways. For finished U-boats or for boats under construction the result was the air intake (schnorkel), which permitted the continued use of the diesel engines even when submerged. For newly designed types a great enlargement of the storage batteries or even the installation of a completely new type of motive power came under consideration.

The renewed preparation of the first series of U-boats converted to use the schnorkel was carried out more or less according to plan and without too much interference from the enemy air force, which did not do too much damage to the U-boat yards during the months in question.

Even the construction of the new types was at first not too badly interrupted in the yards that—quickly and in shelters—undertook the assembly of the various sections. Much more serious were the complication and smashing of means of transport from the interior, which sometimes lasted for days, and the heavy damage to several special factories. As far as the authors know, the construction of boats with larger batteries suffered many delays because the works belonging to this industrial concern were occasionally all idle at the same time after air raids, and a number of storage batteries that had already been dispatched and that took up several goods trains remained lying beside the line or were partly destroyed.

Meyer doubts whether there were any real grounds for optimism based on the new types of U-boat that were being built.

The U-boat high command had great hopes of these new types but, in view of the tremendous advances in the enemy methods of fighting U-boats, there is some doubt as to the justification of these hopes. Furthermore, even if the new types did all that was expected of them, what were the prospects of future construction in view of the enemy's ever-growing power in the air? And would the danger of the passage to and from the Baltic approaches and the North Sea be reduced to within supportable limits? In the event of revivified U-boat warfare becoming really dangerous to him, would not the enemy consider the occupation of southern Norway his best plan and so absolutely close all exits from the North Sea? In these circumstances, would it not have been better to have used the armament potential allocated to U-boats for other important purposes, for example, for surface ships, for tanks, or for the air force and antiaircraft?

I believe that Hitler had not a comprehensive staff competent to judge and decide among all these questions and there is, of course, the question of whether, even had there been such a staff, in view of Hitler's method of deciding everything for himself, they would have been listened to. In actual fact, all decisions affecting the U-boat warfare were made by C in C navy alone, with due departmental support. Hitler did not make decisions on naval matters because they were too remote from him. It may be said that the navy had a special position among the three services, since Hitler allowed it considerable independence. (It was the same with the German air force so long as Goering enjoyed Hitler's confidence.)

Schniewind and Schuster also place great stress on the increasingly dominant influence of the enemy's air power in western Europe.

The authors are of the opinion that the weakening of the German air force through its battles over England and through withdrawals to the east was the main reason why it lost its superiority in the west and why England gained that superiority. A really effective continuation of the U-boat war with successes similar to those gained in 1942 would have contributed to hinder the growth of British air strength and air superiority. The authors think that the whole course of the war would have been influenced by such a continuation. Even the reinforcement of the RAF by American help and the arrival of the American air force on British soil would not have been possible on the scale on which it took place in the years after 1943. Certainly it would have been liable to extremely heavy losses over England if the German air force had been able to operate against England in the same, or in even greater, strength than in 1940. Without enormous British-American air superiority the attacks on German industry and communications—and even the invasion —would have been impossible. Finally, the war against Russia stultified the maintenance and growth of the striking power of the German air force for the battle in the west and hindered the arming of stronger forces for the U-boat war so that the latter could be taken up with better means.

Operations with surface ships were also seriously hampered by enemy aerial reconnaissance and radar, as Dönitz recounts.

The result of the increased air and sea reconnaissance was a sudden deterioration in the situation for German surface craft in the Bay of Biscay, the North Atlantic, and all other seas from spring 1943 onward, due to the superior enemy radar. . . . Raiders, supply ships, and blockade runners were lost in such large numbers that mercantile warfare and surface shipping in foreign waters had to cease. The most vital traffic of personnel and goods to and from Japan was reduced to a minimum and carried out from that time onward by U-boats, including a number of Italian boats.

German naval forces stationed in northern Norway seemed to have the best chance of achieving some success, because the Allied Arctic convoys to Russia were compelled to make a long passage within easy range of German air and naval bases, and the German navy and air force felt that they had to make special efforts to interrupt the flow of supplies when the Russians were inflicting such heavy damage on the German army along the whole length of the eastern front. There were few opportunities in the summer, when the German navy could only conduct operations that amounted to little more than training exercises and sideshows.

Schniewind and Schuster: The U-boats were employed during the summer months in minelaying operations off Murmansk, in the Kara Sea, and in the shipping channels near Nova Zembla. A long and successful operation by a number of U-boats supported by aircraft in the Kara Sea in the summer of 1943 should also be mentioned here.

Dönitz: During the summer [1943] in northern waters the German naval forces had few opportunities for action as the Russian convoys only sailed during the six winter months. In the meantime there was evidence that the bays of Spitzbergen were being frequented by enemy ships. As it seemed desirable to give the German naval forces an opportunity to keep in training, in autumn 1943 the Spitzbergen operation was carried out by the battleships *Tirpitz* and *Scharnhorst,* with a number of destroyers: this achieved the desired purpose and passed off without any particular incident.

Schniewind and Schuster: An expedition by heavy ships against Spitzbergen in the autumn of 1943 served to destroy some enemy bases that were supposed to be there, but it only achieved a partial and temporary success.

Schniewind, then serving as commander in chief northern group with headquarters at Kiel, does not seem to have been very impressed by the bombardment of the small, mainly Norwegian establishments on Spitzbergen on 8 September 1943. It could equally well have been carried out by a couple of destroyers and amounted to little more than a workup cruise to prepare the German battleships for the more serious business of attacking the Allied convoys when they resumed in the winter of 1943–44. Schniewind and Schuster point to one of the serious disadvantages under which the German navy had to work.

In 1943–44 the lack of fuel made itself as painfully felt among the surface vessels as in the air force. The already weak air support was reduced again because of this shortage, and it became impossible to move ships about continually to different bases or fiords to protect them from the increasing enemy air and other attacks. Naturally naval training activities also suffered from this shortage. Operations (e.g., Spitzbergen) were always delayed until a sufficient stock of fuel had been built up so that stocks should not have too heavy demands made on them, the reason being that these were never allowed to sink below a certain level in case of a possible stoppage of sea traffic to Norway (e.g., enemy landings in central or southern Norway).

The Royal Navy was acutely conscious of the threat posed by the German heavy ships, especially the very powerful *Tirpitz*. The mere threat of a sortie by her had been enough to provoke the disastrous scattering of convoy PQ 17 in July 1942. Only two weeks after the Spitzbergen operation, British midget submarines, called X-craft, penetrated Alta Fiord and crippled the great battleship by placing explosive charges under her hull. She did not sink, but she would be in no fit state to attack convoys for some time. When the Arctic convoys were resumed in November 1943, they were able to complete voyages in both directions without losing any ships before the year's end. On 26 December 1943, the Germans did, however, succeed in bring the *Scharnhorst* into action against convoy JW 55B.

Dönitz: An operation by the battleship *Scharnhorst* with a destroyer group in December, which, after a successfully concealed start, seemed to have good prospects of success in view of enemy dispositions and the weather conditions that were encountered, proved a failure, apparently through a misjudgment of the local situation. *Scharnhorst* was lost. In these actions the superiority of enemy radar once more became very evident.

Schniewind and Schuster: This loss was incurred through the failure of our own reconnaissance and through the enemy's superiority in radar and in the use of radar-controlled gunnery. In view of the very precarious situation on the eastern front, a great risk had consciously been taken.

The admirals were quite right in giving credit to the radar-controlled gunnery of the British ships. Twice driven away from the convoy by the escorting cruisers, *Scharnhorst*'s attempt to withdraw had been harried by cruisers and destroyers until she was intercepted by the main British covering force led by the battleship *Duke of York*. Then under a hail of shells and after suffering several torpedo hits, the *Scharnhorst* finally sank. Dönitz completes the account of the contribution of the major German warships to the war on commerce.

The only battleship now left was the *Tirpitz,* as *Gneisenau* was so heavily damaged by bomb hits during her refit in Kiel that in the circumstances further attempts to repair her were not justified.

In northern Norway during 1944 the battleship *Tirpitz* was on many occasions the object of attack by enemy aircraft, armed with giant bombs (5.5 tons), and especially trained for this particular type of task. In September 1944 the enemy succeeded in scoring a heavy hit on the for'ard part of the battleship. It seemed hardly feasible to bring the ship back home for repairs, while to employ her as a mobile floating battery in the Norwegian fiords appeared of some use. The supreme commander of the navy therefore ordered her to move to another anchorage, which in contrast to the former berth in Altafjord, had so small a depth of water that if further bomb hits were sustained it would be less likely that the ship would capsize and become a total loss. Another reason for the shift was the withdrawing of the German front line in northern Norway back to Lyngenstellung, which had already begun as the result of the Finnish cease-fire. A suitable position was found in the neighborhood of Tromso. Shortly after the shift a new English air attack was made. Two direct hits and four near misses assisted by the soft nature of ground caused the ship to capsize. With that the last battleship of the German navy was gone.

The sending of cruisers to northern Norway was also stopped as there was now a great variety of operational tasks for these ships in the Baltic, which previously had been largely employed for the training of new entries. One destroyer flotilla remained in northern waters, whose task it was, in conjunction with the coastal forces, to cover the seaward flank of the retreating [German armies in northern Norway].

The role of the German heavy ships in attacking the convoys to north Russia had been singularly ineffective, if one judges by the number of ships and cargoes they succeeded in destroying. Perhaps in a broader strategic perspective, their very existence had posed such a serious threat that Britain (and to a lesser extent the United States) had been forced to counter it by deploying ships and aircraft that would otherwise have been available for service in the Mediterranean, the Indian Ocean, and the Pacific. Perhaps, also, without the threat of the heavy ships, the Allies would have felt able to dispatch an even greater volume of war supplies to the Soviet Union. By 1944, however, the task of attacking the convoys could only be carried out by U-boats and aircraft. There was no shortage of targets. In all more than 530 Allied merchant vessels were sailed in convoy on the Arctic route, either eastbound or westbound. Of those the German air force did not sink a single ship, while the U-boats sank a total of 7. That figure may be compared with 1942 when, from a total of 434 vessels at risk, the German air force sank 36, U-boats accounted for 24 and surface vessels just 3. The difference in 1944 was brought about by radar, better intelligence from decoded signals, improved antisubmarine weapons, and more numerous escort vessels, including the regular inclusion of escort aircraft carriers. They not only ensured the protection of the merchant ships but also sank a total of 19 U-boats that attempted to attack the convoys. Attacking properly escorted convoys had become little more than a suicidal enterprise for the orthodox U-boats. For Grand Admiral Dönitz and for the whole German U-boat service, the tantalizing question was whether the revolutionary new U-boats, capable of submerged attacks at speed, would be commissioned in time to tilt the balance back in their favor.

11

Invasion and the Long Retreat

ON LAND THE German reverses continued during the first few months of 1944. In Italy their stubborn defense of the Gustav Line and containment of the Anzio bridgehead were finally overcome, and the Allies advanced toward Rome in May. In Russia the German armies had been forced back from Leningrad to a front line running more or less along the eastern frontiers of the former Baltic States of Estonia and Latvia before bending eastward to enclose a substantial German salient, including the city of Vitebsk, in White Russia. South of that the Germans were driven out of the Ukraine, with the Russians beginning to push forward into eastern Poland and northern Rumania. The Russians also overran the whole of the Crimea except for the naval base of Sebastopol, where the Germans were withstanding a siege. Meanwhile, in western Europe and Norway, something like seventy-five German divisions were doing no fighting at all. Desperate to hold back the Russians from the borders of the Reich and to prevent them capturing the vital oil fields at Ploesti in Rumania, the German high command would have welcomed the opportunity to throw into the battle some of those "idle" divisions from France and elsewhere, but they were kept back to meet the threat of an Anglo-American assault in the west. In one sense that assault was already in progress, in the shape of the round-the-clock Allied bombing offensive, but everyone knew that a seaborne landing must soon follow, and the conquests that had opened up such glittering strategic possibilities for the Germans in 1940 now left them with a very long coastline to fortify and defend. Krancke, who was serving as naval commander in chief west, describes the problem from his point of view.

The Allied invasion preparations as a whole were well known. However, with such long stretches of coast the defender was at a disadvantage since he had to be everywhere, whereas the invader could concentrate on one area only. Intercepting reserves had to be placed centrally so as to move them quickly to any front that was being attacked.

The extension of the defense positions (west wall) had been ordered as early as 1942, but was not nearly ready. During the winter of 1943–44 much was built, but at the mouth of the Seine, which was particularly endangered from the naval point of view but was regarded as unimportant by the army, very little had been done. The installation of launching sites for rockets south of Cherbourg and in the Pas de Calais had exhausted the building capacity that was necessary just here. Only three new naval batteries (1 x 21 cm, 2 x 15 cm) were installed. Otherwise this sector of the front was the weakest on the Channel coast.

The army expected the landing east of the Seine, at the mouth of the Somme; this suspicion was responsible for the coastal defense; the navy, however, could only voice an opinion. The navy was in the main concentrated at the larger harbors and had the tactical direction of the entire coastal artillery for sea warfare, while inshore fighting the army worked on its own.

To the high command and to all positions in the west, it was perfectly clear that the failure or success of the invasion would decide the outcome of the war. All available reserves of the supreme command (newly formed troops or replacements, especially armored divisions) were transferred to France. It was hoped to repulse the landing, so as to be able to send the troops thus made available to the eastern front and readjust the situation there. The navy reinforced the coastal defenses by laying mine barriers as well as coastal mines.

Heye's essay shows that the German high command's anxieties about possible invasion points extended far beyond the Channel coast in France.

With the continual strengthening of the enemy war potential, the landing in Italy and the approach of the Russians to the German eastern frontier, one had to reckon on the certainty of an invasion of the French coast. As early as the winter of 1943 the probabilities of various landing points were discussed. Many authorities, including the army, thought a landing in Denmark possible, either simultaneously or as a subsidiary operation. An entry into the Skagerrak and Kattegat and the occupation of adjoining territory and perhaps an alliance with Sweden were also considered. In Norway the area around Narvik and Trondheim appeared to be in special danger. In the opinion of the navy, a landing on the west coast of Denmark was only possible in summer. A landing in the Kattegat, where there were several ports available, also appeared technically possible. A landing in Norway was considered unlikely to have any strategic value; a foothold on the coast and the cutting of our sea communications was, however, possible at any time. In the opinion of the navy, Anglo-American sea and air superiority would, nevertheless, have permitted any of these alternatives.

The navy considered, however, that the main danger of a landing lay in France. The high command had built at huge expense the Atlantic wall, which was to support decisively the German defense in the expected battle with superior enemy forces. It was to be assumed that enemy preparations would be thorough and complete. Exact information about these was, however, so far as I know, not available, and even information from various other sources gave no clear picture. The approximate date of the invasion was, nevertheless, certainly correctly appreciated.

The possibility of invasion also figured prominently in the decisions of Dönitz, as supreme commander of the German navy.

The decisive event of this period of the war was the invasion of France by our western enemies. In view of the general development of the war situation, it was expected to be in spring or summer 1944. Exact information regarding the intended date of the attack was not available. From April onward aerial reconnaissance over the south coast of England confirmed that increasing preparations for the assault were taking place in the areas of Portsmouth-Southampton-Isle of Wight and Plymouth-Dartmouth-Torquay. In the ports of southeast England, including the region of the Thames, nothing remarkable was observed.

The naval command considered the area east of the Cotentin Peninsula as far as Boulogne to be the most probable place for a landing. The coast of the Pas de Calais was regarded as the second possibility on account of its short distance from the English coast, but prospects of success for the enemy appeared possible in this area only if he succeeded in obtaining an efficient port in his first assault. Other possible invasion points were also considered; most of the reports received, which predicted possible invasion points on nearly all the coasts of Europe in turn, were attributed to systematic enemy attempts to mislead.

No detailed information was available regarding the nature of the invasion preparations. The experiences of Dieppe, Salerno, and Nettuno, however, permitted a number of inferences. The very efficient types of enemy landing craft were well known. Aerial reconnaissance had identified a large number of square pontoons in the southern English ports. They were thought to be sections of landing stages. We did not anticipate the production of prefabricated harbors.

Above all, the coastal defenses on the land were further developed and improved in order to meet the imminent invasion. New types of beach and foreshore obstacles were laid in large numbers. The view was held that it was of paramount importance to repel the invasion on the beaches themselves. Appropriate battle orders were issued.

Offensive measures by naval forces against the invasion preparations were precluded owing to lack of suitable means. The precautionary laying of mines, apart from those already laid, was rejected so as not to paralyze prematurely our own freedom of movement in the narrow coastal waters that were still unmined, and to prevent the limited number of mines fitted with new fusing devices being laid in wrong positions, while the laying of mines equipped with old type fuses, which could be easily swept by the enemy, seemed to serve no further useful purpose. The new type fuses were used in the oyster and acoustic mines, which are considered unsweepable. They had hitherto been brought into operation in isolated cases only with the greatest precaution, so as to prevent their falling into the hands of the enemy and being copied by him. The use of these mines by the enemy in the shallow waters of the Baltic would have had a catastrophic effect. Torpedo boats and E-boats in the Channel were strengthened as far as possible, midget craft held in readiness, and U-boat operations in the Channel prepared.

Given his own personal preoccupation with ocean warfare against merchant shipping, Dönitz had shown considerable foresight, soon after he took over the supreme command from Grand Admiral Raeder, in ordering equipment for the kind of inshore warfare that would be entailed by an invasion.

In the European theaters of war the German army was forced into defensive positions everywhere. The whole situation had developed into a war to defend the fortress of Europe. The defensive duties of the navy now rose in importance to a similar degree, even though the offensive U-boat warfare was still its foremost task. To facilitate this, in spring 1943 the supreme commander of the navy had a new plan of shipbuilding drawn up and put into operation. This envisaged, by strict concentration on the more important types, a considerable increase in the building of E-boats, minelayers, and minesweepers, as it was expected that the need for these coastal forces would increase enormously with the enemy's approach to the German frontiers.

For the same reasons, the supreme commander of the navy ordered the construction of midget craft, the building of which in large numbers started as soon as the most useful types had been designed. The types concerned were one-man torpedoes, long-range torpedoes, the smallest type of E-boat and particularly midget submarines with two torpedoes and a two-man crew. In this class were the so-called sea fighters [*Meerskämpfer*] equipped with special swimming suits, whose duty was to take floating explosives to suitable targets; they were to be used chiefly in narrow coastal water and rivers. The personnel for these duties was drawn entirely from volunteers who were forthcoming in large numbers from all branches of the navy as well as from other sections of the armed forces. This keenness to volunteer for jobs known to be dangerous and lonely was a magnificent proof of the spirit, idealism, and love for action of the fighting forces.

The carrying out of the shipbuilding plan and midget craft program, as in the case of the U-boat building, was entrusted to the minister for armament and war production [Speer] who, because of his responsibility for all raw materials and the armament program of other sections of the armed forces, was in a better position than the navy itself to obtain what was necessary for the extensive new plans and, by careful adjustment, to eliminate all interruption. This measure entirely justified itself.

Heye, who was put in command of the midget submarines and other types of small battle units in April 1944, writes with enthusiasm of their potential if there had been enough time to develop them systematically.

Because it was impossible to build larger vessels and because it was appreciated that in an invasion the enemy would have to approach the coastline we occupied, the small battle units were planned. The Italian and British successes (e.g., against the *Tirpitz*) were an example of the effect that could be expected. The planning extended to various models of midget U-boats and E-boats. The intention was to manufacture as many craft of this kind as possible in the shortest possible time and to be able to send their crews out on operations after a short training. A large number of these vessels showed the marks of improvisation. Many of our intentions—for instance, the continual changing over to weapons of various sorts—had to be renounced because our industry was no longer in a position to produce them. Despite lack of experience and far from complete trials, the [situation] compelled the use of small battle units of various types. Trials were, virtually speaking, made against the enemy. Personnel requirements could mostly be met by volunteers who, like fighter pilots, saw the possibility of distinguishing themselves personally. I believe that with the further development of small battle units, especially effective weapons for inshore warfare—up to about four hundred miles from land—could be created. Losses will be smaller than with larger units. This development that we planned was only just beginning at the end of the war. Very valuable small battle units of the most varied types could perhaps have been expected by autumn 1945, if further development had been undisturbed.

As the Allied invasion became imminent, the German armed forces had not really managed to achieve a professional consensus on where the blow was most likely to fall or what strategic dispositions would be most effective against it.

Schniewind and Schuster: The authorities were strongly of the opinion that the enemy was preparing large-scale landings. The most likely places for these were considered to be, first of all, the area between the mouths of the Seine and the Somme, then the Belgian-Dutch coast and Jutland (perhaps with a diversionary attack in south Norway). In the opinion of the naval war staff, the areas of central and western Channel and central and north Norway were only of secondary importance.

In relation to the limited range of the enemy's fighter aircraft, the most likely place for a landing appeared to be between the Seine and the Somme. But the navy and the local army authorities differed sharply as to how an efficient defense against any landings should be built up. The navy, which was directly responsible for the defense of the coastal waters and which had numerous army coastal batteries at their disposal for this purpose, took the view that the main emphasis of the defense should be placed on the defenses right on the coast, in order to be able to attack the enemy at his weakest point (disembarking and landing) provided, of course, that sufficient forces were at their disposal for this purpose in the areas most threatened. The army preferred to concentrate strong forces farther inland so that, in the event of a landing, they could attack the threatened area concentrically. These differences and quarrels, in which the navy's opinion was finally upheld by a decision of the Führer, came up at all points along the threatened coasts, and in some places continued until 1944. Whether the execution of the Führer's decision was everywhere carried out practically and to the best possible advantage is not known to the authors, but they doubt it very much.

This decision became even more important when, with the ever-growing aerial activity of the enemy over the occupied countries, and with the destruction of or damage to roads and railways, the movement of troops became more and more difficult. And indeed, in the opinion of the authors, this question played an important part in the invasion of western France in 1944.

Schulz: I, personally, am of the opinion that such an important area as the Bay of the Seine, and above all the east coast of Normandy—which in view of the normally prevailing west winds of the Channel were the only possible coasts available—should have been much more powerfully defended by numerous quick-firing naval coastal batteries. The completion of coastal batteries under construction is, however, said to have been hampered to some extent, directly and indirectly, by enemy aerial activity. The construction of prefabricated harbors was, at all events, a surprise to us, as I later learned.

> When writing that criticism in 1945, Schulz was well aware of where the Allied landings actually took place. Whether he was blessed with such certainty before 6 June 1944 seems more doubtful. Schniewind and Schuster admit their own surprise, while Krancke obviously feels that, with a little more luck, his defenses would have been better prepared.

Schniewind and Schuster: The enemy began the invasion in the west on the coast of Normandy. This had, of course, been foreseen, but not at that particular point. Weather conditions and the state of the tides during the landings were, in the Germans' opinion, not favorable for the enemy. The time and place of the landings were, therefore, all the more surprising.

Krancke: The mouth of the Seine was due to be mined from the middle of June. The mines were [ready] in Le Havre at the beginning of June. I intended to strengthen the defense of the mouth of the Seine by numerous sea-mine barriers. Preparations were made and orders given. Unfortunately the transportation of the mines was delayed for more than four weeks on account of railway dislocations. At the end of May the mines eventually arrived but the minelayers employed ran into mines en route for Le Havre during E-boat and air engagements. Damage and the loss of two boats occurred, so that minelaying could only begin on 5 June. Owing to weather conditions it could not take place. Therefore the approaches to the coast were unmined on the day of the landing.

The 38-cm battery at Le Havre was not ready for operations, owing to successful air attacks. Battery Marcouf was the only heavy battery at the mouth of the Seine.

Despite heroic efforts on the part of our naval forces, despite bitter defense actions on land, the enemy forced a landing with colossal concentration of troops, assisted by airborne troops, bomber and fighter attacks, and the operation of ships' batteries of all calibers. The bringing up of our own replacements was delayed on account of air action. Within a short time the enemy gained numerical superiority, [in addition to] support from the air force and ships' batteries, especially in motorized forces. All our own action came to a standstill. The outcome of the battle was against us.

Heye: After the success of the landing, which came partly as a tactical surprise, further landings were, as far as I know, expected at other places. For this reason no troops from the adjacent parts of the coast where no landings had been made were transferred to the invasion area. Our defensive front was, therefore, visibly weaker and broken up.

In sharp contrast to the ramshackle improvisations to which, four years earlier, the Germans had resorted when planning their own cross-Channel invasion, in 1945 the British and Americans had available a great variety of specialist landing craft, enormous superiority in ships and aircraft, and all the techniques developed from hard-won experience of earlier landings in North Africa, Sicily, Salerno, and Anzio. Schulz, who became head of the Intelligence Division of the German Admiralty soon after the landings in France, reveals one important aspect of the whole invasion machinery.

With the almost unlimited Anglo-American air supremacy, not only in the invasion area but over the whole of northern France, the further development of the military situation in France was regarded with heavy foreboding. Any movement of troops and their supplies was almost impossible during the hours of daylight. Railway traffic, too, was almost completely crippled, so that the naval bases along the entire west coast suffered from the most serious shortage of coal because the coal trains did not get through. The saturation bombing that ploughed up our defense positions and that, in conjunction with naval gunfire, destroyed the positions of our troops prepared for counterattacks, had a particularly bad effect.

It is an interesting point that we were taken by surprise by the effect of the naval guns of the invasion fleet, both by their multiplicity and by their accuracy even at extreme ranges. The firing technique of British naval guns, developed in order to support the army during the invasion, certainly fully justified itself and was responsible for a great part of the success.

As during the invasion fighting we had succeeded in capturing a series of documents concerning this firing procedure, these were able to be translated, collated, and sent to the German surface forces as soon as possible. They rendered a valuable service later, when our surface forces were frequently compelled to take part in the land fighting both during the evacuation operations in the Baltic and in support of the army.

Within a few days of the initial landings, the Allies had secured a viable bridgehead and succeeded in building one of the prefabricated mulberry harbors through which more men and supplies could be put ashore. The German navy did not have at its disposal the kind of reserve power the Royal Navy would have thrown into the struggle if the German invasion of Britain had gone ahead in 1940. Nevertheless, Dönitz recalls that it was called upon to make some attempt to interfere with the enemy's traffic to Normandy.

When the enemy succeeded on 6 June, in spite of failures at various points, in establishing a few bridgeheads and extending and uniting these immediately, the situation was regarded as extraordinarily grave by the naval high command. All forces were summoned to put difficulties in the enemy's way by disrupting his supplies. . . . The first U-boats fitted with schnorkel were ready at the beginning of the invasion and were used between the Isle of Wight and the mouth of the Seine. They operated here in very difficult conditions with strong currents in shallow waters and powerful fighter and radar defenses on the sea and in the air. In spite of this, the boats fitted with schnorkel were able to operate, and the losses were bearable. The U-boats returned from this area after approximately three weeks' sea time without surfacing; three to five ships had been sunk, a result that would have been good even at the peak of U-boat warfare in 1940. The operations of the U-boats . . . , of the torpedo boats and E-boats with torpedoes and mines, of long range torpedoes—and especially, one-man torpedoes—in conjunction with powerful Luftwaffe operations achieved to our knowledge considerable success but were nevertheless unable to bring about a change in the situation.

In an air attack on Le Havre in the middle of June, in which the A/A defenses did not come into action owing to a mistake on the part of the local Luftwaffe command, three torpedo boats, ten E-boats, and a considerable number of other vessels were sunk and the base installations destroyed, so that operations were no longer possible from Le Havre.

The great mass of Allied shipping crossing and recrossing the Channel—and sometimes lying at anchor in the Bay of the Seine—was bound to suffer a significant number of casualties, many from mines, but the performance of the schnorkel-equipped U-boats must have been something of a disappointment to Dönitz, despite what he says in his essay. The schnorkel equipment had only been installed for two or three months; it was temperamental in use; and the U-boat commanders had not had much practice in using it. In the two months immediately following the D-Day landings, U-boat successes in the English Channel amounted to five naval escort vessels and two naval landing ships, but only four Allied merchant vessels—and three of those were smaller than 2,500 gross tons. That was a far cry from the heady days of 1942 when Dönitz had directed the "tonnage war." The one-man torpedoes and other small battle units achieved some successes, the most noteworthy being damaging the Polish cruiser *Dragon* so badly on 8 July that she became a constructive total loss. On the night of 2–3 August small battle units were sent out in a mass attack on shipping in Seine Bay. They sank a small British destroyer, a minesweeping trawler, and a landing craft, but forty-one *Neger* one-man torpedoes were lost out of fifty-eight, and twenty-two *Linsen* explosive motor boats out of thirty-two. The German naval effort in the Channel was brave and determined, but it amounted to little more than a gesture of support for the hard-pressed soldiers in France. Eventually the British and American buildup reached the point where they were able to break out of the restricted bridgehead. By the end of June they had overrun the whole of the Cotentin Peninsula and captured the important port of Cherbourg. By the end of August they had broken through at Avranches, occupied Brittany, and raced to Orleans on the River Loire and Paris on the River Seine. Landings had also been made in the south of France on 14 August. In danger of being enveloped by fast-moving armored columns, the German armies conducted a precipitate retreat from France. By the middle of September the Germans had given up Ostend, Antwerp, Brussels, and Liège in Belgium, and the American front line was on the whole length of the German frontiers with Belgium and Luxemburg. As commander in chief of the German navy at that time, Dönitz could see very clearly the consequences of this retreat for the navy.

When the enemy, in the land fighting, had pressed on to the north of the Seine, long-range torpedoes could no longer be used, while the one-man torpedoes could reach the Seine Bay only with difficulty. Thus the possibilities of attack on the enemy's supply traffic dwindled gradually.

The premature surrender of Cherbourg by the local army command was considered a grave error by the naval command as well as by the supreme command. After the city and its fortifications had fallen, the heroic stand of the naval officer in charge on the outer mole could only delay for a short time the final loss of the port. Consequently the first efficient port fell prematurely into the enemy's hands. The damage to the harbor installations could still hold up the full working of the port for a limited time but could not prevent it in the long run.

When in August 1944 the American troops succeeded in breaking through at Avranches, France was lost to Germany. The garrisons of the harbor fortresses on the western and southern coasts of France were strengthened; their defense was ordered to deny the enemy the use of these harbors as long as possible. This was successful in the case of the western ports and the Channel Islands until the end of the war, with the exception of the fortifications at the mouth of the Gironde, which fell shortly before. On the other hand, the ports in southern France, where meanwhile a second successful landing in the region of the Maritime Alps was made, were lost at an early date. The U-boats were withdrawn from the French ports, the remaining naval vessels being left there to help in their defense. The personnel not needed for defense were brought back overland as part of the withdrawal of the army and the majority reached German soil after taking part in much hard land fighting.

After it proved impossible to form out of the retreat a defensive line on the Seine, the rapid advance of the enemy continued as far as the edge of the Vosges and the German frontier. The loss of Antwerp, with its undamaged port installations, through the surprise thrust of the enemy to the north was regarded as a strategic setback of grave consequences. Thus, after the clearing of the Scheldt minefields, which naturally could delay operations only for a short time, the enemy had at his disposal near the front line an efficient port, which was to be most useful to him for further operations.

The loss of France was a setback of the utmost gravity for the conduct of the war at sea. All the strategic advantages arising from the possession of the Biscay ports were lost with one blow. The U-boats had to fall back on the Norwegian and home bases. The long passage swallowed up a disproportionately great part of the boats' endurance and, as previously mentioned, had to be made submerged.

Other German admirals comment on aspects of the retreat that they consider significant.

Schniewind and Schuster: The enemy air force played a decisive role in these defensive battles. Even before the invasion it had succeeded in almost completely disrupting transport facilities in northwest France and made the rapid movement of troops into threatened areas almost impossible.

Krancke: After the Cotentin Peninsula had been cut off, and after the breakthrough at Avranches, the situation was the reverse of the western campaign of 1940. Evacuation of troops on the Biscay coast was only partly possible. The naval bases, with numerous submarines for repair in their pens, had to be held. With the exception of Brest, which fell after weeks of fighting and tremendous enemy losses, the other "western strongholds" were held. Not one U-boat fell into the hands of the enemy; all of them were able to put to sea again after repairs had been completed.

In the Channel, the navy, using all available weapons against supply lines, did achieve some success, but could not, however, alter the situation as a whole.

The Allied landing in the south of France was bound to succeed, after several divisions had been transferred to Normandy. Thus the south of France had to be evacuated too. I attribute the catastrophe of the German army in the west to the destruction of the railways, lack of trucks, and lack of fuel. Our own air force hardly put in an appearance. The army was without supplies and was immobile; direction by radio was only possible to a limited degree; and road traffic suffered constant attacks from fighter bombers. Thus the renewed pincer operations could be successful up to the capture of Antwerp.

The French opposition movement had, in my opinion, no appreciable share in the Allied victory. Perhaps, however, France gave the enemy valuable assistance through the service of agents and spies.

The routed German army could not be intercepted again until it had reached the west wall. The loss in the west had brought about . . . the heaviest of losses in material and personnel. Only 120,000 men remained in the western fortifications, and the German frontier was directly threatened. The whole of France and Belgium was available as a base for the superior enemy air force. The belief of the soldier in a victorious ending to the war was shaken, since his own air force was so completely lacking. The high command was still hoping for newly formed, well-equipped divisions, for the new weapons that were being prepared, and for the last man to be brought up into battle, in order to retrieve the position.

Heye: Owing to lack of reserves we . . . had to retreat as far as the Rhine. During this retreat signs of disintegration and lack of leadership among the troops became more apparent. Not only the front line troops but also the lines of communication troops left the area formerly occupied. At the frontier, the retreating troops had to be reorganized by rigorous measures. All available naval resources, including the small battle units, were concentrated on the operational area of the Channel in order to relieve the severe fighting on land.

While the British and Americans were inflicting these serious defeats on the German armies in western Europe during the summer of 1944, Allied forces in Italy had driven forward as far as Florence and Rimini, and the Russians had also made sweeping gains. Although the Germans were still managing to hang on to the Baltic coastal plain all the way from Estonia to East Prussia, in the center the Russians had advanced by September 1944 into Poland as far as the River Vistula opposite Warsaw and up to the Carpathian Mountains on the prewar Czechoslovak frontier. Russian armies poured into the Balkans and quickly overran Rumania and Bulgaria. Both countries deserted Germany and made a separate peace, as did Finland in the far north, while Hungary was only prevented from taking the same course by the large number of German troops in their territory. Fearing that they would be cut off, the Germans also began to withdraw from Greece, the Greek islands, and southern Yugoslavia. On 4 October British troops began to land in Greece. Schulz, who served as sea defense commandant in the Crimea until May 1944, writes of the final loss of the whole coast in the Black Sea.

At the evacuation of the Crimea in April–May 1944, [we undertook] the transporting of the German-Rumanian troops from Sebastopol to Constanza. The execution as planned of this difficult evacuation operation was unfortunately interrupted by an order from highest quarters that arrived on 25 April when the evacuation was in full swing, according to which the defense of Sebastopol was to continue. In this way the enemy gained time to form up in such strength that he was able, with his greatly superior numbers, to break through our main line between Lapun Heights and Balaclava, thereby forcing us to a precipitate evacuation of the remainder of the fortress in four days, which in view of the length of the sea passage to Constanza (about 140 miles), the limited amount of shipping that had to be called up for this purpose, the effects of enemy gunfire on the embarkation points, and the activity of Russian fighter-bomber and bomber formations entirely unhindered by any German aircraft, could be carried out only with considerable losses. Of the 41,000 men embarked during these last days, a good quarter met their end at sea, practically all the larger merchant ships employed were either sunk or torpedoed, and 13,000 to 15,000 men must have been left behind in the fortress. Our successes in transport were achieved only by the utmost exertion and most courageous activity on the part of all the naval forces involved. In particular, the light landing craft flotillas distinguished themselves beyond all praise.

Mention should be made that in this difficult evacuation, Royal Rumanian naval forces were, like their German comrades, fully engaged and proved their worth—a fact recognized by Germany in the award of the Knight's Cross to the Rumanian C in C, Rear Admiral Marcelarin.

The reaction on German powers of resistance of the loss of Ukraine and Rumanian oil can be better described by experts on the subject than by me.

I personally regretted the breach with Rumania and the events that followed as, by reason of my close cooperation with colleagues of the Rumanian navy and army, I had learned to appreciate the Rumanian armed forces and had become a warm friend of Rumania.

The strange lack of activity by the Russian Black Sea fleet during the final stages of the war in that sea came as a, no doubt pleasant, surprise to Dönitz.

When in February–March 1944 land communications with the Crimea were cut by the Russian advance in the Ukraine, the navy had the task of supplying the Crimea from the sea. This was carried out successfully to the end. Even here the activity of the Russian Black Sea fleet was, in comparison with its size, remarkably small. In the evacuation of the Crimea in June, which was necessary as a result of the Russian breakthrough in our land front in the Perekop isthmus and the unsuccessful defense of Sebastopol against the advancing Russian troops, the Russian naval forces again only appeared in small numbers. Serious losses were however, caused by the Russian air force and artillery fire on the advancing land front.

The German admirals could see that the loss of so much territory in

both the east and the west was bound to have a serious impact on the German war economy.

Schniewind and Schuster: Naturally giving up all these countries with their extremely valuable economic resources as well as their factories and stocks of raw materials, which up to that time had been working at full capacity to strengthen German armaments and ensure a supply of food, had a tremendous effect. How great the effect was in single instances, and how far—expressed in production figures—the manufacture of arms, ammunition, food, and other goods was jeopardized, is not known to the authors. In retrospect, however, it can be seen from appreciations by high-ranking officers at the front that they exercised a decisive influence. Reinforcements to the front in the form of men, arms, and ammunition diminished continually and the influence of single causes grew and multiplied [because of] the loss of factories in the evacuated territories, the loss of sources of raw materials, destruction of supply lines, and damage to centers of production at home.

The consequences can be clearly seen of the inadequacy of the defense, for example, of the air force, which was revealed not only in insufficient production, but in the strength and numbers of operational units, and in a fuel shortage. It may be concluded, therefore, that without his enormous air superiority, neither the continually growing damage to German industry, nor the invasion, nor land operations would have been possible in the form they took.

Dönitz: The loss of the Rumanian oil country reduced the already small fuel supply of the German forces and led in the navy also to a strict reduction in consumption. The fuel necessary for the U-boat war remained, however, unreduced.

Heye: The loss of the Ukraine was bound to have an economic effect, even if not immediately. The evacuation took place so quickly that very large stocks of grain could not be brought back. Heavy equipment was also lost, as everywhere during the retreat in Russia, owing to a lack of heavy transport, bad roads, and strong partisan activity. The lack of prepared rallying points and reserves made itself felt. The collapse of Rumania put an end to German naval activity in the Black Sea. An attempt was made to hold the Crimea as a base. The breakthrough at Perekop ruined this plan too. The loss of the Rumanian oil alone would certainly have had a decisive influence within a measurable time. Until now the Rumanian oil was primarily used by our allies, especially Italy, and for the campaigns in Europe. The Rumanians had, moreover, caused considerable difficulties about delivery, which were connected with our financial settlements with Rumania. Germany had considerable debts, as she did almost everywhere in the countries allied to the Axis, since everything delivered there had to be paid for. The collapse of Rumania brought about the loss of our former base in Bulgaria as well.

For Germans the autumn of 1944 represented a depressing contrast with their prospects two years earlier. In 1942 they may well have thought that their seemingly unstoppable armies would win a decisive victory over Russia at Stalingrad and in the oil-rich Caucasus; in Egypt they looked to be on the brink of breaking Britain's hold on Suez and the whole Middle East; and on the ocean highways of the world the Axis powers were sinking Allied and neutral merchant shipping at the average rate of three-quarters of a million tons each month. Two years later they were struggling to keep enemy armies from the very frontiers of the fatherland, while at sea, sinkings were running at an average of about 70,000 tons a month. That was no way to win a "tonnage war," when American ship-yards alone were averaging a million tons of new building every month throughout 1943 and 1944. It would hardly have been surprising if, at that time, Germany had produced a group of resolute military and po-litical figures determined to depose Hitler and sue for peace, in the same way as the Italians had rid themselves of Mussolini in 1943. Such a move-ment had been simmering in Germany for some time, especially among senior army officers who blamed Hitler for bungling the campaign in Russia. Following the Allied invasion of Normandy they thought their moment had come. On 20 July 1944 they had made an unsuccessful at-tempt to wipe out Hitler and his leading supporters with a bomb ex-ploded under the table during a regular staff meeting. The failure of that plot—and the subsequent hunting down and execution of various field marshals, generals, colonels, politicians, aristocrats, and theologians connected with it—undoubtedly deterred others from voicing the opin-ion that the time had come for a change of government and a peace ini-tiative. Many Germans felt they had no choice but to fight on.

12

Fortress Germany and
Unconditional Surrender

LOOKING BACK TO the autumn and winter of 1944, the German admirals attempt to explain why Germany chose to fight on when any rational assessment of Germany's parlous military position would have been forced to the conclusion that any hope of victory was no longer realistic.

Dönitz: The war situation in all theaters and on all fronts, in the autumn of 1944, had an extremely grave appearance. After losing the greatest part of the territories previously occupied by us in the west, south, and east, Fortress Europe had become reduced to Fortress Germany, with the exception of Norway, Denmark, and Holland, which were still firmly held by us.

Heye: From autumn 1944 it was clear that it was only now a matter of fighting for Germany itself. The hopes of wide circles of the armed forces and of the civilians were maintained because [of] a belief in new weapons, and the large number of troops still available did not allow their resistance to flag. All measures against defeatist talk were, moreover, naturally tightened up to an unusual degree, as had already happened after the 20 July [plot].

The invasion and Russian successes were often so represented as to suggest that treachery, primarily on the part of the officers' corps, was at work. Whether this propaganda was introduced by the Germans or from the other side, I cannot judge. Internal supervision increased to an extraordinary degree.

The hopes of intelligent military circles rested solely on the possibility of a political termination to the war. The widespread ignorance of the political situation and of any negotiations that existed even among the highest authorities, hindered any stronger opposition to the measures taken by the government. No one, for example, wanted to be responsible for disturbing negotiations already in progress by overhasty measures.

Our propaganda bore to the last a strong positive and suggestive stamp. In the last instance a large section of the people, especially the youth and the young soldiers, thought and believed in the possibility of a better outcome. Other circles were considerably influenced by the thought that the fearful fate of continuing the fight, and in particular the air attacks, would be still better than unconditional surrender, which would end not only with the destruction of National Socialism but also of the whole German people.

The final battles in the east and west can only really be considered as a desperate struggle to maintain frontiers that were still to some extent tenable with the last ounces of our strength. Soldiers and civilians wanted in the main to do their duty in spite of the events that were overwhelming them and were driven on by ever-confident propaganda and the hope of a better solution than they could logically expect from events.

Krancke: The loss in the west had brought about . . . the heaviest of losses in material and personnel. Only 120,000 men remained in the western fortifications, and the German frontier was directly threatened. The whole of France and Belgium was available as a base for the superior enemy air force. The belief of the soldier in a victorious ending to the war was shaken, since his own air force was so completely lacking. The high command was still hoping for newly formed, well-equipped divisions, for the new weapons that were being prepared, and for the last man to be brought up into battle, in order to retrieve the position.

Unless political events occurred that would alter the situation entirely, victory no longer seemed possible. The constantly reiterated war aim of the Allies not only to destroy the German Reich but the German people, as well as the boundless hate that was directed against us in their press and radio, and the unconditional surrender terms laid down in the Casablanca charter made it impossible for the high command and the German people to give up the struggle before it was hopeless.

The last phase of the war can be likened to a desperate defensive battle. The explanation of the fact that it was morally and physically possible to carry on for such a long time, despite devastating enemy air activity, which we could only watch helplessly, can be explained by the belief of the German people in the righteousness of their cause, by the fact that they still believed in the high command and feared the outcome of defeat.

Dönitz: In the east and the west the opposing armies stood on the frontiers of the Reich or had in places actually crossed them. The ever-increasing air offensive of the western forces on the German homeland had already seriously reduced the industrial and economic resources, both by direct destruction and by the annihilation of means of communication, and threatened them in an ever-mounting degree. The German air force had failed with the available types of aircraft to bring it to a standstill. Thus the prospect for Germany of a successful conclusion of the war appeared very slender.

All thought of an earlier conclusion of the war was, however, destroyed by our enemies. Leading figures of the opposing side repeatedly declared that only an unconditional surrender by Germany was acceptable. Enemy propaganda painted a gloomy picture of the intended treatment of Germany after defeat. For this reason, therefore, our leaders had no alternative but to maintain resistance as long as in any way possible in order to exploit any possible opportunity of saving the German people [from] the fate painted in such fearful colors by the enemy press.

The German people themselves, through the continual air attacks and the numerous restrictions on their daily life, had become, here and there, somewhat weary but for the great part stuck to their task faithfully and with admirable determination. The terror raids on open towns with no military or even industrial significance brought horror and misery to all, which produced in the defenseless population of women, children, and old people on the spot rather a stiffening of the inner will to resist than the contrary. Men and women carried on grimly and obstinately with their work bringing unbelievable energy to the rebuilding of their places of work so that they remained in production.

Schniewind and Schuster: The majority of the German people trusted the high command, and still hoped for a finish to the war that, if not victorious, would at least not be a complete defeat. The hopes—based on the effects of new weapons (V-weapons), on the rebirth of the U-boat war with new types, on the raising of new army units (People's Grenadier Divisions), and on the strengthening of SS units, et cetera—played an important part in this attitude. It was hoped that the enemy would at least be prepared to compromise with a negotiated peace, after these new defensive and offensive weapons had been brought into operation.

Meyer: Following the successful invasion of Normandy, the loss of the whole of France, the terrific losses in the east during the summer of 1944, and the heavy air attacks, a large and important body of German opinion had scarcely any hope that the war could still be won. Hitler, however, still believed that he could turn the tide.

Perhaps most Germans continued the struggle out of an unshakeable patriotism that refused to accept the Allied demand for unconditional surrender; perhaps some of the better informed fought on out of fears about the retribution that a repressive Nazi regime could still wreak on those whose words or conduct might be assessed as defeatist; perhaps some still harbored hopes of a last-minute political and diplomatic solution that would be skillfully engineered by the Führer, who would persuade the Americans and British that total victory over Germany would be bought at too high a price if it meant handing all of eastern and southeastern Europe over to Russian communism. As for the influence of propaganda, optimism was kept alive by the myth that Hitler was working on some great master plan that could yet bring victory if the German people were steadfast enough to be worthy of his genius, and that new and powerful weapons would shortly be unleashed that would tilt the balance decisively in favor of the German armed forces. Heye points to the way in which, even under the weight of the Allied air assault, the German people were still able to believe that new weapons would be able to hold the bombers at bay.

The enemy air attacks on German industries and communications assumed increasingly greater proportions. Beginning with the mammoth attack on Hamburg, in which very large numbers of civilians lost their lives, the effect of these attacks became apparent. They led not only to the destruction of valuable industries but also to the lowering of production through the loss of their houses and of the workers themselves. This mounting air activity naturally had an effect on morale. The continued endurance of the already sorely tried population is only to be understood as developing from their belief that there could still be a successful outcome of the war, and in particular from the feeling that, as the propaganda stressed, the fate of a capitulating Germany would be much worse than the fiercest air bombardment.

Three of the admirals mention the kind of air force developments that helped to sustain morale among the civilian population.

Dönitz: Serious as the situation was, there were still grounds that encouraged the hope of a last-minute turn of the tide. The fighter program with its new types of "beam fighters" (*Strahljäger*) and jet-propelled fighters promised

Hitler's Admirals

the possibility of checking or even putting an end to the enemy's uncontrolled air supremacy over the whole German area.

Meyer: Mighty efforts were to be made to again "put a roof" over Germany (to use the expression then current); antiaircraft defenses—fighters and A/A guns—would be increased tremendously by a colossal effort.

For a few months we were successful in turning out an increased number of fighters (to my knowledge up to twenty-five hundred a month) but it proved on the one hand that the old types of machine, which were the only ones that could be produced in numbers, were in effect of no more use, and on the other hand that the ever-increasing attacks from the air on Germany had gradually became so catastrophic that even with the utmost concentration of all energies, it was no longer possible to increase any kind of armament production.

Schulz: In . . . July and August 1944 we were continually being told on high authority that the German production of fighter aircraft was increasing so rapidly—monthly production figures of from three thousand to four thousand were given—that the German air force would have recovered its air supremacy over German territory in November at the latest. Under these conditions the fuel situation, which was becoming more and more acute, continued to be a grave source of anxiety, particularly as the transportation of existing fuel supplies became increasingly difficult owing to damage to traffic installation.

One important way of sustaining morale was to show that the enemy was being effectively counterattacked. In the air war that function was served by the so-called V-weapons, first launched against England in the summer of 1944. The V-1 was a small, pilotless flying bomb propelled by a jet engine, and the V-2 was a rocket that could be fired to a height of fifty miles before crashing to explode in enemy territory. They both carried about a ton of explosive and neither could claim to be very accurate. Although the V-weapons caused considerable, if indiscriminate, damage in Britain, especially in such a huge target as London, the German admirals do not write about them with any great enthusiasm.

Heye: The V-weapons were generally expected to have a great effect. They were used for almost a year as propaganda to increase the power of resistance of our own people and troops and to make an impression on the enemy. The period of this propaganda was so long that the belief in an effective V-weapon was already diminishing in many circles. As far as I know, the weapon originally developed as V-1 was in the experimental stage for years, without being developed into a usable weapon. Propaganda relied on this weapon, but it was delayed from month to month. As I understand it, it was by luck that a different self-steering V-weapon was discovered, which became the later V-1 and took over the part of the V-weapon that had been originally announced but that was still not ready.

The so-called V-2 only appeared much later. It was clear in many military circles that the best V-weapons could, under the most favorable circumstances, only represent a substitute for the failure of our air force. In general their effect will not exceed that of a bomb.

Krancke: The V-weapons were completed, unfortunately, only after much delay. Technical hitches, rather than the [enemy air] attacks on Peenemünde, delayed the use of this entirely new type of weapon, which was not employed until after the invasion [of Normandy]. The hoped-for effect upon the morale of the enemy was diminished by the news of victory in France. The day drew near when the launching sites would be in Anglo-American hands. Even if this did not stop the use of the V-weapons, the concentrated use of all V-weapons, as originally planned, became impossible with the loss of the main launching sites, and the V-weapons did not have the decisive effect anticipated.

Meyer: The V-weapons were considerably less effective than had been promised for months by the German propaganda, and their development and manufacture were considerably hindered by the air attacks and the advance of the enemy in the west. This was a terrific disappointment for the mass of Germans who, until shortly before the end, believed in the coming wonder weapons. This had a great deal to do with the collapse of morale.

For a few days toward the end of 1944 the German people could even hope that their army was still capable of inflicting a serious reversal on their Anglo-American opponents. On 16 December, twenty-five German divisions under Field Marshal Gerd von Runstedt unleashed an offensive against a thinly held Ardennes sector of the U.S. front in Luxemburg and Belgium. They broke through and rolled on toward the River Meuse and—a more distant objective—the port of Antwerp. A great bulge was punched in the Allied front, and memories of the decisive breakthrough in 1940 were briefly revived, but the bulge was sealed off, the forward momentum was lost, and by mid-January 1945 the British and Americans had recovered most of the lost ground. The offensive had cost the Germans 100,000 men and 1,000 aircraft. The admirals are fiercely critical when writing of this attempted offensive.

Heye: Although military circles were, from the first, of the opinion that the intended operational area was extraordinarily unfavorable, the hopes that were attached to this offensive by the supreme command were nevertheless very high.

Schniewind and Schuster: In the west events seemed to have temporarily taken a turn for the better during the Ardennes offensive in the middle of December 1944. After initial successes, however, lack of striking power both in the army and in the air force brought the attack to an early close; though if it had succeeded in breaking through to its goal, Antwerp, it would have caused serious repercussions both on the Allies' northern and southern fronts in the west. Retreating step by step the army had to give up all the ground that it had won.

Meyer: The German offensive in the Ardennes came . . . as a great surprise. Hitler had expected a lot from this. I was told by C in C navy that Hitler even hoped to reconquer the whole of France. How this was to be done in the face of the overwhelming air superiority of the enemy is a puzzle; the sky would not remain forever overcast and the ground would not always be smothered in fog. Other considerations were the extent to which the army had been bled white and the great drop in its morale due to the continual reverses at the front and the air-bombardments of homes and property, and wives and children.

The offensive in the Ardennes was an absolute failure; it hastened the defeat of Germany since the divisions that took part came out very badly mauled and were yet badly needed for the defense of all fronts. Their movements, moreover, took much longer than in normal times because of the widespread damage to railways.

Schulz: Our offensive in the Ardennes—of which the navy was not previously informed—must, when taking the long view, be regarded as a mistake because we used up almost our last reserves, which we had withdrawn from other hard-pressed fronts, and owing to the air superiority of the enemy, our attack achieved little success. If the forces kept for this operation had been sent in their entirety to the eastern and southeastern fronts and had been joined with an army group withdrawn in good time from Courland, they would probably have been sufficient to prevent the catastrophic result in which the Russians' German offensive ended, and at least have made it impossible for the Russians to penetrate far into Germany in their fighting advance.

Krancke: [The offensive was] an attempt to destroy the enemy and change the situation in the west by making a thrust through the Ardennes toward Lüttich, perhaps to Antwerp, to oppose the great offensive that was being prepared against the Ruhr. The best of everything that was available was prepared for this.

After a successful beginning, however, which gave Germany a temporary respite, this offensive came to a standstill. Again it was the shortage of fuel (where the air force was concerned), tanks, and replacements, in contrast to mobility and air superiority on the part of the enemy, which denied us success. Not even the withdrawal of the motorized units, which was ordered after the failure of the offensive, could be carried out on account of the fuel shortage and the destruction of the railways. Thus the offensive not only proved a failure in the west and brought only a short respite from the enemy offensive, but also the reinforcements for the other threatened fronts came too late.

> The German navy still clung to the hope that the U-boat war would once more turn in their favor as soon as the older boats equipped with the schnorkel device and the new boats with more powerful motors began to enter operational service in considerable numbers. The scope of German plans for a renewed U-boat offensive may be judged by the fact that, in the second half of 1944, 31 of the smaller type XXIII U-boats and 62 of the larger type XXI were newly commissioned into the Kriegsmarine, with a further 31 type XXIII and 57 type XXI entering service in the first four months of 1945. Only a handful of the type XXIIIs and one type XXI were actually sent on offensive patrols, and they sank just five small ships, all under 3,000 gross tons. A number of other boats were nearing completion when the war ended. No one was better qualified than Dönitz to write an account of the hopes that rested on these new U-boats and the way those high hopes remained unfulfilled.

The new types of U-boat led to [the] expectation of a powerful impetus to U-boat warfare. Therefore the Führer's task was to hold out, concentrating all forces in the most important tasks, and to work for time until the new weapons could be brought into operation.

By the end of 1944 practically all available old type U-boats on operational work had been fitted with schnorkel. They were operated on the English east and northwest coasts, off the north Channel, off the Bristol Channel, in the invasion area, and in the Irish Sea. The results were good and the losses acceptable.

The loss of the Bay of Biscay ports as operational bases was of enormous disadvantage to the U-boat war. The land communication to these ports had been severed by the advancing Anglo-American armies in France, and thereby all possibility of further supply of fuel and torpedoes [had been] removed. In spite of the favorable opportunities for attack close to the English coast, there was only a moderate increase in total sinkings. The reasons were obvious: the number of boats present and able to operate was very small and never exceeded thirteen. The great majority were on the long trip to or from Germany or Norway. This entirely submerged passage at very low speed reduced the economy of the U-boat warfare considerably, by comparison with earlier times. Even if each boat in the operational area reached the same daily average of sinkings as in the best days of 1942, at that time, given an equal number of boats at sea, there were three times the number in the operational area than at present, because of the time saved by the short distance to the Bay of Biscay ports and the faster surface passage.

That even the old boats fitted with schnorkel could operate again close up to the enemy coast, with its powerful defenses, was a proof that we were on the right lines with our new U-boat types. With these by virtue of their high speed submerged, the dead cruising time would be halved. Over and above this, their length of stay in the operational area was expected to be shorter, since with this high speed, they would be able to attack more quickly and move often. Therefore, it was expected that the economy of U-boat warfare would once more become extremely favorable.

In the meantime the construction of U-boat types XXI and XXIII was pressed on with all vigor. After completion of all construction plans the boats were put into construction as follows. The construction of the engines and accessories was given over to industry spread over the whole German area for production in the most widely diverse factories. The hulls of the boats themselves were manufactured in sections inland and then transported to the building yards: here all the parts belonging to the single sections were installed and the completed sections then welded into the U-boat in the assembly yards. In this manner, in spite of the heavy air attacks on German industry, which necessitated a continual diversion and transference of manufacture, the production figures planned were on the whole maintained up to the end of 1944. Only then, as the result of intensified air attack and the destruction of lines of communication, did a considerable reduction take place. For all that, at the beginning of 1945 there were already a considerable number of both new types of boat in commission.

In March 1945 several type XXIII boats were, for the first time, sent to operate on the English east coast. The operation confirmed to the full the hopes entertained. Out of seven trips, five were successful. All boats returned to base in spite of the strongest opposition. By virtue of their high speed submerged the boats came easily to the attack and thereafter withdrew from enemy countermeasures by making off at high speed. After withdrawing some miles they then observed, from safe range, the concentrated and extensive depth charging of the attack area, without themselves being located. The personnel had great confidence in the new type. This applied equally to type XXI. The first boat, commanded by Korvettenkapitän Schnee, an experienced U-boat officer, had already been placed in operation in April. Monthly increasing numbers of both types were to be operated against the enemy in the coming months.

We were entitled to assume that the U-boat war would enter a new phase. Considerable successes had already been achieved by old type boats fitted with schnorkel on operations of long duration, without a single surfacing being necessary. The strain on crews, who remained up to seventy days submerged, was surprisingly small. Thanks to the schnorkel the atmosphere remained fresh during underwater cruising and considerably better than in former circumstances. But the most important easing of strain came from the removal of the continual nervous tension in U-boat crews caused by surprise attack by aircraft.

Type XXI, with its great range of twenty-two thousand miles, was capable of scouring all waters of importance for the U-boat war without once having to surface. It was obvious that this would bring about a turn in the naval war. Control of the sea by great sea powers was exercised through surface craft supported by aircraft. A warship whose primary operational sphere lies beneath the surface, immediately renders the greater part of this control of the sea impossible. If in addition this warship has a high top speed under water, which makes possible an easy approach to the enemy, it is obviously a very valuable instrument of war.

The final requiem for Dönitz's high hopes is delivered by Schniewind and Schuster.

The attempted reconstitution of the striking power of the U-boats, and Grossadmiral Dönitz's hopes of breaking previous sinking records, suffered such setbacks through the decisive influence of the continuous attacks of the enemy air forces that, even with the attainment of a minimum of new armament, the strategic situation of Germany and the position at sea had already deteriorated appreciably. . . . Before the new U-boat types came into operation against the enemy and the hoped-for improvement in the general war situation could be brought about, the whole basis of the conduct of the U-boat war collapsed, together with the armed forces on land and in the air, under the blows of the enemy air force.

During the final months of the war, the German navy could only play various subsidiary roles while the army was pounded into defeat. Meyer emphasizes the crippling fuel shortage:

[By early 1945] the position . . . was everywhere catastrophic; it was worst of all in the matter of fuel-oil supplies, which fell very heavily as a result of the retreats. This was the reason for the offensive in Hungary, for without the Hungarian oil, the war was certainly lost. This offensive was carried out, therefore, although it seemed crazy in view of the defeats sustained on all fronts. Like the Ardennes offensive, this also failed because the German army, without sufficient cover from the air, was far too weakened, and because morale had collapsed in the face of all the reverses.

The question of fuel was critical for the navy, too, in the spring of 1945. Stocks were completely exhausted when the war ended. In the last weeks and months operations at sea had to be more and more limited and ships had to be laid up, all on account of the lack of fuel. German sea power was at its lowest ebb, and had the war continued for a few weeks more it would have had to cease operations altogether, solely through lack of fuel.

Minor war vessels and the small battle units achieved a few successes, where the courage of the sailors involved was squandered in minor operations that had no chance of affecting the final result of the war.

Heye: All the resources of the armed forces were now thrown into defense. Explosive boats and swimmers from the small battle units command were used on the Rhine, as well as in Hungary and on the Oder. The effects of the mounting enemy air offensive were daily becoming more visible to the general populace, although the immediate results can only have been clear to the government.

The last emergency program within the four-year plan confined the production of armaments, which had already been decreasing for two years, to a few absolutely essential weapons, and then only in such small numbers that it would have been impossible on the basis of this program to carry on the war longer than the summer of 1945. One must bear in mind that, even when Germany had control over large areas of Europe and over their industries, she was unable to keep step with the productive capacity of the enemy countries. Herein lies also, perhaps, the best proof of the impossibility of Germany ever being able to rearm herself inside her remaining territory.

Dönitz: The sending of cruisers to northern Norway was also stopped as there was now a great variety of operational tasks for these ships in the Baltic, which previously had been largely employed for the training of new entries. One destroyer flotilla remained in northern waters, whose task it was, in conjunction with the coastal forces, to cover the seaward flank of the retreating [German armies in northern Norway].

In the North Sea, small craft, together with U-boats and E-boats, bore the burden of our operational activity. The most important target was the enemy supply traffic to the Scheldt. Meanwhile, the latest type of midget submarine, the so-called *Seehund* had become operational. These boats had an enormous endurance of up to five days at sea, a noteworthy performance bearing in mind the enormous strain on the crews. A series of satisfying successes were achieved against the Scheldt traffic.

Schulz: The later operation of the small battle units and E-boats from the Dutch area, which was conducted with real fanaticism by C in C navy, could, owing to the strong enemy countermeasures at sea and in the air, only be regarded as pinpricks that could in no way decisively affect the sea communications between England and Antwerp or Ostend.

For the river crossings that became necessary in the course of the campaign, the navy took over to a very great extent the task of ferrying the army. The highly successful transportation across the Scheldt to Flushing of the army that had been cut off on land in Belgium deserves special mention; it was carried out with comparatively small losses in spite of enemy air superiority. Many naval units also fought within the framework of the army as infantrymen and were later incorporated in the army. During the last year frogmen, saboteurs, and other demolition units of the navy had, moreover, been used continually in support of the army. For this reason the navy was compelled more than before to keep itself informed of army operations.

After the Russians had broken through to the coast in the Baltic States and East Prussia the Baltic Sea was, as Schulz describes, transformed into a war zone instead of the fairly quiet training area it had been since 1939.

Here too the navy was very much concerned with military operations, as this further withdrawal of the eastern front greatly endangered the irreplaceable ports between Windau and Gdynia, with their dockyards and supply depots and their various training activities, especially those in connection with U-boats. The central Baltic was an unequaled training area for our U-boats, because the western Baltic was too extensively mined, and the training of U-boat crews was fanatically maintained, so that the new U-boat types could be put into operation as soon as possible. Later, when the front was in East Prussia, this gave rise to really extraordinary circumstances. When, after the loss of Memel, Russian E-boats were operating against our extensive transport off Danzig and Gdynia, our U-boats continued to put out of both ports to carry out their exercises, so that things were made very difficult for our own anti-U-boat defenses, because of the possibility of confusion.

In places like Courland, Memel, and Königsberg where German forces continued to resist after the main Russian offensive had passed them by, the German navy found itself obliged to shoulder the burden of ferrying in supplies, providing artillery support from seaward, and ferrying out to Danish or north German ports very large numbers of wounded, surplus servicemen, and civilians fleeing in fear of the fate that might await them at the hands of the Russians. During these operations, Russian submarines torpedoed and sank, with enormous loss of life, the passenger ships *Wilhelm Gustloff* (on 30 January 1945), *Steuben* (on 9 February), and *Goya* (on 16 April). In the confused circumstances of the hurried evacuations, accurate figures for the number of people on board were not kept, but it seems probable that from those three ships more than fifteen thousand people were drowned. More than thirty-five hundred men in training for U-boat service were on the *Wilhelm Gustloff* when she was sunk. Dönitz also had to suffer other painful losses as surplus U-boat men and seamen from other branches of the navy were pressed into service as stopgap infantrymen.

All new construction, reconstruction, repairs, and developments that could not be made ready for front line operation in the shortest time were abandoned; the authorities and staffs concerned were then reduced or dissolved and the personnel turned over to operational duties. The manpower of the navy was continually and more carefully than ever supervised, so that personnel rendered superfluous by the shrinking of the theaters of war could be transferred immediately to the army. To maintain naval tradition, to which there was great devotion among these superfluous ratings, naval infantry divisions were brought into being that were destined purely and simply for land warfare. Just as with earlier naval formations that took part as required in land operations, as for example during the retreat from the west, from Leningrad, and from the Balkans, the traditional naval fighting spirit was preserved in these new divisions. To compensate as far as possible for the lack of land fighting experience, these new divisions were provided with the greatest possible number of battle-tried army officers and NCOs. As the result of the short period of training permitted by the development of the situation, losses were relatively high.

The U-boat and small craft construction program was maintained as long as possible. But here too the increasing destruction of industry and means of communication, together with the loss of building yards and production units, compelled a gradual decrease until, finally, shortly before the capitulation, new construction was given up entirely and only boats already working up were available to supply the front.

The final disintegration of the defense of the German homeland could not be long delayed. By the end of March 1945 the Americans and British had driven forward through the Rhineland as far as the Rhine itself; and they had established bridgeheads on the eastern bank of the river across a wide front. The Russians had thrust a huge salient into Germany as far as the River Oder, where their spearheads were only forty miles from the suburbs of Berlin. On 13 April the Russians took Vienna, and three days later they launched their final assault on Berlin. On the twenty-fifth, advancing U.S. and Russian troops met in central Germany, and the Russians had Berlin completely encircled. On the last day of April Hitler committed suicide in his besieged Führerbunker under the chancellery in Berlin, after appointing Grand Admiral Karl Dönitz as his successor, a thankless task that left the admiral with no alternative but to try to end the war as best he could. Without entering into a detailed account of the final debacle, the admirals provide a rather poignant assessment of those last days, which were, of course, very fresh in their minds as they wrote their essays in captivity during the summer of 1945.

Meyer: Hitler's efforts to hold out along the Rhine and the Oder were condemned to failure by the utter material, physical, and moral exhaustion of the people. The masses had lost faith in their leaders, and the army no longer cooperated. The political retainers failed one by one and the war came to a quick end.

Krancke: The big Russian offensive swept over our troops in the east and reached the Oder, where it was brought to a temporary standstill. The German people were unable to stand up to the all-round offensive that was now beginning. Everywhere there was a shortage of weapons, equipment, ammunition, and fuel. The armament industry still remaining and the lines of transport were destroyed. Internal resistance collapsed; one army after another fell; one part of Germany after another was captured by the enemy. Refugees fleeing from Bolshevism poured into territories not yet taken by the enemy.

When the English and Americans stopped at the Elbe, one more attempt was made to free Berlin and stay the Russians. But it was in vain; the economic chaos of the Reich, which was now so split up, and the final end could no longer be prevented. Germany was forced to capitulate, as well as those sections of her army that were still untouched and able to fight, but that nevertheless could not alter the fate of the German people by continuing to fight; it would only have been an unnecessary sacrifice of blood. The German people fought to the last, in order to escape the awaited destruction. Their achievements and the deeds of Germany's soldiers only history will be able to judge.

Schniewind and Schuster: Soon the armed forces were engaged in a battle for the Rhine. The direct attacks and the encircling moves by the enemy west of the Rhine, undertaken in order to endanger our positions on the Saar and in the Palatinate, became fiercer and more effective; and our own defense, which lacked any fresh supplies of men and materials, became more and more inadequate.

It is not to be wondered at that the fighting spirit, the will to defend, and the holding power of the troops should finally have been broken in the face of continual failures, of an almost hopeless inferiority that was quite clear even to the soldiers on the fighting front, and of a complete lack of every kind of supplies. High-ranking officers from the fighting troops told me later, however, that this was not the case. But, all the same, some other people have expressed a completely contrary opinion to me.

The German defense reached its last stages on all fronts. In face of the complete disruption of all lines of communication and supply routes, the shrinkage of all types of arms production, the almost complete breakdown of supplies, and the ever-growing difficulties of a coordinated command, the

German soldiers' defensive actions took on the character of a last battle of despair. To a sober judgment the continuation of the war at this point, when there was no resistance to the enemy air forces' growing attacks, must at last definitely appear hopeless.

Even if the defense could have been successfully stabilized along the new fronts, in the long run it was obvious that collapse must follow because all the important armaments centers . . . had either been destroyed or else were too near the front line, and because of the impossibility of transporting, for example, coal, arms, ammunition, or food safely or according to any pre-arranged timetable in order to supply the area of central Germany where the population, increased by thousands of refugees from the occupied territories, had risen far above its peacetime proportions. I have been told that, in official circles, the consideration of holding out boldly, at least against the western Allies until the last moment, in order to reach a more favorable settlement in connection with at least the eastern areas of Germany, played a large part.

There was fighting for the capital of the Reich, and the eastern part of the industrial area in Saxony and the Ruhr was lost; the enemy was advancing at all points and meeting with practically no effective resistance. The Führer died in Berlin. An attempt by the new head of the state to throw in all available forces against the eastern enemy while abandoning the west to the western Allies failed. The eastern and western Allies met on the Elbe, and the whole of Germany except for a few small areas in the northwest and southeast lay in the hands of the enemy. On May 8 the capitulation of Germany was complete.

Against the disastrous battles on land, the final destruction of what was left of the German surface fleet was not even mentioned in the admirals' essays. In addition to large numbers of smaller warships that were mined, bombed, or scuttled in the Mediterranean and in home waters during the last two months of the war, the remaining major units ended their careers in rather pathetic circumstances. The pre-1914 battleship *Schleswig-Holstein*, bombed and aground off Gdynia, was later scuttled, and her sister ship *Schlesien* was mined and sunk off Swinemünde. The pocket battleship *Admiral Scheer*, once proudly commanded by Krancke on her commerce-raiding voyage in 1940–41, was bombed and capsized in Kiel, and her sister ship *Lützow* was eventually scuttled after being sunk by bombers at Swinemünde and then refloated. The hulls of the never-completed aircraft carriers *Graf Zeppelin* and *Seydlitz* were also scuttled, the former at Stettin and the latter at Königsberg. Of Germany's remaining cruisers, the *Köln* was bombed in Wilhelmshaven, the *Emden* was run aground at the same port after being severely damaged in a bombing raid, and the *Admiral Hipper* was also scuttled there after suffering bomb damage. The *Leipzig* was a constructive total loss after being damaged in a collision the previous autumn. The *Prinz Eugen* and *Nürnberg* were the only major warships that were seaworthy enough to be formally handed over to the victors when the surrender was signed. Heye excuses himself from commenting on this phase of the war, on the plea that "special work and unrestricted research would be required in order not to write superficial history"; but the magnitude of the German tragedy weighed heavily on the conscience of some senior officers. Schulz, for example, obviously feels the need to pen a very personal explanation.

In the last few months any senior officer who possessed some kind of general view of the military situation could regard only with increasing inward wrath how resistance, now militarily senseless, was continued despite the enemy's numerical and material superiority and his complete mastery of the air, which every day added new wounds to the German people—a resistance continued without any prospect of a change in the situation unless a miracle were to occur. Nevertheless orders were issued on the highest level for the destruction of irreplaceable German industrial, transport, and harbor installations that, had the orders really been carried out, would have meant the destruction of further invaluable assets of Germany's economy.

In its own province the German Admiralty made successful efforts to bring about an alteration in this situation; the destruction of German harbor and shipyard installations, of the remaining German merchant ships and of warships [that had been] originally merchant ships or convertible to merchant service purposes, as well as of all minesweepers, was canceled. This was not simple to attain in view of the psychosis reigning in high and very high levels, and [it] demanded a personal concentration of the first order from our officers concerned.

In the last six months, after the inevitability of further developments was to be foreseen and after our belief in new V-weapons with an annihilating effect had disappeared—even though hopes of this were again and again raised by the "high-ups"—there was much in evidence among senior officers the view that, now the war was after all lost, it would be practical to stop the war against the Anglo-Saxons and to throw in all our troops from the west on the eastern front to save the Reich and the greatest possible area of

Europe from a further advance of Bolshevism into the sphere of western cultural influence, until Anglo-Saxon troops had occupied these areas behind the back of our own eastern front.

Nevertheless, this viewpoint was most strongly opposed by those in charge, and I know that individual officers expressing themselves in this sense were set for court-martial, a thing not only very bad for those concerned but also having the gravest consequences for members of their family, for in the last few months so-called kin-arrest—extending to parents, wives, and children of those in question—was constantly threatened.

It is very difficult for the nonparticipant, and especially for the foreigner, to understand the conflict of conscience arising for every officer between the dictates of common sense and the duty to obey the head of the state as a result of a religious oath of allegiance—a conflict made keener by worries regarding the fate of family, nation, and homeland—for naturally people were to a certain extent clear as to the catastrophic consequences of unconditional surrender as demanded by the Allies.

Dönitz quickly realized that, unpalatable though it might be, there was no alternative to unconditional surrender. Further organized resistance was impossible, and his despairing effort to negotiate separately with the British and Americans was brusquely rejected. His essay offers no detailed analysis of why he felt compelled to send his representatives, General Jodl and General Admiral von Friedeburg, to sign the surrender that came into force at midnight, 8–9 May. His essay merely notes:

The entry into force of the unconditional surrender in northern Germany at 0800 on 5 May 1945 and the total capitulation of the German armed forces that followed on 9 May 1945 brought the war to a close.

The surrender terms included provision for the handing over of the very large number of U-boats still in commission. Sources differ as to the precise numbers, but one of the more recent calculations lists 168 U-boats as being surrendered, 6 taken over by the Japanese in the Far East, and 222 scuttled or dismantled. In other words, more than half the U-boat commanders and crews defied the terms of the surrender and Dönitz's own orders. Instead they chose to put into effect Operation Regenbogen, an earlier doomsday contingency plan for destroying the U-boat fleet. No doubt they reasoned that whatever Dönitz might have accepted under pressure from the enemy, they were acting in accordance with their old chief's innermost wishes. With an eye to possible war crimes trials in the offing, Dönitz penned a sincere and comprehensive tribute to the way the men of the Kriegsmarine had fought under his command.

[The] new effectiveness of the German U-boat war was cut short by the German capitulation, which had become inevitable through the occupation by the enemy of the whole German area.

The battle of the U-boats had come to an end. Self-sacrificing and courageous, unstained and honorable had been the conduct of the crews in battle. Of an approximate strength of 38,000 men in the U-boat arm, around 30,000 had fallen. On the other hand their successes were unique; far more than 2,000 ships—according to enemy figures—of at least 14 million tons, numerous escort vessels, destroyers and cruisers, 2 aircraft carriers [in fact, 3, and 2 escort carriers], and two battleships sunk, and many other naval and merchant vessels damaged.

The German navy fought honorably and courageously, afloat and ashore, on all the seven seas and in all European theaters of war. The fighting spirit and high idealism that inspired both officers and men remained unbroken to the bitter end. No stain sullied the German ensign when it was hauled down with honor after a lost war.

13

Some Conclusions and Verdicts

MOST OF THE admirals offer some kind of comment on why the war turned out so badly for Germany. Boehm, the oldest admiral at sixty-one, simply blames Hitler for relying too much on old political associates, and he pays off an old score with one of them, with whom he had clashed in Norway.

The fall of Germany was largely due to the fact that Hitler placed confidence in men who had assisted him to power but who, both in regard to their lack of understanding of the great constructive tasks of the future and because of their own characters, were incompetent. Terboven is one of these men, greatly to the misfortune of Germany.

Schniewind and Schuster point to political miscalculation and an unworkable arrangement at the very top of the German war organization:

I realize today that the main reason for the failure of the expectations of the naval war staff was the early entry of America into the war on the side of England. . . . The scope and power of their [ability] to render assistance was not known either to the naval war staff or even to the economic experts in Germany before the war or even up to 1941–42—and it was, therefore, underrated.

A fatal series of false estimates of our opponents' "political aims and military capabilities" was, in my opinion, the reason for the disaster that overtook Germany. These estimates also obviously failed to take into account the last most important fact—that the attitude taken up by the western Allies was fundamentally opposed to a rebirth of German power.

It is fundamentally wrong that the head of state should be himself the commander in chief of the armed forces and also, accordingly, of a part of the armed forces—the army. The interposition of a minister of war or C in C of the Wehrmacht is necessary.

Meyer is critical of both Hitler's personal leadership and the competence of the high command to run the war.

Hitler, who had all the power in his own hands, frequently did not or would not come to decisions that would best serve the cause. For example, until late in the war he was disinclined to oppose Göring's views with regard to the use of the air force for one of the other services; on this account, our cause suffered a good deal.

The supreme command of the armed forces (OKW) was frequently not brought into consultation by Hitler, and on account of its composition was frequently not in a position to handle all-embracing questions. It thus lost prestige and the power to have its orders accepted, even on unimportant matters, by the supreme command of the individual services.

Even toward the end of the war, owing to its composition, the OKW could not, even though it was the highest authority, deal on its own with all questions of the war as a whole, make decisions, or advise Hitler.

During the years previous to the war, an attempt was made at the so-called *Wehrmachtsakademie* (armed forces academy) to train staff in matters appertaining to all three services so that they could serve on the OKW. Apart from the fact that too few officers received this training, the scheme never really became effective because the army considered this as their own domain and, on the other hand, the high commands of the navy and air force were disinclined to have a kind of parallel command or to allocate too many of their officers for this purpose.

These commands always endeavored to obtain independence of action and only to get their orders direct from Hitler. A good example of this is the fact that, as late as the beginning of 1943, the naval position was explained at the daily consultations with Hitler by a general staff officer. It has to be asserted that the lack of a really competent OKW that could advise Hitler had very serious effects on the general direction of the war.

During 1943 and 1944 the chains of misfortune became more and more tightly bound round Germany . . . [as] the result of the overwhelming superiority of the enemy and of the many mistakes of the leaders of Germany in all spheres. Had these errors been avoided (e.g., by a greater use of the general staff in the execution of the land war, by a really comprehensive and sufficient high command of all the armed forces together, and no less important, by a change in the command of the air force) then, in my opinion, Germany could have carried on a defensive war for years; a policy of exhaustion could have been used; and after several years the war might have ended on terms that Germany could support.

Heye argues that Germany should have built on her military successes by making great political efforts to organize a united Europe under her leadership.

I believe that Germany would have been more successful [in trying to establish a self-sufficient Fortress Europe after 1941] if she had attempted to realize the concept of a "United States of Europe." This would have meant putting no one nation within such a Europe at a disadvantage, making no boundary changes, and steering a similar political course. There is no doubt that there existed everywhere in Europe, including the occupied countries, conceptions of this kind that were in no way connected with the idea of National Socialism. Perhaps there were no suitable politicians who could pursue a farsighted policy of this kind and who possessed the necessary insight into the character of other nations.

I considered it a mistake then, too, that we did not make known any clear war aims, since this was bound to lead to uncertainty as to German intentions and mistrust of possible changes of those intentions dictated by the current situation. We did not reply to the Atlantic Charter with a single aim that could have induced a unifying conception in every one of the peoples of Europe. As the strength of Germany's enemies increased and her own great offensive successes steadily decreased, the willingness to work with Germany toward a common European future was bound to flag.

The admirals are inclined to lay much of the blame for Germany's failure on the narrow continental outlook of so many politicians and soldiers.

Heye: In my opinion the political as well as the military development of this war would have taken a different course if the German government and the German people as a whole had looked upon problems less from the point of view of the Continent than of the whole world. I think, however, that this development was a logical consequence of Germany's history. The time had unfortunately not yet come to enlarge the field of vision of this nation, which, crowded together in a small area, had undergone such numerous political developments in the last sixty years. Internal political problems were always so pressing and important that our foreign policy, and those who could pursue it and who understood other nations, proved inadequate.

All these problems are closely connected with the preparations for the war, its direction, and the tasks of the navy as part of the armed forces. These questions, moreover, strongly influenced the gradual development of our political methods after 1933, although the German people could not realize this fact in 1933. Overestimation of one's own internal problems plays, in a certain sense, a great role in foreign policy. Factual historical research, particularly in the history of the war, will in many cases lead to different opinions than clearly exist at the present moment in many parts of the world.

Krancke: The influence of the navy was comparatively slight with the supreme political command and the supreme military command. The German way of thinking was still on continental lines.

That theme also bulks large in Weichold's analysis. He writes by far the most extensive critique of the higher direction of Germany's war effort, but one must make allowances for the fact that he was embittered by the way his advice about how to win the war in the Mediterranean had been ignored, embittered about the way that advice had ultimately led to his replacement as naval commander in chief in that sea, and embittered by the way Dönitz had later appointed Heye to supersede him as commander of the small battle units.

[By the spring of 1942] the importance of the sea and of the naval operations as a fundamental basis for the whole of the war plan (as was so clearly shown by the developments in the Mediterranean for those who could see) was not even now universally recognized. The silent effects of sea power still remained in the background, overshadowed by the more spectacular successes of the other services on land or in the air.

This was the fruit of the fundamentally "continental"attitude of the high commands of the German nation and of the forces. It was this one-sided view and the weaknesses arising from it that led to all the mistakes and failures of war operations. It was not this or that particular failure, nor the loss of any particular battle, which was responsible for the collapse of the Axis powers, but the fundamentally wrong ideas of those in command during this world war, in that they underestimated the importance of war at sea and declined to accept any objective views, criticisms, advice, or warning, and were presumptive enough to believe that they understood these matters much better than the experts, from whom they removed all responsibility by suppression and elimination.

Those are the reasons for the military defeat of Germany. This military aspect, however, was but a part of the generally false basic attitude of National Socialist Germany, especially in the sphere of worldwide ethics. Because it was totally wrong, it was bound to lead to collapse.

When planning the strategy of the war, the German high command did not take the initiative and marshal all Axis forces against Britain. On the contrary it concentrated to the full on continental warfare and thereby let the time factor operate to the advantage of Great Britain.

This false decision was typical of the leading men of Germany's government and armed forces. They were all landsmen and soldiers accustomed to the land. As in the policy that led to the war, they attributed the decisive importance to conditions and forces on the continent and underestimated the size and powers of the world, as they did everything that lay on the other side of the sea. Above all they failed to recognize the demands of the sea itself and the invisible strength of sea power. This underestimation led to a postponement of the solution of the pressing maritime problem until all the aims considered as desirable on the continent had been achieved. From a purely military point of view, however, one of the most important military maxims was thereby violated: the immediate exploitation of existing opportunities. The German high command believed that the favorable opportunity presented by Britain's isolation and weakness could be put on ice until Russia had been completely defeated on the continent. This preference for continental desires and the postponement of naval necessities were the fundamental errors of the German supreme command. It cost Germany the war.

The blame for the undervaluation of the fundamental naval character of this war must be carried not only by the highest political leaders but also by the supreme command of the armed forces. It was entirely under military influence. On all the Wehrmacht staffs the commanding positions were held by army and air force officers who directed a world war, and the operations arising therefrom, from their own continental point of view. There was no admiral in the position of commander in chief or chief of a Wehrmacht staff in the whole organization of the German Wehrmacht high command of the war. Thus were the decisive positions of command filled in a war, which, being a world war, was intrinsically a naval war. It should therefore have been conducted from the ocean-maritime point of view, no matter how small the navy or how great the army and air force were as war factors.

It is now obvious that a military education on land and activities within the frame of continental conditions and limits develop a comprehension that may be suited to the problems of a land war; but for the direction of world war such schooling is inadequate. This has been the teaching of history for centuries, recently proved again by the results of the past two wars. The outcome of every war is, however, not a question of powerful means, war material, and war potential in themselves but is dependent on the mental capacity of the high command.

This holds true not only for warfare but to a greater extent for the politics of war, indeed even for the influence of peace politics. The historical development of Germany in the past fifty years, particularly in the period of reconstruction after 1918, is a convincing proof of the accuracy of this fact. The continental outlook was the dominating factor in the Reich's policy.

Weichold's whole essay is devoted to expounding the strategic significance of the loss of the Mediterranean.

The Axis powers' loss of the Mediterranean war freed Britain from danger in the Middle East and so made possible the Allied landing in Italy and the breaking of the Italian ally. The German position was thereby much worsened, both from the standpoint of geography and deployment of her forces. It was these operations that enabled the Allies to make the decisive attack against the German fortress in Europe. However heavy the Russian pressure in the east, the additional weakening of the German forces on the western front in Europe decided the war.

Without its Mediterranean positions secured, the British command would, however, not have had the freedom of movement in its rear [nor] the forces to spare to carry out a landing in France. The loss of the Mediterranean was therefore the turning point of the war. The importance of this position, and the effect it could have on the whole war, was not recognized by the German command, although there was no lack of representations and warnings on this matter.

In looking to Germany's future, Weichold lays stress on the educational value of the sea.

In future the natural land-bound outlook of the Germans must be broadened to grasp a more far-reaching and general relation to world problems. The sea is the best teacher for this.

In contrast to the land, with its narrow territorial, material, and spiritual boundaries, the sea is the great element that binds the peoples together. It is common to all, everybody's road. It demonstrates that the nations form one community, that they are interdependent, that cooperation, respect, and considerateness are necessary, and thus it encourages a feeling of community. Without wishing to misunderstand or alter the national foundations of the peoples, the sea is nevertheless, with its work of education, the highest class in the school of mankind. It broadens one's thinking, frees it from the restrictions of partiality, and leads to a comprehensive view of the life of men and nations.

Such education has as its result a development of individualism, which leads to the further development of democratic principles. It is an unquestionable fact that among all peoples individualistic and democratic achievements have developed from a way of life connected with the sea and seafaring.

The value of the sea within the framework of man's development is one of the greatest experiences of the lost war.

Weichold is scornful of the blinkered attitude of the German high command and the insidious effect of stifling any professional dissent.

It is evident that Germany did not lose the war through the enemy's superiority in men and material, but in the military sphere principally through mistakes of the high command. The military situation was for the most part wrongly appreciated; naval possibilities were overlooked; the military operations on land were a failure; and the people were bled beyond the loss of the war.

The cause of these mistakes lay in the one-sided and uninspired attitude of the supreme command, against which different ideas, suggestions, or warnings could not prevail. They were either not listened to or rejected. That this one-sidedness of the high command, without intellectual exchange of viewpoints, was possible, was due to the systematic degradation of intellectual values, the destruction of freedom of thought, the exclusion of all criticism, taken together with the standardization of the mind in accordance with the ruling conception of a one-sided high command.

Thus those who were appointed to key positions in the armed forces lost any responsible participation. They sank to the level of handymen, whose ideas possessed only small value. Faith, trust, and unquestioning obedience had to take the place of mental capacity, judgment, and responsibility. Thus all ideas that differed from those of the high command were judged at best as deviations from the so-called absolute truth, or as presumptions on the part of individuals, or at worst as lack of loyalty, undermining of the armed forces, or treason. The advocates of other opinions were relieved of their positions and incurred degrading treatment, or even danger to life and limb.

Weichold does not hesitate to heap blame on the philosophical basis of National Socialism.

The question of the value of the National Socialist system in waging war can only be answered, after a close examination, that it proved to be not a source of strength but the ruin of Germany's military power. Whatever positive results it may have produced in the forming of personal or material strength are far outweighed by the diminishing and destruction of the value of the spirit and personality, the foundations of real leadership. From the lack of these qualities resulted the loss of the war, for without such leadership the greatest assembly of force remains a dead mass.

This negative result in the military sphere coincides with the effects [that] the system had on other spheres of life. By striving to adapt himself inwardly to National Socialism, the German can only arrive at a fundamental rejection of it.

The attachment manifested by the German people to National Socialism and its founder rested on a lack of discernment, false promises, and sham values, and arose from and was spread by an unscrupulous propaganda. A change of inward attitude is therefore no alteration of convictions in the normal sense. Such an alteration is certainly no betrayal of faith, since faith always has to have an ethically and morally unobjectionable medium.

It is however not the opinion of the writer of these lines that the course and outcome of the war, that is to say military events, or even success or failure, are the best yardsticks by which to judge the National Socialist system. On the contrary, the military side is only an outcome of the ethical and human fundamental characteristics of the system and its leaders. The more searching and more comprehensive judgment of National Socialism will therefore cover those provinces that will furnish the main arguments for its valuation. But besides judging its inner nature, it is just as necessary to consider all the other spheres connected with it, in order to estimate the value of the principles from the phenomena they produce. And the military province, one of the most important sides of the National Socialist system, was actually made the core of its ideas and organizations, as it was the most readily employable "means to an end." It is therefore not superfluous to occupy oneself with the results of these efforts. But a sketch of the course of the war is not merely a collection of bare facts or their military significance, but a recognition of the forces releasing them, the forces that characterize the existing system. Every system and its representatives must at some time submit to criticism, however long they may have enforced its suspension.

Many sections of the German people have already had their eyes opened considerably to this state of affairs, but it is necessary to enlighten them all. Only out of the conviction of the whole community can the foundation for a new spiritual revival arise. The military sphere plays a part also in the problems that have to be dealt with now. At first many objections will be urged to discussing military questions of the past at all, at the present time. But if this did not take place, advantage would not be taken of an important field in the recent past, and no lessons for the future would have been gained in a sector that has always played a large part in the minds of the German people, whose outlook has always been militaristic. If the examination of the content and value of National Socialism were restricted to the political or ethical-human sphere, the belief could be sustained that in the military sphere at least National Socialism had achieved something positive, and that only the material superiority of the enemy crushed the German people. Such a contention, which toward the end of the war was widely disseminated on the part of the National Socialists, must be refuted if dangerous seeds for the future development of the German people are not to remain.

Knowledge of the true facts leads, on the other hand, to the recognition of the fact that National Socialism corrupted soldiering, warfare, and the war leaders as much as it did the other provinces over which its influence extended. Only by such instruction will considerable numbers of the German people, who are born and bred to a genuine soldierlike attitude, be enabled to come to the conclusion that the National Socialist system was fundamentally unsoldierly, and that it had nothing in common with real soldiering, as existed among all peoples. National Socialism only made use of the external forms in order to misuse a source of strength latent in the people.

Such realizations are of the greatest importance, but it is very difficult successfully to bring home their truth. After a defeat inflicted by the enemy, the average German is not very willing to accept voluntarily the knowledge of his own shortcomings. All those of their own people who have gained this knowledge in the past must, therefore, take up the struggle for the soul of the people. They must take upon themselves the duty of pointing out to the German people the error of the way that they have consciously or unconsciously followed. The individual will thereby have to undertake a great sacrifice; hard struggles, [and] misunderstanding of the motive, and every kind of attack will be the inevitable accompaniments. This risk must be run by everyone who experiences a complete upheaval of life. Whatever experiences have of necessity been called forth by the recognition of facts have been disclosed in this essay. To make them accessible to a wider range of people is the duty of a man who feels a responsibility for the general fate above that of his own. Only thus can a blessing for the future arise out of the unhappiness of the present time.

Meyer's essay also tries to strike a note of optimism about the possible good that would emerge from the war.

The end of the war brings with it a renewed common attachment of the peoples of the world to a peace organization that appears to offer a lasting and effective peace. In this connection another recent event—the dropping of the first atom bomb on Japan—seems to me especially important. A weapon of this destructive power makes future war completely senseless. On the other hand, this new discovery offers unimaginable possibilities for increasing the well-being of humanity through peaceful exploitation.

Perhaps that was the reason for the fall of Germany . . . so that the nations should combine in a new peace organization and so that out of war should come a discovery that really can guarantee the peace of the world and become a new source of benefit for the whole of mankind.

For their part in planning and conducting the war, Grand Admiral Erich Raeder and Grand Admiral Karl Dönitz were included among the twenty-six German leaders accused of war crimes before the International Military Tribunal set up by the victors. The trial opened in November 1945, and when the court delivered its verdict in October 1946, it indicated that the admirals were considered less culpable than their army counterparts, Field Marshal Keitel and General Jodl, both of whom were executed. Dönitz was sentenced to ten years' imprisonment. Raeder was sentenced to life imprisonment, but he was released in 1955 on account of his age and state of health. During the trial the two admirals spoke out boldly in their own defense, and in defense of the service they had led. Dönitz insisted: "Men are killed during wars and no one is proud of it. . . . It is a necessity, the harsh necessity of war." And there was no hint of apology when he told the tribunal: "You may judge the legality of German submarine warfare as your conscience dictates. I consider this form of warfare justified and I have acted according to my conscience. I would have

to do the same all over again" (International Military Tribunal, *Trial of the Major War Criminals* [Nuremberg: Tribunal Secretariat, 1948], 13:356, 12:390). Raeder spoke on behalf of the whole German navy, which he had led from 1928 to the end of 1942:

On the basis of the evidence the German navy's cleanness and decency in battle were fundamentally confirmed. The German navy stands before this Court and before the world with a clean shield and an unstained flag. . . . The naval operations staff and its chief . . . made an honest endeavor from the first to the very last moment to bring the conduct of modern naval warfare into harmony with the requirements of international law and humanity, on the same basis as our opponents. (International Military Tribunal, *Trial of the Major War Criminals* [Nuremberg: Tribunal Secretariat, 1948], 12:391).

Written at a time when so much attention and argument was focused on the tremendous conflict that had just ended in Europe, General Admiral Boehm's essay is a valuable reminder that, unlike most novels and many history books, history itself does not reach a final chapter when all problems have been neatly resolved and all loose ends neatly tied off. With almost Wagnerian bravura, Boehm makes a bold attempt to adopt a very much longer perspective from which to discern some justification for Germany's role in the Second World War and to argue that Germany still had an important contribution to make to the future well-being of Europe.

Filled with anxiety about my country, I feel that I cannot conclude this review without some consideration of the future.

It is neither proper, nor is this the place, to discuss the real and deeper reasons for the antagonism between England and Germany that led to the war. Germany now has to face the hard fact that she has lost the war and to realize the terrible danger that lies before her of utter destruction. The words Clemenceau spoke after the First World War, "The war was merely the preparation . . . the destruction of Germany now begins," apply to us now, but to an even greater extent.

One of the main reasons for the loss of the war—probably the greatest among the many errors that were made—is in my opinion the fact that the Führer of the German nation, as [an] "inlander," ignored the Anglo-Saxon mentality and underrated sea power. He believed that by his generous offer made in 1935 he had pacified England, and that France would follow on account of his offer of a twenty-five-year truce and the cessation of Germany's claims on Alsace and Lorraine, and that he could settle the unbearable pressure from the east by military means seeing that other measures had been unsuccessful.

How very badly Hitler erred in his judgment of England has been shown by the history of events and by the tragic misfortune of the German people. History can only prove, however, whether British statesmen have not made equally big mistakes during this period (in that they interfered with Germany in her fight for her own interests on her eastern borders) and to what extent England will suffer for these errors. For now we are all—Britain included—faced with a tremendous and threatening danger; what I call the Asiatic danger.

Since early historical times, throughout the centuries, this danger from Asia has existed. The Asiatics, with their uncurbed increase of population, have overflowed toward the west from time to time with primitive force, and it was the Germanic peoples who, primarily, brought them to a standstill and fought them off. In the year 375 the Huns penetrated the kingdom of [the] Ostrogoths on the Dnieper and, in 451, under Attila, forced their way as far as Gaul where they were beaten by the west Goths under Theodoric, with Germanic auxiliaries, on the Catalaunian Plain. Then again, came horsemen from the Urals—the later Hungarians—who in 933 were beaten by the German kings on the Saale and [beaten again] in 955 on the Lech Plain. Further, there were the Mongolians under Genghis Khan, who overran the whole of Asia as far as Turkey, and the nephew of Genghis Khan, who got as far as Silesia, where he was beaten in battle with the Silesian knights near Liegnitz in 1241.

Then the Asiatic Mohammedans spread over Africa and Spain to France, where they were stopped by Charles Martel, the grandfather of the German emperor Charlemagne in 737. This was followed by the Turks, who in 1683 were beaten near Vienna by Charles of Lorraine. And finally, there were the mixed Russian races who, in the two world wars stormed—with guns and tanks instead of horses—against the sons of Germany. I heard in 1941, from Hitler himself, that according to certain information he had received, the Russians were going to march against us in 1942 and, on this account, he wanted to forestall them. Historical events show that Hitler's views were not unfounded.

However this may be, the fact remains that Germany, attacked on both fronts, has this time succumbed and the Asiatics have now forced their way as far as the Elbe. This state of affairs concerns not only Germany but also England. Recently the *Daily Telegraph* wrote: "It depends on events in Potsdam whether we shall have a Third World War." I am in full agreement with this last thought: we are, in fact, faced with a Third World War for, should the Russians wish to march forward, England and America will not be able to stop them, with the result that the Russian-Asiatic wave will overflow into the Atlantic and, in Asia, into the Indian Ocean.

Russia has always shown herself to be land hungry in spite of her size, no matter whether it was under the czars or the Soviet Union. And now, to this land hunger is added the idea of Bolshevism. Superficial observers say that there is but a slight difference between Bolshevism and National Socialism. They completely ignore that the latter will have nothing to do with class warfare and taught the unity of all German peoples in a common striving for Germany's future, while Bolshevism desires class hatred and demands the dictatorship of the proletariat. This had been attained in Russia but there exists the further idea, and plan, of "proletariats of all countries unite!" This is nothing more than a striving for a world revolution and even if, for political convenience, this may be camouflaged at the moment, it is the essence of Bolshevism.

Thus we have a combination of land hunger, desire for power, Bolshevistic aims, and Asiatic hate against the superior European races and *Kultur* still expanding in the same direction and with the destructive force of an upheaval of nature. The Balkans, Poland, and the eastern half of Germany is now in the power of the Asiatics. France is ripe for Bolshevism, especially in the south; Italy was only saved from it by Mussolini, and Spain by Franco. Who is going to stop the Asiatics if they get Germany, the heart of Europe, into their power? As once, in the dark ages of the migratory period, the Germanic races, with primitive means, forced their way toward Italy, Gaul, Spain, and Africa, how is Russia to be stopped? With her inexhaustible Asiatic races, her modern-equipped war machinery, [and] the latest technical developments at her disposal, who can hinder her? What it means for England to have Russia at her gates and in her most valuable colony—India —I need say nothing further. It is a battle for existence. This affects Germany, seeing that to have Germany used as a battlefield will mean the final extinction of her people. There lies our community of interest with England.

The words in the *Daily Telegraph* article would be very satisfying to us Germans were the occasion not so tragic. [This] English statement, two months after the end of the Second World War, that one is faced with a

Third World War is the best proof, even if it is undesired, that Germany is not the disturber of world peace but that it is an entirely different problem —Asia versus Europe. The real fact is that National Socialism wanted nothing more than to secure for Germany and her compressed population a clearance of her eastern frontiers and more *Lebensraum* in that direction, after the Treaty of Versailles had taken all from us. And, even here, an extension of her territory toward the east could never have constituted a warlike threat to the British Empire, such as now exists from Russia. With this thought in mind, Hitler's words, "I cannot imagine that any British statesman would bring England into the war in these circumstance" are quite comprehensible.

World history sometimes moves very fast. The statesmen of our time have got to utilize the time they have—and that before it is too late. Natural forces such as the Asiatic pressure to expand will not be held up by treaties but only by force. For many centuries Germany was the wall against this pressure; now the wall is down. England alone cannot hold up the danger, but only with the help of Germany, if that is still possible (which I almost doubt). If that which is still remaining to Germany is finally physically and spiritually smashed, then this factor will be eliminated from the balance of nations. Discernment and action are necessary, for it is not only for Germany, but also for England, that these words apply:

> *To be, or not to be,*
> *That is the question.*

World history did, indeed, "move very fast." American and British statesmen were already coming to the same alarming conclusion as General Admiral Boehm. On 5 March 1946 Winston Churchill told an audience at Fulton, Missouri, that an "iron curtain" now stretched "from Stettin in the Baltic to Trieste in the Adriatic" and that Russia was planning "the infinite expansion of [its] power and doctrines." By 1948 the Americans and British were compelled to mount a giant air lift to supply Berlin as a counter to Russian efforts to pressure them out of Germany's former capital. In the following year the North Atlantic Treaty Organization was established and America, Britain, and France combined their occupation zones to set up the Federal Republic of [West] Germany. Before Grand Admiral Raeder's release from Spandau jail in 1956, the Allied occupation of West Germany had been terminated and that country had been admitted as a valued member of both the European Defense Community and the North Atlantic Treaty Organization. Among the German naval officers who subsequently rose to flag rank within NATO were the Second World War convoy expert Friederich Ruge; the former captain of the disguised commerce raider *Atlantis*, Bernhard Rogge; and the former U-boat aces Otto Kretschmer and Eric Topp. As for the admirals whose essays form the basis of this book, Otto Schniewind died on 26 March 1964 and Theodor Krancke on 18 June 1973. Hellmuth Heye died on 10 November 1970, after serving as a member of the West German Bundestag between 1961 and 1964. Karl Dönitz was released from prison in 1956 and published his memoirs in 1958. An English translation, *Memoirs: Ten Years and Twenty Days*, was published in 1959. Dönitz died at Aumühle, near Hamburg, on 24 December 1980, when he was eighty-nine. The last Führer of the Third Reich was buried with full military honors in the presence of many former U-boat commanders who had served under his leadership.

Index

Italy, 75, 103–21, 148, 176; Air Force, 108,
114; Italian Army, 108–9; Italian Navy,
8, 108–10, 112–16, 119, 148, 175, 187.
See also ships' names
Italo-Greek War (1940–41), 133

Japan, 120, 126, 132–35, 137
Jodl, Alfred, 224, 235
Jugoslavia. *See* Yugoslavia
Juminda, 128
Jutland, Battle of (1916), 25, 111, 196

Kara Sea, 107
Kattegat, 193
Keitel, Wilhelm, 235
Kerch Straits, 171, 175
Kesselring, Albert, 150, 151, 154
Kharkov, 175
Kiel, 17, 142, 187
Kiev, 127, 175
Kirkenes, 77, 129
Königsberg, 219, 227
Kramer, Otto, 7
Krancke, Theodor, 16–17, 21, 39, 43, 46,
50, 54, 58, 64–65, 67–68, 76, 78, 80,
83–85, 87, 92, 96, 98, 100, 104, 107,
122, 124, 134, 159, 163, 178, 184, 192,
202–3, 208–9, 212, 214, 221, 240
Kretschmer, Otto, 89, 240
Kriegsmarine. See German Navy
Kristiansand, 68
Kronstadt, 128, 131
Kuban River, 172–73, 175
Kummetz, Oskar, 144
Kursk, Battle of (1943), 175

Laconia Order, 4
Langsdorff, Hans, 65
La Pallice, 75
Le Havre, 199–200
League of Nations, 33, 37
Lebensraum, 239
Lend-Lease Act (US) (1941), 191
Leningrad, 127–31, 191
Libya, 77, 105, 112, 115, 118–19, 150, 153,
158
Liège, 200
Linsen, explosive motorboat, 200
Loire River, 200
London, 83
London Naval Conference (1936), 36

Luxemburg, 212
Luftwaffe. See German Air Force
Lütjens, Günther, 68
Luxembourg, 200
Lyngenstellung, 189

Maikop, 170, 172
Malaya, 119
Malta, 105, 112, 114, 117, 119, 126, 150–54
Maquis, 160
Marcouf battery, 198
Marschall, Wilhelm, 16
Martienssen, Anthony, 15
Massawa, 114
Matapan, Battle of (1941), 152
Mediterranean Sea, 77, 85, 103, 21, 127,
136, 145–46, 149–70, 176, 189, 231
Memel, 219
merchant shipping, Allied, 148, 156, 176,
178, 190, 206; Axis, 90–91, 118–19,
147, 204
Mers el Kebir, 106, 159
Mersa Brega, 119
Mersa Matruh, 157–58
Meuse, River, 212
Meyer, Hans, 7–8, 35, 40–41, 43–44, 47,
63, 67, 76, 83, 85, 125–26, 133–34, 145,
159, 173–74, 180–81, 185–86, 209–13,
217, 220–21, 227–28, 235
Middle East, 77, 105, 117, 151, 169–70, 206
mine warfare, allied, 67–68, 74–75, 89;
axis, 37, 58, 62, 64–65, 89, 92, 128,
143, 194, 197, 199
Minsk, 127
Moravia, 46
Morocco, 107
Moscow, 5, 126, 130–32
Mozdok, 170
Munich crisis (1938), 45–48, 52, 103
Murmansk, 129–31
Mussolini, Benito, 103, 109, 133, 166, 206

Namsos, 70
Napoleon I, 126
Narvik, 67–69, 193
National Socialism, 32, 208, 233–35; value
of in waging war, 233–34
Near East oilfields, 104
Neger, one-man torpedo, 200
Nettuno, 194
Newfoundland, 97

About the Authors

Roy Bennett joined the British merchant navy (Andrew Weir & Co.) as an apprentice in 1944. He stayed with the company until 1947, when he went into teaching and eventually teacher training at Bishop's Lonsdale College in Derby, England. He gained his Ph.D. from the University of London in 1964.

George Henry Bennett (Harry) received his Ph.D. in history in 1992. He became a historian at the University of Plymouth in the same year, later becoming head of American Studies and then head of Humanities. In 1999, after the death of his mother, Harry published his first book with his father on wartime accounts of shipwrecked British merchant mariners. This second book by Roy and Harry Bennett continues their collaboration on maritime history.